IN AN INSTANT

IN AN INSTANT

A Family's Journey of
Love and Healing

Lee and Bob Woodruff

 RANDOM HOUSE | NEW YORK

Published in the United States by Random House,
an imprint of The Random House Publishing Group,
a division of Random House, Inc., New York.

RANDOM HOUSE and colophon are registered
trademarks of Random House, Inc.

Except where noted, all photographs courtesy of
the Woodruff family.

Title-page photograph by Cathrine White

ISBN 978-1-4000-6667-4

Printed in the United States of America on acid-free paper

www.atrandom.com

9 8 7 6 5 4 3 2 1

FIRST EDITION

Book design by Dana Leigh Blanchette

To our four children, Macklin, Cathryn, Nora, and Claire.
Love is in the heart, not the head.

—MOM AND DAD

About This Book

Writing one book with two voices is a challenge, especially with your spouse. This manuscript began as my personal therapy over the summer. Throughout our marriage I have always picked up a pen when life got difficult or confusing. When Bob was injured, I began keeping a daily journal, knowing that the reporter in him would want to learn every detail of his time after his injury and during the early fog of his recovery.

As I began to write, it became clear that we had a story to tell. And it was obvious that there were places where Bob needed to tell the story in his words. There were numerous memories and feelings that only he had experienced.

Writing the book became part of Bob's therapy too. We remembered together. Sometimes I wrote what he dictated and he edited what I wrote. And while my voice and perspective appears more frequently on the pages, what we've ended up with, we hope, is a panoramic view of a marriage and a family, a crisis and a recovery.

The two perspectives are not so much a "he said/she said" as perhaps a little Mars/Venus. I'm the raw emotional writer who likes to dissect my feelings, and Bob's tendency as a journalist is to stick to the facts. Probing his emotions on the page did not always come naturally. "But how did you *feel*?" I often asked him when I read his sections. I sometimes got eye-rolling in response.

The fact that Bob could focus at all on writing the book, a mere seven months after his traumatic brain injury, is a testament to his will to recover and his persistence and determination to drive his own recovery.

What started as a therapeutic exercise for me, intended at first only for our family, has become something we both hope can inspire and help other families, who will find their own strength to rise to challenges, crises, and tragedies if their lives are upended—in an instant.

Lee Woodruff

IN AN INSTANT

Lee

Orlando, Florida, January 28, 2006

There is a ride at Disney World called the Tower of Terror, and on the weekend of January 28, 2006, my four children, even the twin five-year-olds, begged me to go on that ride over and over again.

Housed in a re-created aging Hollywood hotel, the ride begins where you climb into a creaky elevator that snakes its way through the creepy premises. An electrical storm kicks up, and right on cue something goes wrong with the power. The elevator in the eerie hotel suddenly drops. The descent is so rapid, so sudden, that it almost sucks your diaphragm up into your throat, and right before the drop there is a moment where you are literally suspended in air, too stunned to scream. It feels as if speed, motion, light, and time literally freeze.

We must have taken that ride a half dozen times. And then the feeling returned the following morning as I rolled over in my king-sized hotel bed. The day before, the kids and I had been to the Animal Kingdom in Disney World. We'd marveled at the African safari ride, ridden rapids in Asia, and gotten soaked as we howled our way down the man-made white water. After an early dinner we'd rented a pedal bike with another family and laughed until we cried as we raced other bikers around the lake, while fireworks from Epcot exploded overhead.

Tucking four kids into bed that night, I silently congratulated myself on a good weekend. I'd come to Disney to shoot a pilot TV show for

Family Fun. We'd spent two days on set and then the rest of the time had been the kids' reward: combing the parks for Disney character autographs for the twins and thrill-seeking rides for the older two. We'd planned to fly back home on Sunday and get ready for school.

Toting around four children by myself was not new. That weekend my husband, Bob Woodruff, the newly anointed co-anchor of ABC's *World News Tonight,* was thousands of miles away in Iraq. We spoke to him briefly that day, in between the safari and the rapids ride. He and his crew had had a tiring day covering the Palestinian elections before flying on to Baghdad in advance of President Bush's State of the Union address. The plan was to bolster ABC's Iraq coverage at an important moment in the war. The pace was blistering, common to any foreign correspondent who must keep moving and file stories from faraway places in time zones eight to twelve hours ahead of our own.

Bob and his crew were operating on an aggressive schedule with only a few hours' sleep each night. As usual, the itinerary was punishing. Get in, get the stories about the Iraqi military, anchor from Baghdad during Bush's address, do some pieces for *Good Morning America,* and, on the way back, try to finalize an interview with the King of Jordan in Amman, the Jordanian capital.

Our conversations with him from Disney World had been short and tough. The cell service in Iraq was spotty and the time difference was frustrating. We had one conversation midday Saturday, as he and his crew were going to bed in a military compound somewhere in Baghdad. He exhaustedly mumbled something about getting much-needed sleep the next day. Exactly what he said didn't register with me at the time. My daughter Cathryn was determined to buy a puka shell necklace. With my shoulder cradling the cell phone, I negotiated some cash from my wallet while keeping an eye on the twins, who were dangerously close to a fence in front of a bamboo grove.

Later, Bob would swear that he told me has was going to embed with the military for some exercises, while I would swear he said only that his team was going to relax for the day. At the end of our conversation I passed the cell phone around so the kids could say hi. This was common practice in our house—good-nights, kisses, homework help, all via satellite. When your father covers news around the world, the phone becomes a primary communication tool, for better or worse.

"Do you feel safe there?" I asked absentmindedly, collecting the change from Cathryn. "Are you okay?" It was a stupid rhetorical question, made more absurd by the fact that we were currently standing in Disney World, "the happiest place on earth," while he was somewhere in the most violent place on the planet.

"I do. We're surrounded by the military. It's fine," he reassured me. He and his cameraman, Doug Vogt, couldn't know that the elevator was about to drop. In the ocher-colored sands on a godforsaken highway outside Baghdad, they were about to enter their own Tower of Terror.

That night I called the front desk to request a 7 A.M. wake-up call. With the bigger kids sleeping next to the twins, perhaps I could slip downstairs the next morning and take a quick swim in the pool before breakfast. Even though it was January in Florida, the water was invigorating and it would be a great way to start our last day in Orlando.

In a few days Bob would be home and we'd be a family again. His new appointment as co-anchor had set a grueling pace for the past month, even the weekends. His days had been crammed with photo shoots, press conferences, and ad campaigns. The new program with Bob and Elizabeth Vargas was committed to go to the story, to have one anchor on the road and one in the studio as often as possible. Bob relished the challenge. It was a new era at ABC News. There was an excitement at the broadcast that was a welcome tonic after the months of sorrow following Peter Jennings's illness and then death from lung cancer. Bob and Elizabeth would give the news department something to rally around, after feeling like a ship without its beloved captain.

"Just get through January," I had told Bob, as he left for the Middle East on that fateful trip. It had become a kind of mantra for us after the announcement, as he shot out of the gate as a newly minted co-anchor.

"I really don't want to leave you guys," he said, as he leaned into the door frame of my home office, rolling suitcase in hand. He looked exhausted, distracted, and not eager to get back on a plane to return to

Iraq for the sixth or seventh time in three years. The town car was already idling in the driveway.

"Just get through January," I repeated, "and life will take on a more normal pattern. We'll have weekends again, and we can be a family."

He reeled off everything he'd packed, hoping I'd figure out what he might have missed. This was familiar territory, this nonchalant leaving. It should have had more weight, but to give it any more importance would have jinxed it in my mind. Pakistan, Afghanistan, Iraq, the Gaza Strip: give him a kiss as always, treat it like a normal morning, and he will come home safe and sound. I had a work deadline that day, and the sooner I got him on the road the faster I could finish my task.

Frankly, I didn't think a lot about Bob over the Disney weekend either. The days had been full and the kids eager to pack in as much as possible. Bob drew sustenance from being on the road; the stories, the energy, the adrenaline rejuvenated him. He loved being a journalist, and that meant leaving us for stretches of time. We may not have always liked it, but we had made peace with it as a family. Periods of being intensely together were interlaced with periods of being apart.

As I rolled over and turned off the bedside light that Saturday night in Disney World, I thought we would all rise to this new challenge of Bob's career as well. "Co-anchor." It was good and bad. Good because he had reached the pinnacle of his profession, a plum job in television news, a successor to one of broadcast journalism's icons. Bad because we would see him even less. Our definition of family time would need some revising.

The Sunday morning phone call pierced the quiet and I jolted awake to a bedspread of floral and chintz in a totally unfamiliar room. It took me a second to register where I was. Ah, right, I thought. Disney World. The wake-up call.

I rolled over and picked up the receiver. "Thank you," I said, and lazily began to set it back on the cradle. I had decided to lie there for a few more minutes before I snuck out the door.

"Lee?" A faint voice came from the receiver, now almost back in place. Geesh, I thought. Personalized wake-up calls, how very Disney. I brought the phone back to my ear to thank the man.

"Lee, it's David Westin," the voice said.

He had my immediate attention. My brain fired signals to my body as I bolted up on the pillows. The president of ABC News does not make social calls to employees' wives at 7 A.M. on a Sunday morning, even a co-anchor's wife. I licked my lips and swallowed. My mouth was dry.

"We've been trying to reach you," he said, in a slow measured voice. He stopped for a beat as if to gauge how he would say his next line. "Bob has been wounded in Iraq."

I sat straight up, trying to process the information I was hearing. Every synapse in my brain was firing. "Wounded?" I said to David Westin, as calmly as I could. "What do you mean *wounded*?"

"He was on an embed outside of Baghdad riding with the Iraqi army. We don't have a lot of information right now, Lee, but we are getting it as fast as we can. We are getting him the best care possible."

"David." I interrupted him. "Is my husband alive?"

"Yes, Lee. Bob is alive, but we believe he may have taken shrapnel to the brain."

I tried to digest what that meant and couldn't comprehend it. He was alive; I'd start with that. The rest was gravy.

"What was an anchor doing on a military exercise?" I asked, voice rising. "The last thing I knew he was doing a story about an ice cream shop in Baghdad. I thought they were sleeping!" My mind grasped for facts, searching for what I knew or thought I knew. I was back in the Tower of Terror.

You can't know how you would behave in a crisis until it drops out of the sky and knocks you down like a bandit: stealing your future, robbing you of your dreams, and mocking anything that resembles certainty. Sudden tragic events and even slow-burning disasters teach us more about ourselves than most of us care to know.

I felt the panic in my voice as I spoke to David Westin, and slow tears streamed down my face. At the same time, I began to feel a cool steely calm seep into my brain. It slowly formed a cocoon in which I could think and react rationally, disembodied from my emotions. In the months to come, this cocoon would allow me to handle the very public nature of this crisis, synthesize information, deal with teams of doctors, communicate with family, and take care of the business at hand without collapsing into a mass of spineless marrow.

For now, that steely calm began to morph into the part of me that became "the General." The General would make important decisions, hold things together for the troops, lead the charge, and—most important for our team—ensure we didn't lose a single man on the battlefield. The General was beginning to take over.

"Lee, we have a plane waiting to take you and the kids home to Westchester," David said. "You just have to tell us what time. It's fueled up and ready to go."

I felt I needed to keep him on the line for some reason. I wasn't ready to start making decisions. I didn't want to take my first step into this new world. I wanted to relish my old life for just a minute more. All four of my children were blissfully sound asleep beyond my door. Inside my room their secure little lives were being hacked apart while they dreamed, oblivious to the chaos.

"Okay," I said in a small voice. "Tell me what you know. Please tell me what happened."

"Bob and the crew were traveling on a road in Taji on a routine ride," David said. "Bob was in an Iraqi armored vehicle. We believe he was doing a stand-up at the time, and they were hit by an IED [improvised explosive device] in an orchestrated attack on the convoy. There was gunfire after that, but neither man was hit. Bob and the cameraman, Doug Vogt, have been taken by helicopter to Baghdad and are going into surgery.

"Apparently he asked Vinnie, his producer, if he was alive; he did come to." David spoke coolly and rationally, but he was clearly rattled.

So he spoke, I thought. He spoke. This is going to be okay. The General in my brain dictated that nothing less than recovery would be acceptable. There were no other options. Bob would be okay. He was always okay. He was lucky and bright and hardworking and a good man. Things like this didn't happen to good people. I could feel hope in my heart, on its simplest level, as clear and bright as the streak of a shooting star. Hope is the most basic human emotion. It was the hope that wives have had since the days of the caveman, when they sent their mates out past the campfire to fight marauding tribes. Hope was good. It was a brain-stem reaction. The General in my brain moved hope into the front lines, preparing for the next maneuver.

"Lee," David gently reminded me, "there are security people on the ground to escort you out of there. The plane is standing by; you just need to tell us what you want to do. Let us know what time you want to go. When you get home, we are working on getting you to Germany, where Bob will be transported."

For one moment the silliest thought flashed through my mind. I thought about how much my kids had wanted to ride the Soarin' attraction and see the rest of Epcot. The part of my brain that was still in shock weighed the option of not ruining their perfectly planned morning for about a tenth of a second before I clicked into action.

"David, let me process this," I said. "I have to call Bob's folks and my family, and then I have to wake up the kids and pack. And I need to think. Let me just get outside of this hotel room so I can talk, and then I'll call you back as soon as possible."

I slipped on some clothes and grabbed my cell phone. No one stirred on the pull-out couch or in the second bedroom. Four innocent heads dreamed kid dreams. I sucked in my breath and eased the door shut behind me. How would I tell them their father had been hurt in Iraq? Was there a right way to do this? It was all their worst fears boiled down into one phone call.

There was a small lake outside of our hotel, and I immediately set off around it at a fast pace, heart racing, lungs pulling in fresh air. I dialed the number for Bob's parents' house without thinking through what I would say.

"Hello?" Bob's mother, Frannie, answered on the first ring, her voice slightly tense. It was 7:20 A.M. on a Sunday.

"Mom?" I said.

"What's wrong?" she asked immediately. After seventeen years, my mother-in-law could read my voice almost as well as her son's. Days later, one of Bob's brothers reminded me it had been their dad's birthday.

"Bob has been hit in Iraq and he may have taken shrapnel to the brain," I said matter-of-factly. The General was in full swing. I was already thinking ahead to the next call. I had completed one lap around the lake already and was keeping my voice low as I passed other joggers and early morning walkers.

"Oh, God," Frannie said. It was half moan, half cry. It was the visceral pain a parent feels when something tragic happens to a child, the upending of the natural order of the universe. Then my mother-in-law's own inner General took over. It was the last time I would hear or see anything resembling weakness. She was a master at pulling it together. This was a woman who had raised four boys with sports teams and ER visits, crazy schedules and reams of laundry. She'd gotten them all into navy-blue blazers for Sunday-night country club dinners. Yet somehow she never let anyone see her sweat.

Frannie would call Bob's brothers, so I moved on to my family, with a simple plan for fanning out information. I would make only two calls and then get back to the room to pull us out of here. I was on lap two or three around the lake. Moving felt better than inertia. It felt like I was taking action.

Bob's elder brother, Dave, heard the news from his mother and collapsed on the kitchen floor with a cry. Brother Mike, the third son, heard the news on NPR while driving in Ann Arbor, Michigan, with his cell phone turned off. He headed immediately to his parents' house in the Detroit suburbs. Youngest brother Jimmy was setting up a ski race course for his sports marketing company at the X Games in Aspen. Frannie Woodruff called while he was in the shower. When he saw the message on the phone Jimmy instinctively knew it was about Bob. He turned on the TV and saw a photo of our family flash on the screen. From the moment they first heard the news, each brother began a journey toward Bob and our family that would spin a web of love and protection around us for months to come.

I called my own parents next. They were calm and rational and concerned. They would call my two sisters. Calls begot calls. Aunts, uncles, dear friends, cousins: like a dye spreading through tissue, the horrible news began to trickle out to the people we loved.

As I rounded the edge of the lake, my cell phone lit up. It was Melanie Bloom, the one person I knew in the world who could understand what I was going through. Her husband, David Bloom, an NBC correspondent and good friend, had been embedded with the army during the 2003 invasion of Baghdad. He had died of a pulmonary embolism on Iraqi soil. Melanie understood the cost of being married to a journalist. She was also the only person outside of Disney World who knew what hotel I was in. We'd had a long chat on the phone the evening before, as I had watched my kids swim in the pool.

"Lee," Mel said, in her breathy, almost Marilyn Monroe voice. For her, this must have felt like raking up all the pain of her own initial phone call about David three years earlier. This was, as she and I used to say so many times after her husband died, a "fresh hell."

"Mel." I collapsed into tears. "Can you believe this? What is happening? I'm outside, and right now I have to go back in and get my kids up. I have to tell my kids. How did you do this?" I moaned.

"Lee, it's going to be okay. It will be okay. Bob is going to be all right, I can feel it." Mel began calming me down. "One foot in front of the other," she said. "Just take one task at a time. First you have to pack, and then you tell the kids."

I called David Westin back at home. I figured I could get out in an hour and a half. I'd need to give the kids some food, talk to them, and get on the road. I silently congratulated myself for having organized our things the night before and laid out some clothes. I would need to appear as calm and in control as possible. No matter what size blaze was raging around us, I was determined my children would not smell smoke.

"We're having a hard time keeping a lid on the story, Lee," David told me. "We're going to need to release it to the media." It was already midafternoon in Iraq. The attack had happened around noon; surely Baghdad was already buzzing with the news. The media was only holding off in deference to the family.

"Go ahead," I said, understanding a firestorm might follow. "Our two families have been told."

"Okay," David replied, his voice heavy. It would be a dreadful and emotional day at ABC bureaus all around the world, and David Westin knew it.

"David, what do I say to the kids? I have to go tell the kids now." A wail began to creep up the base of my throat. I was circling a set of stairs right outside the hotel entrance, and was crying softly. A fresh wave of morning walkers with coffee cups eyed me with skepticism, no doubt convinced I was a hysterical type, a woman with a hormone imbalance.

"Do you want to talk to Sherrie?" David's wife was a onetime PR person for ABC who worked at Sesame Workshop. I knew her to be a calm, measured person. Surely she'd know what to say, I reasoned.

David handed the phone to Sherrie. She outlined a strategy for dealing with my two different-aged pairs of kids and gave me some phrases that would let the kids know it was serious but that I was in control. Her empathetic yet confident voice made me cry again. I felt terror rising in my throat but the General choked it back. I hung up and proceeded to the hotel elevator. I took a deep breath as it rose and marveled that this was actually happening. My husband had been hit by a bomb in Iraq. I was about to tell my children. I let out my breath, feeling a pressing weight as the elevator doors opened and I headed back to our room.

Bob

Taji, Iraq, January 28, 2006

Heavy rains had turned the dung-colored earth into a thick ankle-sucking mud at Camp Taji, one of the largest military staging areas in Iraq. Everywhere we stepped, our boots were covered in an ocher-brown paste. The landscape surrounding the base was flat and desolate and each building looked much like the next. There were few trees, and although the base was located close to the town of Taji the area seemed more like a large village surrounded by wide, chaotically busy roads.

The army base, about ten miles northwest of downtown Baghdad, had been an old Iraqi facility that the Americans had taken over and refurbished after the invasion. It boasted the largest post exchange, or PX, in Iraq, with a Subway, Burger King, and Pizza Hut on the premises. The newly built dining facility offered soldiers a remarkable array of food, given the circumstances, and a new gym gave the men a place to work out, watch movies, and play games.

The soldiers' quarters were in air-conditioned and heated trailers; the temperatures fluctuate to extremes in Iraq, from blistering heat to chilling desert cold during the winter months. You don't actually see the cold because the landscape remains forever the same, dusty and flat, during every season of the year.

This was my fifth time in Iraq since the invasion in 2003, and the situation had changed dramatically since the heady days of riding in tanks into Baghdad to topple the government. Central Iraq, especially, had continued to degenerate into a dangerous region for coalition forces and Iraqis alike.

Along with my three crew members, I had spent the night on the base as an embed, as reporters living among the military were called, in preparation to go out with the Raider Brigade, part of the army's Fourth Infantry Division, for a day of observation. For the past six days I had been traveling with Vinnie Malhotra, a New York–based producer; our Canadian-born cameraman, Doug Vogt; and Magnus Macedo, our Brazilian soundman. With President Bush's 2006 State of the Union address just two days away, the war in Iraq would be center stage. At ABC News we wanted to get a first-hand look at the handover of U.S. military activities to the Iraqi forces.

Vinnie Malhotra and I had worked together for a long time. He was the son of Indian immigrants, but Vinnie was as American as the Gap. Although I often treated him like a kid brother, he was sharp as a tack and ambitious, a solid producer with a wonderful sense of humor. On the road we kept up a comfortable and often humorous banter.

Our first assignment together had been in Pakistan after the September 11 terrorist attacks, and later that fall we moved to Kabul, Afghanistan, living in a small house on the outskirts of the city and covering the events after 9-11.

Vinnie had spent years as a producer largely for Peter Jennings, but he began to work with me when I was on the road. We had made several trips together to Iraq, winning an Emmy Award for our coverage of the state of southern Iraq. Doug Vogt had been our cameraman for that assignment and we had fanned out around the southern region of the country, which in those days was much easier to do. We had traveled by car from city to city, checking into hotels and interviewing people we met on the streets. The extreme sectarian violence that was such a hallmark of present-day Iraq had not begun in earnest.

Vinnie had traveled extensively with me, covering the shuttle launch at the Kennedy Space Center in Florida and Pope John Paul II's death in Rome. I had also worked with Doug numerous times. Doug was one of the best cameramen—or "shooters," as they are known—in the business. He intellectualized a story and knew instinctively what to shoot. He had accompanied me on my third trip to Iraq in 2003. Doug was smart and reserved, with a soft Canadian accent we loved to imitate. At age forty-six he was a tennis fanatic and had beaten me handily in a hard-fought tennis match in Quetta, Pakistan, just before the U.S. invasion of Afghanistan. Ironically, shortly after our competition, the hotel was attacked by a mob angered at our coverage of the Taliban.

Our soundman, Magnus Macedo, was a charming, charismatic, always smiling Brazilian. I had never heard Magnus utter a negative word about anyone. He seemed intrinsically happy and his longish curly hair made him a chick magnet.

At bars the women always seemed to find Magnus. When I reported from North Korea in 2005, Magnus was my soundman. He was dedicated and hardworking, and his Brazilian roots had taught him never to miss a good party.

We had come to Baghdad, having just covered the Palestinian elections, where the Hamas party had unexpectedly defeated the rival Fatah party. The Palestinian elections were exhilarating; breaking a story like this was everything that made me love what I did for a living. The chance to be in the moment while history was being made was the reason I had switched careers from lawyer to journalist fifteen years before. The previous night, as I walked among the triumphant people celebrating on the street with Hamas, yelling slogans and pumping their fists in the air in excitement, I marveled again that I was actually paid to do what I loved.

We hit the ground running in Baghdad and put together what would turn out to be my last news piece for over a year. It was a story about a Baghdad ice cream shop, of all things, a slice of real life in the midst of a chaotic and violent city. With many news stories about the horrors of war, there is no real context for Americans to get a sense of what daily life is like for the Iraqis, and we wanted to find a way to convey that. This little ice cream shop was an oasis in a land pockmarked by war. It was a simple story, an example of how life goes on. Over time, the shop had had some close calls; car bombs had exploded mere blocks away. But in the evening, Iraqi families gathered there with their kids and shared an ice cream, and for that brief moment they could try to forget that they were standing in the middle of the worst war zone the world had seen in a long time. It was an unexpected story of resilience amid a terrible backdrop. We fed the story to *World News Tonight* and set our minds ahead to the next day.

Arriving at the bureau sometime after midnight, we prepared for our trip with the military the next morning. We each grabbed body armor from a pile on the floor of the Baghdad office. Doug had his own helmet and flak jacket that he carried into every war zone. I grabbed a helmet and flak jacket with a neck guard. Somehow, the next day, too tired to think much about it, I would end up with a different jacket, the one with no neck guard that I was wearing when the convoy was attacked.

It had been nearly two years since I had last been to Iraq, and much had changed. I needed to get up to speed quickly. I was to anchor a live broadcast from Iraq around President Bush's State of the Union address, while Fareed Zakaria, international editor for *Newsweek* and an ABC political analyst, would provide political commentary and act as a sounding board for questions. Elizabeth Vargas would anchor from Washington, D.C., with George Stephanopoulos providing in-depth analysis at that end. I felt considerable pressure to take in as much as possible during our short time on the ground.

On Saturday, January 28, at Camp Taji, I interviewed Colonel James Pasquarette, commander of the First Brigade Combat Team of the Fourth Infantry Division, at the base in Taji. Under the colonel's command, American soldiers were fanned out among the Iraqi army as "military transition teams," a kind of advisory unit. These small groups of Americans lived and worked with the Iraqi units, helping to speed their evolution into an effective fighting force. Due to the violence in that area, the American soldiers often would have to assume the lead with certain tasks, but they were working hard to pass day-to-day security over to the local Iraqis.

In order to see as much of this cooperation as possible firsthand, we would travel with the military and watch their daily rounds. I am a firm believer that to cover a story you have to get out in the field and see it with your own eyes. We needed to know what the military was thinking about their circumstances. We wanted the best possible assessment of how effectively the Iraqi troops were assuming responsibility for the security of their own country. We were looking for concrete examples of the cooperation between U.S. and Iraqi troops. The American troops felt positive that Taji was a good model for what the rest of the country could become. American troops were letting the Iraqis take the front seat in the security of the country.

In one instance, the American soldiers had the name of someone in the village who they believed was running guns into Taji. The Iraqi soldiers had been ineffective in shaking people down, so the Americans felt they had to take the lead. The advisers started grabbing civilians and asking questions through the translator. There was a clear intimidation factor when U.S. soldiers were asking the questions, and it seemed to get better results.

Driving along the road, we saw the dead body of an Iraqi man. We were told that he was a bus driver, an informant for the U.S. Army who had been shot forty-five times. He was soon dragged in front of an Iraqi police station as a somber warning, and by the time we circled back to the area the man's body had been put in a crude coffin and placed in the outer courtyard of the police station. There was a long trail of blood leaking out from the coffin's seams and the Iraqis were rounding up suspects. The American troops had surrounded the Iraqis so they would not be harmed. I went over to try to talk to some of the suspects through a translator. Each one assured me of his innocence.

The sun was dropping and at about 6 P.M. we finally stopped filming and headed back to the base, where I bought a black long-sleeved nylon shirt and some new Ray-Ban sunglasses, since I was constantly losing mine. My ability to misplace things like keys, sunglasses, and passports had long been a joke with my family and was fast becoming one with my crew as well. Our group turned in at about 11 P.M., and we joked that the next six hours of sleep would be the most we had gotten in an entire week.

Bob

Taji, Iraq, January 29, 2006

Early the next morning we four packed our gear in an SUV and drove to the mess hall. We were in great spirits. We had gotten some terrific interviews from the soldiers and we'd gained a greater understanding of what was happening on the ground on the eve of the president's speech, where we knew he would address the issue of training Iraqi troops for an ultimate handover at this critical juncture of the war.

Over breakfast we talked about how much footage we already had and how we probably didn't really need to do this final part of the embed. But we had pushed hard for access to the military and the Fourth Infantry Division had been gracious enough to set up this opportunity for us on short notice. They had gone out of their way to make room for our crew, and it would have been rude, we thought, to have canceled on this last leg. Besides, we were relying on a military helicopter to take us back to Camp Victory in Baghdad that afternoon. We would get some last shots and interviews on the road to Taji and get back to Baghdad to cram for the live State of the Union broadcast. I needed to memorize notes, information, and talking points. I was nervous but excited by the challenge. Broadcasting live during big events is like the Super Bowl of TV news. You need to be firing on all cylinders and access information immediately.

That morning the military wanted to take us to an Iraqi water treatment plant, which provided fresh water for the

IN AN INSTANT | 19

town. Insurgents had attacked the facility while it was under U.S. protection and now it was in the hands of the Iraqi soldiers, who were doing a good job of securing it. A huge hole had been blasted through the center of the plant by a rocket-propelled grenade and the station grounds were muddy. It was the first time the sun had shone in a week.

"Man, I hate driving over this shit. You never know what's underneath there," the driver of our Humvee muttered under his breath. We knew he meant improvised explosive devices, or IEDs. The insurgents had been clever about placing these bombs, and the number of IED blasts had ratcheted up in the past few months. The men had good reason to be jittery. I was too.

I interviewed the Iraqi in charge of the mission that day and he seemed confident in the Iraqis' ability to secure their own facilities in and around Taji. I knew that to some degree he was underplaying the level of danger and violence. I also saw that he was a proud Iraqi commander and appreciative of the American efforts to help them.

Doug wanted to walk out toward the road to film the treatment plant from another angle. Immediately First Sergeant John McFarland and another soldier walked over to Doug and Vinnie, guns up, to scan the area. They seemed unusually tense about any one of us being in an open space and searched the tops of nearby buildings with their eyes. When Doug and Vinnie came back off the road, the soldiers seemed to relax.

Our convoy continued on its planned route, stopping at another water access point and then on to a checkpoint along another corridor, where a great deal of control had been turned over to the Iraqi army. The next step was to take a drive down a dual carriageway road toward the town of Taji, which was one of the success stories for the military.

The road was being patrolled by the American Fourth Battalion, along with the First Brigade, Ninth Iraqi Army

Division, and it had been a major IED attack area. With an aggressive coalition campaign to root out insurgents, intelligence had improved in the area and it was now considered a successful example. The road was still pocked with blast craters, and we were warned to keep our protective gear on at all times. We were told that an advance team had just swept the road minutes earlier for IEDs. It would be a five- or six-minute ride and we decided I would try to do a stand-up—where the reporter talks on camera—as we rolled along. I wanted to be on top, where some of the Iraqi soldiers rode.

Waiting at the checkpoint, I saw Iraqi vehicles patrolling the street and I began peppering the commander with questions.

"What are those APCs doing?" I asked. "Is it possible to go in one?" That way I could talk to Iraqi soldiers patrolling the highways. This was where the rubber met the road in terms of the handover. This was the critical part of the story that was impossible to tell from sitting in the Green Zone or even from an American Humvee.

Each Iraqi brigade mixed old Soviet tanks with smaller armored personnel carriers, or APCs, mostly holdovers from Cold War days. When Saddam Hussein had been in power, he had had warehouses of tank parts, but they had been ransacked and destroyed during the invasion. Now much of the army's efforts were spent keeping these old dinosaurs running in the desert sands. But with their hulking metal frames and mounted guns, they were still an imposing sight for the enemy and usually had the desired effect.

Major Bill Taylor green-lighted our decision to ride in an Iraqi vehicle to get a view of what was happening through the eyes of the Iraqi troops on patrol. Doug fixed a camera on the front of the tank, and Major Taylor placed an Iraqi interpreter in the vehicle with us to help translate for the soldiers. One Iraqi soldier manned a mounted gun in the right hatch.

Doug and I decided we would position ourselves together in the left hatch when we came up above.

All four of us climbed into the darkness of the tank. The doors closed and the vehicle started its slow rumbling forward.

With the tank in motion, Doug climbed up through the hatch with his other camera and realized with a jolt that as the convoy vehicles had peeled off from the jumbled mass, our Iraqi vehicle was now in the lead. He yelled down into the hatch to let us know. We were all surprised and even concerned, as this was not standard procedure for journalists traveling with the military.

I had hoped to do a stand-up in the top of the hatch where I would speak and Doug would film as we were moving, but Magnus warned me that the roar of the diesel engine might override my voice on the sound track. Doug and I decided to give it a try and, at the very least, get some pictures of the Iraqi soldiers on top of the vehicle. I climbed up to the top of the APC to survey the road. As expected, it was tough to compete with the rumble of the engine. I popped back down into the hatch to confer with Magnus and Vinnie about the sound. We looked at some digital pictures Vinnie and I had taken. I climbed back up onto the second hatch; on the opposite side of the tank an Iraqi soldier sat watching the road. Magnus was having some issues with his sound equipment, so I went down below again and came back up next to Doug to confer with him. Doug was filming the Iraqi soldier in the front of the tank and I was behind Doug, gazing straight ahead. Doug remembers that the interpreter was advising us to go below as we were approaching a stand of palm trees where insurgents had positioned themselves. I have no recollection of that conversation.

All told, we had traveled only three miles or so when there was a giant explosion, a deafening, horrific blast that rocked the tank. What the hell was that? was the first thought Vinnie and Magnus had below, followed quickly by the certain knowledge of what it was.

Hidden behind some trees, a band of Iraqi insurgents had detonated a crude roadside bomb with a remote-controlled device. The IED was a 155-millimeter shell, one of the biggest artillery shells available. Often a vehicle merely running over a bomb will initiate the blast, but this was a well-planned complex attack. The bomb was set off to the side, on the left of the roadway, about three to five yards from the tank. Rocks and stones had been packed around the shell in the dirt to magnify the damage.

Hundreds of rocks shot upward with the force of bullets. The white heat of the firepower ripped through the air like an apocalypse. The explosion shot up and under the tank, powerfully showering the side of the vehicle, the angle of the blast effectively saving our lives as most of the shrapnel flew over our heads.

I took a direct hit to the left side of my head and upper body. More than a hundred little rocks and countless fragments of black dirt were blasted into my face, peppered around my eyes, tattooed onto the bridge of my nose and ear, and shot into my jaw and under the helmet. One marble-sized rock sheared off the bottom of my jawbone, cracked two teeth, and entered the soft flesh of my neck. A second marble-sized rock ripped into my cheek and up into my sinus, coming to rest up against the eggshell-thin bone of the eye socket. Another rock tore into the chin strap of my helmet, blowing it off my head and into the sand several yards away. The force of the blast was so strong that it crushed my skull bone over the left temporal lobe of my brain. Small shards of my cranium were driven into the outer surface of my brain, and the force was so great that my left eyeball was slightly displaced in the socket.

Three large rocks and dozens of smaller ones shot under my flak jacket in the back by the armhole, slicing into the flesh and cartilage of my scapula like tiny dulled knives, coming to rest just a millimeter from my chest wall, heart, and lungs.

Doug was still filming as his skull absorbed the concussive blast from the front, but his helmet stayed on. The force of a giant rock slamming into his helmet shattered his skull. Only a few rocks hit Doug, though, as the force of the blast slammed him onto the top of the tank on his back. In shock from the concussion, he could not move and lay staring up at the blue cloudless sky. The Iraqi soldier riding at the front of the tank had one of his hands blown off.

Below the hatch, Magnus had been holding Doug's legs as he filmed. The blast caused Magnus to fall back and lose his grip. Vinnie and Magnus looked at each other for a split second and screamed. Doug's camera fell down into the hatch and instantly Vinnie looked up and saw my body sway and crumple down into the tank in a kind of macabre slow motion, blood streaming down my face. As I fell into the vehicle, my helmetless head and the back of my neck ricocheted off the hard metal on the sides of the hatch like a child's rubber ball.

Vinnie grabbed me by the flak jacket and began screaming, "Open your eyes, Bob! Bob, open your eyes for me!"

Omar, the translator, who had lived through dozens of IED blasts, yelled at Vinnie to cover my neck with his hands where a giant shrapnel hole was pumping out blood. Seconds after the bomb went off I was completely unconscious and Vinnie, unsure if I was even alive, immediately followed instructions. The sound of Omar's commanding voice snapped him out of shock and pressed him into action.

Outside the tank, the convoy was now engaged in a complex attack. This was increasingly becoming a signature maneuver of the insurgents; they would set off an IED to draw the troops out to help the wounded and then barrage the scene with small-arms fire and rocket-propelled grenades.

Other army vehicles immediately circled our personnel carrier to protect it, and some of the soldiers hopped out to fire back. Major Taylor's men began driving the insurgents back with weapons and another group of Iraqi soldiers took the lead, peeling off on foot to go after the enemy.

Although the vehicles had circled our own, it was several minutes before the arms fire was under control enough for the soldiers to come to our aid. Doug could still not move. Pinned on top of the tank, he was semiconscious and bleeding from the head. Magnus, terrified that Doug would be hit in the gunfight, climbed up the hatch to pull him in.

On the hard floor of the APC I suddenly came to, opened my eyes very wide, and began spitting blood as I tried to focus. There was so much blood on the left side of my head that Vinnie told me later it looked like syrup. He could see only my left eyeball through the blood. Vinnie remembered later how odd it had seemed that blood in such massive quantities looked black and not red.

My eyes opened and closed again, and I rolled to the side and spat out more blood. Vinnie was still bravely trying to stanch the blood from the gaping wound on my neck.

"Put your hands on his neck," screamed the Iraqi interpreter again. "Stop the blood with your hand and push against the vein."

Vinnie kept screaming at me to stay awake. He was convinced I was dying.

"You're going to be okay!" Vinnie and Magnus shouted at me. Pinned inside, Doug remained in shock, staring straight ahead. The two hatches were open on top and Magnus and Vinnie could hear gunfire all around. Our only way out was the back hatch, which remained closed as the firefight raged on outside. Until the situation was stabilized, no one could get to us.

There was yelling all around outside the tank. Many of

the soldiers in the division were new arrivals and this was their first conflict experience. It was chaos and confusion, blood and tissue, adrenaline and the smell of gunfire and fear.

Relief overtook Vinnie's rising panic when a Bradley vehicle pulled up next to the APC. John McFarland suddenly opened the back hatch of the APC. "Bring him out, bring him out now!" he yelled. Omar helped Vinnie pull me out of the tank, one man carrying my feet and the other my head. It was a painstaking process, given my wounds, but within a few minutes I was safely on the other side of the vehicle, in and out of consciousness on the ground, lying in a patch of sunlight on a litter. Magnus helped Doug, who by now could walk on his own.

"Medic, we need a medic," Vinnie shouted. "Get a medic!"

"We don't have a medic. There is no medic," answered a soldier nearby.

Another soldier atop the closest Humvee, holding an M-4 rifle, looked over and said calmly, "Just keep talking to him. Keep the words coming. Just keep talking to him to keep him conscious." He was only about nineteen or twenty but spoke in such a measured, authoritative voice that it allowed Vinnie to focus. It was the only thing that made sense to him in the midst of all of that chaos.

"Stay with me. You're going to be okay," Vinnie said. I began to come to again, and the reality and confusion of what had happened hit me hard. "You are going to be okay, you are going to be okay," said Vinnie, leaning over me.

Suddenly, awake again and confused, I began to scream. "Am I alive?"

"Yes, you are alive," Vinnie screamed back. "Hang in there, you are going to be okay." At the time, Vinnie didn't really believe that. We were in the middle of a gunfight on a godforsaken dusty Iraqi road. I was bleeding profusely; we were miles from the closest hospital and scared as hell.

"What happened?" I screamed.

"It was a bad accident," Vinnie replied, squeezing my hand to keep me focused. "Stay with me, you'll be okay."

The blood on my head and neck was cascading down my body. I began to feel the pain of my wounds and as I reached up toward Vinnie I saw the blood on me, everywhere, and it scared me.

"This hurts," I screamed, kicking my legs and flailing on the ground. "This fucking hurts." I tried to stand but Vinnie held me down.

"We need to kick somebody's ass," I yelled, as gunfire rang out somewhere in the distance.

It was a ridiculous thing to say, given my position, but a trace of a smile crossed Vinnie's face. Bob is still in there, he thought, and fighting back. If we can just keep him alive until we get medical attention. But there was so much damned blood, Vinnie thought. So much blood. It was now pooling on the litter. It was on everything. Vinnie knew he would see my blood in his nightmares for years to come.

"We're getting you out of here, buddy." Vinnie squeezed my hand again.

I rolled over on my left side, the injured side, and rolled back immediately, screaming in pain and spitting more blood. My orthopedic surgeon told me later that he could have put his entire fist through the hole in my back. Vinnie had not known I even had a wound on my scapula, he was so focused on stopping the blood pouring out of my head and neck.

"Oh, no, oh, no," I moaned, watching blood stream from my mouth. To Vinnie, I seemed unusually calm. I kept trying to pick myself up, spitting blood again and again and pulling my knees to my chest in a fetal position to deal with the pain.

Soon after that I passed out, and for more than a month I would be completely unaware of anything that was happening around me. My mind would journey to a place that to this day I cannot describe or even remember.

Lee

Orlando, Florida, January 29, 2006

As soon as I came down the hallway back to my hotel room, my twelve-year-old daughter, Cathryn, rushed toward me, a look of spooked panic in her eyes. "Where have you been, Mommy? Has anything happened to Dad?"

"Why?" I said, in my calmest mommy voice.

"Well, the phone kept ringing and woke us up. Alix called from *Family Fun* and asked if you were all right, and then Melanie called and said she is praying for you and loves you," she said breathlessly. With loving honey-brown eyes, a huge heart, and long coltish legs, Cathryn was her father's daughter.

"Come on," I said. "Let's get out of the hallway and into the room."

"Mom, tell me," she demanded, planting her feet.

"Let's get Mack first," I reasoned. Miraculously, the twins were still asleep on the pull-out couch. This would make my life easier, as our two teams of kids, as Bob called them, Team A and Team B, were six years apart. The dialogue between the two teams would be very different.

Mack, our fourteen-year-old, was awake and studying my face as I walked in. I began talking immediately.

"Guys, Dad has been hurt in Iraq. He was riding in a tank with the army and something blew up. We don't have a lot of information, but he is getting some great medical care."

"Is he alive?" Cathryn asked. Her eyes narrowed a bit.

"Yes, absolutely," I said immediately. "I think your dad is going to be fine. He's tough, he's a fighter. And I have a feeling in my heart that everything is going to be okay, I really do. But we're going to pack up and leave now to get back home."

"Mom?" Mack asked softly, rolling over in bed to look straight at me. "Is Dad really going to be okay?"

My words stuck in my throat. I never wanted to lie to my children or give them unrealistic hope. "I believe Dad will be okay, Mack. He has some wounds, but they are treating them. And your dad always thinks about safety. I'm sure he had on his helmet and all of his gear, so whatever happened he was protected as much as he could be."

Mack grabbed the remote and flipped on the TV, which just happened to be set to CNN. As if on cue, the blond anchor said, "ABC anchor Bob Woodruff was wounded in Iraq with cameraman Doug Vogt." A picture of Bob flashed up on the screen. I rushed to the TV and turned it off. It was the last time I would watch the news, or any other TV program, for months.

My cell phone started ringing almost immediately, with calls from friends and colleagues. I turned it off so I could take action. I had four children to pack up and get out of Disney World. I had two children who still had no idea about their daddy's grave injuries, and then I had to get on a plane for Germany that evening, devising some kind of plan for the kids' care in my wake. The clock was running down.

I left Mack and Cathryn in charge of getting the twins dressed. Then I jumped in the shower. Something about the solitude of the big tiled bathroom and the huge luxurious shower stall terrified me. With the door shut my resolve began to fade. I began to sob quietly as the running water masked the sound.

All at once the bathroom door jerked open and Cathryn came in and saw my face. Hard as I tried to pull myself together, her own calm broke and she began to cry.

"Mommy, you're crying," she wailed in a terrified voice. "Are you telling us everything? I thought you said Dad was going to be okay."

"I believe so, sweetie, I really do. But this is scary for Mom, and we are far away from home right now. I'm sad and I wish Dad were here. Everybody needs to have a good cry when something happens, Cath. Now go and help the girls get dressed so we can get on the road, okay?"

Stepping out of the shower I looked hard at myself in the mirror. I saw sad eyes staring back, red-rimmed from crying. I needed to stay strong, I told my reflection. I needed to make the kids feel I was in charge. My job now was to get them back home. From there, I thought, we'd come up with another plan, take the next step.

Lee

New York, January 29, 2006

Bob was already in his black unconscious state. The rest of his news crew and colleagues back at ABC headquarters, however, were in the midst of a crisis. And Bob was the story, as the news spread quickly by television and Internet.

At about 1 P.M. Baghdad time, Kate Felsen, an ABC News senior producer who had been with Bob in Baghdad, reached Martha Raddatz, ABC's senior White House correspondent and previously the network's Pentagon reporter. Martha was one of the most connected journalists in the business when it came to the military. She was also a personal friend.

Kate briefed Martha on what she knew about the attack. "Bob, Doug, Vinnie, and Magnus were on an embed and they were hit by an IED," she said. "It's bad."

"I'll get right on it," Martha said immediately, and dug up some private numbers. Although she would never take credit for it, in those early hours, Martha helped ensure that Doug and Bob were afforded the same lightning-quick care normally given to the military.

Martha felt sick to her stomach. This was a tough story for her, a friend, to be on. Her first call was to General Pete Chiarelli, commanding general for all U.S. forces in Baghdad. Her second call was to General George W. Casey, Jr., the overall strategic commander, a four-star general.

Chiarelli told her that both men had been transferred from Taji to a combat support hospital in Baghdad, where they would be assessed and then flown to a field hospital in Balad that handled severe casualties. He also told her Bob's Glasgow Coma Scale, a routine test performed on

head-injury patients as soon as they reach the hospital to assess neurological function. Although Bob's scale was between 3 and 4 out of a possible 15, General Chiarelli seemed mildly hopeful. Martha made a few
more calls to people in high places.

"The report I gave you about Bob," began the general a short time
later on the phone to Martha, "it is not looking so good now. I think
it's very bad." General Chiarelli spoke carefully and slowly. "He was
hit in the head and the shoulder." Martha's stomach turned over. She'd
been to Iraq dozens of times and understood the fate of most of the
soldiers who suffered head injuries. They called these men "the walking wounded." Most often the scars were invisible, but the damage inside the brain was permanent. It had become the signature wound of
this war.

Kate Felsen called Martha back in Washington at about 2:30 Baghdad
time. She was at the Baghdad hospital in the Green Zone and had had a
glimpse of Bob and Doug as they were being rushed into surgery. She
was sobbing on the phone.

Clark Bentson, another producer traveling with Bob who was with
Kate at the hospital, remarked that there were so many tubes and so
much dried blood on Bob's head that he looked horribly burned. "Doug
is going to be fine, just fine," a nurse reassured Kate and Clark over and
over. No one was saying anything about Bob. A colonel asked Clark if he
had permission to make life-and-death decisions about him.

Back in the *Good Morning America* studios in New York's Times
Square, Kate Snow and Bill Weir, weekend anchors, had begun broad-
casting the Sunday edition. It was 7 A.M. in New York and 3 P.M. in
Baghdad.

Suddenly, Snow heard executive producer John Green's voice in her
ear with the news about the attack. She struggled to maintain some
composure as she began to deliver the news on the air. Kate and her
husband, Chris, were friends and neighbors of ours, and our children
played together. She fought back the urge to cry. She and Bill were visibly shaken.

In Washington that morning, *This Week* with George Stephanopoulos was gearing up to go on the air after *Good Morning America*. George

heard the news in the Washington bureau and immediately called home to his wife, Ali Wentworth, breaking down as he told her what he knew.

Back in the New York studio, Diane Sawyer and countless others had come in early on that Sunday morning after hearing the news. Diane sat silently watching the monitor with the rest of the newsroom, waiting for information. Like everyone else, she would tell me later that she was stunned by the horror and magnitude of what had happened.

From the moment he broke the news to me at Disney World, David Westin began a chain of regular e-mail updates to the concerned ABC staff. From that point forward, he would work to keep everyone informed, while at the same time protecting our family's privacy as well as that of the Vogts.

There was a feeling among the entire broadcast community that day that blended respect, horror, and reverence. For anyone who had spent time in Iraq or any other place of conflict or danger, there was a response I would hear repeated so many times from Bob's colleagues: "That could so easily have been me."

Back in Balad, Vinnie and Magnus had finally made it to the hospital where Bob and Doug had been quickly flown by helicopter from Baghdad. They were still covered in Bob's and Doug's blood. Shortly after they arrived, insurgents began shelling the Balad hospital with mortars. The attack continued while doctors were operating on Bob. Now that the two men were patients in the military's care, a veil of privacy was dropping. The doctors would no longer release detailed information to ABC personnel.

"Your friend is going into surgery and Doug will be next," one of the medical team finally told Vinnie and Magnus after their repeated badgering for more details. "The army has shut down information on Bob Woodruff."

Lee

Orlando, Florida, January 29, 2006

Somewhere on the way to the airport my cell phone rang. It was Dr. Tim Johnson, the ABC News medical editor.

"Bob is going into surgery now," Tim said. "I know you are about to board the plane. Lee, you need to think about whether or not you want to be in the air when he is being operated on. We could reach you in the plane, but it would be difficult."

Bob's life was hanging by a thread and Tim was asking me to think about whether I wanted to be incommunicado during such a delicate time. But internally I was processing things differently. Bob would be okay. Surgery? Fine. Doctors fixed things. Expert doctors would be caring for Bob and making sure that his outcome was good. If the ultimate goal was to get home and get the kids back, why would we sit on the tarmac waiting for news, delaying our return home even more? We just needed to get going. Heading home meant somehow moving closer to Bob and to answers.

It wasn't until later that I would understand that Dr. Tim was gently trying to tell me that at that very moment it was touch-and-go. I would later learn that in the middle of the Iraqi desert in some converted barracks where generators provided the power source, a surgical team that knew not to hesitate was about to cut through my husband's skull with a bone saw to relieve the rapid swelling in his brain. Major Debra Muhl, an OR nurse and air force reservist, was shaving Bob's head. As she prepped him for surgery, she leaned into his good ear to be heard over the commotion and chaos. "We're going to take very good care of you, Bob," she whispered, "so hang in there."

What I would come to understand, weeks later, was that in the midst of the Iraqi desert, miles from the nearest hospital, my husband had a chance for the best outcome possible from a head injury in the hands of the military medical team. Doctors would tell me later that if this kind of head injury had happened in the States, Bob would probably not have survived.

I honestly don't remember how we got on the private plane. I don't recall if we went through security or walked to the tarmac. I do remember the pilot touching my back as I climbed the slim set of stairs. He told me how brave my husband was and that he was praying for him.

Fortunately, the kids were focused on how cool the plane was. I tried to keep it upbeat and make it feel like an adventure. "Look at the screen," I said. "It tells us where the plane is right now and over what state." They seemed amazingly up. I had done a good job so far of appearing positive and in control. In the hotel room I had given the twins a simple explanation that their daddy was hurt and we had to get home. Mack and Cathryn were hunched over homework, and the twins focused on their handheld video games.

Somewhere down below the clouds, thousands of miles away, Bob was lying on an operating table, but the reality of a head injury meant nothing to me. I knew that Bob had briefly been conscious and that was probably a positive sign. I knew he was in good medical hands, and I trusted the military doctors. Every day they treated people in Iraq who would have to redefine themselves because their lives had turned on a dime, in one bleak instant.

I loved my husband fiercely. Our marriage was strong and in a good place and I had come to terms with our life together, living as we did at the whim of breaking news. I thought about his strength and his love for us. I thought about how many producers and cameramen and colleagues had told me over the years how proudly he would talk about his family when he was on the road.

We were lucky. We'd had adventure as a couple and as a family. We'd taken risks for Bob's career and we'd traveled. We understood the importance of comfort without the need for luxury. There were lots of categories in which we could receive better grades, but we'd carved out a life that we loved. That life dangled near a cliff right now. As tears rolled down my cheeks I hugged myself and pulled my knees up to my chin in the plane seat. I wasn't good at the unknown. Improvising wasn't my strong suit.

All at once Cathryn was next to me in the aisle with what seemed a trumped-up question about some schoolwork. She was checking up on me, gauging my every move. Darned if she hadn't caught me crying again! I smiled through the tears, as if that might tell her not to worry.

"Mom?" she asked. "Are you okay?"

"I am, sweetie," I answered, willing my tears to stop. "I'm just having a moment. This has all happened so fast and I'm just emotional. It's a lot to take in, isn't it?"

"Uh-huh. Can you quiz me on the names of the thirteen colonies?" she asked. I was grateful for the distraction.

As the plane began to descend, my cell phone rang. It was Vinnie, calling from the hospital; the army neurosurgeon, Major Hans Bakken, was on the line "in the theater," as they called it.

"Mrs. Woodruff?" An authoritative, decidedly military voice launched into a rapid-fire monologue of medical terms. "I've just finished operating on your husband. He suffered a concussive blast and had a penetrating brain injury due to the explosion. His skull was fractured, so we had to do a hemicraniectomy. The original material was contaminated, so we were unable to save the bone. We do not know the extent of the damage. We are unsure about the function of his left eye and ear. He has a serious head wound and we are going to prepare to transport him to Landstuhl, Germany, as soon as he is stable."

"I . . . uh . . . will he live?" I asked feebly, fighting a fluttering feeling of terror.

"Yes, ma'am, he is alive," said the doctor more softly, after a pause, afraid, I was sure, to say anything more. In the coming months I would live on this delicate seesaw: doctors offering some kind of hope while reciting the potential for cold hard outcomes.

In order to survive my journey and to maintain that flame of hope, I would need to tell myself that Bob was different. That through sheer force of will and love for his family, he would control his own outcome. There were many, many times when I tried to tell people that they simply "didn't know Bob." Sometimes I would have to avert my eyes from the pitying, knowing looks that told me I was too shocked or stunned or naive to know what a pockmarked road lay ahead.

"I'm going to hand you back over to Mr. Malhotra now," said Dr. Bakken.

I was stunned. What the heck did the guy just say? I thought. Half of it had sounded like medical code, and it was delivered at a machine-gun pace. I was still dazed when I heard Vinnie's voice, fighting his own fear to reassure me.

"Lee? Are you there?" Vinnie asked. Something about his familiar tone made me feel connected to the events and to Bob.

At some point during the conversation with the doctor the plane had landed and taxied down the runway. As I stumbled out the door, I registered a look from the pilot and co-pilot as they stood at attention on the tarmac. It was a mixture of respect, sorrow, and empathy. It was a look I would come to recognize many times.

"Vinnie, what was that?" I screamed into my cell phone. "What is happening? That was horrible. What the hell did he just tell me about my husband?"

The kids were piling out after me and Cathryn was rapidly approaching, with her built-in X-ray vision and bionic round-the-corner hearing.

"What's wrong, Mommy?" she asked, eyes boring into my face.

"I just talked to the doctor, sweetie, and Dad's operation went fine. They are very optimistic," I said, fighting the urge to let my knees buckle and drop to the asphalt, sobbing.

Mimi Gurbst, vice president of news coverage for ABC and Bob's friend and mentor, piled out of her car with Bob's assistant, Lauren Lipani. Behind them was a van. Mimi was gesturing to me, ready to whisk us away.

I needed some space to process what had just happened and what was going to happen next. My life was zooming out of my control. There was a ticket waiting for me to fly to Germany, and I needed to think about who would accompany me. Who would care for my kids? How would I airlift myself out of a jam-packed life and abandon my responsibilities? As all these thoughts swirled around me, one thing became crystal clear. I had to get to Bob. Everything else was insignificant.

"Mimi, I need a moment," I said, giving her a bear hug and battling back tears at the sight of a familiar face. "Can the kids go with Lauren?"

I fell into the front seat of her car, hugging my purse. My children were redirected into the van with Lauren, who would become fresh meat for the twins' volley of questions and stories from Disney World.

"I'll see you at home!" I waved feebly out the window. Somehow on this car ride I would need to recharge sufficiently to calm the kids, pack a suitcase, and get on a plane to Germany to see what was left of my husband.

Lee

Westchester County, New York, January 29, 2006

I was numb. The energy I'd expended to be cheery in front of the kids for that entire morning had completely deserted me in Mimi's car.

Mimi was trying to cheer me up, telling me Bob stories and asking about our trip to Orlando. I robotically guided her to my house from the highway. All too soon we pulled into the driveway and sat for a moment while I gathered fresh reserves of courage to walk in the door and turn the page to some sort of new chapter.

"What did you do the day he left?" Mimi asked.

"Well, I helped him pack." I smiled. "I don't have to tell you how disorganized he is when it comes to things like that. We got everything he needed together for his trip. And then . . ." I trailed off, remembering suddenly that we had made love that morning. Despite how hurried we had been and into our own schedules and demands, we had stopped for a moment of intimacy. And for a brief second I let the inevitable *what ifs* intrude before I pushed them back down and far, far away from my thoughts. I was grateful, grateful that no matter what faced me in the future, we had that moment in our past, like the end of an engrossing book or a movie.

A big gray SUV pulled up behind Mimi's car in the driveway and my friend Karin Kukral climbed out. She had obviously heard the news. Her face was a welcome sight. In the entire journey following Bob's injury, Karin's expression of friendship was one of the most appropriate. She handed me a goodie bag for the plane, with magazines, candy, gum, aspirin, and a toothbrush. She fought back tears valiantly and gave me a giant hug. Then, with barely a word, she jumped in her car and drove away. Just like that.

It was friends like Karin whom I would come to rely on and be amazed by. These were the friends who refrained from calling repeatedly, friends who dropped off meals and food and slunk away. They made Costco runs for toilet paper, took my children for playdates, and drove them to soccer practices, confirmation classes, and countless other extracurricular activities.

Karin had nursed her father through a serious time in the hospital and knew how to behave in the wake of a tragedy. It meant simply letting someone know you were there without any expectation of a response. Even when I pushed them away, my dear friends quietly pushed back.

I don't remember at what point the silent army of good friends began to enter my house that Sunday or how they all formed into efficient units and divided labor wordlessly like a swarm of worker bees. All at once my kitchen was humming. Somehow, everyone seemed to know just what to do. Cell phones were going nuts, food and flowers were coming to the door. Mothers offered to take my kids to various houses and I nodded numbly. Somehow Mack's ride came and he slipped out the door while I was upstairs. None of us could know it would be almost two weeks before I would see my children again.

Once they were all gone, I felt relieved to focus solely on the trip to Landstuhl. We decided that my brother-in-law Shawn McLoughlin, Melanie Bloom, and Bob's brother David would go with me.

"I'm coming with you, Lee," Mel had insisted on the phone. "You don't even have a say. You were with me every step of the way for a year after David died, and I'm going to be with you for Bob."

My sister Nancy's passport had lapsed, so her husband, Shawn, was elected. A loving bear of a man with a heart the size of a football field, Shawn was exactly the kind of guy you would want to be with if there was anything that needed fixing. Mel would offer me the solace of a best friend and be my rock as a fellow journalist wife, and Shawn would provide the fierce protective flank.

David Woodruff, Bob's older brother, almost didn't come. Our initial thought had been to leave him in charge of Bob's parents, who were flying with him from Detroit to New York to be with the kids and await more information. But it was important that he come as a member of Bob's family. In the end it would prove an invaluable decision, for he became the "face of the family" as spokesperson to the media.

As I flitted around the house, somehow my sense of humor was heightened and completely intact. I knew it was a defense mechanism to keep me from thinking or feeling too much in the vacuum of information. My veins throbbed with pure adrenaline and I felt a duty to protect the people around me from faltering or falling apart. I moved from room to room like a butterfly, unable to focus on any task for more than a second.

My sister pressed two prescription bottles into my hands, one for sleeping and the other for anxiety. Somehow she had thought of this critical detail with lightning speed and had already contacted a doctor. My college friend Nora shooed me upstairs. There were only a few hours remaining before I needed to leave for the airport. "You've got to eat something, and you've got to pack a bag," she said, and then she took me by the arm and led me to the master bedroom.

"We'll pack some things for Bob too," she said optimistically.

Mimi Gurbst also came upstairs. Packing my bag for Landstuhl, she soon discovered the answer to one of the questions she had tortured Bob about at the office: boxers or briefs?

"I can't believe I'm rifling through Bob Woodruff's underwear drawer!" she exclaimed. "Do you know how many women would like to be in this position?"

"I'd be wearing gloves made for toxic waste if I were you." I giggled and then turned to face my own closet with a heavy sigh. In Florida, the weather had been balmy and sunny. In January, in the heart of Germany, it would be downright frosty.

"You've got to take some comfortable clothes for the flight," said Nora.

"Ummm . . ." I mumbled absentmindedly. "What about yoga pants?" I yanked open a drawer and pulled out my comfortable cotton workout pants with the flared legs.

For what felt like an eternity I would be forced to live with the poor judgment of my "comfortable clothes" decision. As I pasted myself into black skintight yoga pants and fake Ugg boots, looking like something out of a Josie and the Pussycats forty-fifth-reunion tour, I had no way of knowing that I would be stuck in that outfit as events snowballed.

For the next sixty hours—exactly the time that we were in Germany before heading back—I would walk the halls of a military hospital in skintight black pants with visible panty lines, leaving very little to the imaginations of the armed services members, army doctors, and family members who inhabited the base.

At Kennedy Airport we located Bob Murphy, ABC senior vice president and friend to Bob since his early days as a reporter. Bob Murphy had been assigned to be the ABC liaison for us. His role was to smooth the way and help facilitate anything that needed to be done for Bob and Doug.

As a group we were all slightly awkward with one another at first. I realized that I represented the only connection to each of the other four people and I felt duty-bound to make sure everyone knew one another and got along. It was so very Emily Post that in the midst of my fear and grief I was trying to orchestrate relationships, hoping that everyone liked each other. As with most harrowing events, experiencing it together bonds people to one another.

I need not have worried. The five of us who set out to JFK on that cold crisp January night would return as a cohesive unit. We would dub ourselves "The Landstuhl Survivors" after the popular CBS reality show. Our moniker would provide the framework for many jokes that masked sorrow, terror, and uncertainty. It would be a way for us, and ultimately for Doug Vogt's entourage too, to connect, laugh with one another, and form a community around our tragedy.

Flying through the night, I was unable to concentrate on my book. Ambien provided only a short sleep. I tried to focus on Bob and what he might be doing at that moment. Somewhere in the skies over the Middle East, he and Doug were flying on a military transport plane rigged to carry the injured.

Would I find the man I had fallen in love with or would I find something worse, different, immutably changed?

I had taken an anti-anxiety drug at Melanie's urging, but it only served to make me feel disconnected in a scary way. I was not a person who drank much, and drugs had never held much appeal. I liked being in control, and the pill made me feel unfocused and unplugged from my life. It short-circuited my fighting spirit. I knew I would need to fight for Bob. I understood enough from past brushes with tragedy to know I had to be present for every moment. To blunt it would do no good. I needed to feel it all: the horror, the shock, the grief, the hope. Only then would I be able to begin to move through it.

I tried to focus on the novel in front of me. It was a tale about a sinister misguided kid who massacres some of his classmates Columbine-style. His mother had tried everything to connect, but the child was born with a burning anger.

"Life could be worse," I whispered to myself as Melanie slept soundly beside me. For the moment I took tiny solace in the fact that the hideous pain of the wife and mother in the book trumped mine.

Lee

New York, 1986

It's easy to assume that I married Bob Woodruff because of his "dreamy" green eyes or his cut Ken-doll jaw. There are lots of other attributes I've heard women tick off to me about my husband over the years, but the simple fact is that I married Bob Woodruff because of his brain. Bob was the smartest guy I'd ever met. Somehow, I was wise enough to know that the looks part of the package fades. But laughter, fun, and a shared sense of the world—they make the stuff from which two people can really construct a life together.

We knew each other in passing at Colgate University, where I was a class ahead of him and, for the most part, uninterested in younger guys. It wasn't until our paths crossed in New York in 1986, after we'd both graduated, that we took another look at each other.

It was mid-May, and I was at the South Street Seaport in lower Manhattan helping my sister Nancy with a bridal shoot for a newspaper. We broke for lunch at a restaurant, where Nancy had arranged for a cake to be brought to the table to celebrate my birthday. I was twenty-six. It was the first big stretch in my life where I wasn't dating one special person, and I was enjoying that freedom.

As I lifted my head to laugh at something the photographer had said, I saw Bob out of the corner of my eye. He was dressed in a dark suit and walking through the restaurant accompanied by some very lawyerlike people.

There had always been something very *alive* about Bob Woodruff. His walk had a springy bounce, a way of almost rolling up on his toes, that exuded confidence. His eyes were deep-set but sparkling, and he had a ready smile. He looked, perhaps, like someone you would judge to be a cocky, pompous pretty boy.

In reality, Bob was an extremely smart guy who put little stock in the great genes life had dealt him. He was a bit shy, uninterested in clothes, passionate about playing sports, a friendly but serious competitor, and hugely curious about the world. He had a gift for languages, had backpacked solo in the Middle East, lived and worked on a kibbutz, and in 1986 was attending law school at the University of Michigan. Bob was largely unfazed by almost any situation; he approached life with the awe and wonder of a child. He possessed a single-minded focus, the ability to tune everything else out, including my voice, and zero in on whatever he was concentrating on. I had often thought that if Bob were deep into some intellectual pursuit and a fire started in the building, he might burn up before he detected smoke.

This trait could be enraging at times, if you were his partner, and at other times it was a gift. It allowed him, as a journalist, to stay completely focused on writing a script under deadline, despite the chaos or conflicts raging around him.

I wouldn't learn any of these things about him until later. For the moment he was the guy I vaguely knew who had dated the same gal all through college. One of my only memories of him had been as a sophomore, when he was a freshman. My girlfriends and I were living off campus in an apartment and, too bored to cook dinner, we had snuck into the dining hall to grab a free meal. I remembered seeing a completely green young kid with the most striking eyes. I remembered how he had held his books under his arm, a quaint affectation that somehow seemed out of place. And I distinctly remembered turning to my friends with a superior air. "Look at that guy with the books," I'd said. "Could he look any more like a freshman?"

Buried for years, that image came rushing back. Me with the horrible long-term memory. And now here he was, years later, in Flutie's restaurant just as we were taking a break inside. Like so many moments that hinge on fate, a half-hour difference in either direction and we would have missed each other completely.

As he walked past the opening to our area of the restaurant, I impulsively yelled "Woody!" which had been his nickname on campus. He turned toward the call and, as he would tell the story years later, he "saw a roomful of beautiful models . . . and Lee."

After a brief hello I introduced him to my sister Nancy. "Nan, this is a friend of Phil Foussard's from college, Bob Woodward."

Bob cleared his throat before correcting me. "Uh, actually it's Bob Woodruff," he said, smiling.

For years we would laugh about that first introduction. It became part of our lore, part of our story that we told our children and our friends. When Bob lay heavily sedated, comalike, in Washington, D.C., twenty years after our first encounter, I finally had a chance to tell the story in person to Bob Woodward. He and his wife, Elsa, were guests at an intimate dinner, a gathering meant to get my mind off the horror of my life, to pry me from the hospital and into a warm home. Bob Woodward had laughed and with a gentle humility had said sweetly, "And now his name is more famous than mine."

Somehow during our brief chat among the models in the restaurant, Bob and I set up a dinner date. He was headed for Hong Kong to work in the law offices of Millbank Tweed for a month, but he would be back. "I'll give you a call," he promised.

As he walked away to find his colleagues, my sister Nan muttered, "He's cute, you should go for him." A tiny *zing* of interest went off in my head.

Almost exactly a month later, he picked me up at my apartment in Chelsea and we walked down into the West Village and stumbled on a random restaurant. I recall the night as long hours spent talking and talking and feeling instantly comfortable. Because I knew enough about him to know he was a decent guy, I let my defenses down all the way. There is a natural high that comes from new romance, and as we made our way back out into the night he tentatively slipped my hand into his.

Our summer courtship was a whirlwind, but the weeks were counting down until Bob had to return to Ann Arbor for his last year of law school. Liberated woman that I was, I grabbed Bob on the steps of a church late one weekend afternoon. "Don't say anything back to me right now." I placed my finger over his lips. "I just wanted to tell you that I love you." My heart was pounding, and I figured I'd take a chance. What did I have to lose? He was leaving for Ann Arbor in less than a week and we'd be facing the challenges of a long-distance relationship regardless.

Bob's eyes widened slightly, in the involuntary fight-or-flight reaction of the male animal since the dawn of time. There was no question that he was taken aback, and I watched his face regain its composure.

I don't remember exactly what his response was. He did have the good sense not to parrot back an I-love-you-too. He mumbled something along the lines of how much I meant to him and how I had just surprised him. He hadn't been looking for anything resembling a relationship, and now here I was. I knew he had many things he wanted to do in his life. Getting tied down to one girl wasn't exactly in his personal playbook at age twenty-five, especially a girl who would be hundreds of miles away.

We said goodbye a few days later, immensely sad, unsure of where the next year would take us and not pledging to date exclusively. I may have tipped my cards to Bob early on, but I wasn't dumb enough to make any demands.

Fate intervened that fall as my marketing firm, Porter Novelli, was hired to help auto company Audi of America fight off allegations of unintended acceleration in its cars. I quickly volunteered to work on the troubled automotive account, based just outside of Detroit. It was conveniently located about forty minutes from Ann Arbor, where Bob was living with three other third-year law students in a slum house just two steps away from being condemned. For one entire law-school year we lived apart, Bob as a carefree student and me as the suit-clad marketing consultant. Whenever possible, I scheduled meetings in Detroit on a Friday or Monday so I could stretch my time with Bob over the weekend.

Weekends in Ann Arbor were a lifetime away from the sophistication of Manhattan. They were filled with fall leaves and record snowfalls, attending Big Ten football games and watching Bob play rugby against other midwestern schools. I would drill him in Chinese, and we'd laugh at my poor pronunciation and silly methods for memorizing words. We shared private jokes and smiled way too much. I was more than smitten. The early stages of our love affair, as with most young couples, were the best kind of opiate.

Back in New York, my daily routine was to get to my office extra early after my morning swim and type a letter to Bob. He received at least four a week and began to look forward to them as a ritual. In many ways those letters provided the extra glue that kept everything together until Bob accepted an offer to work for Shearman & Sterling in New York City. His interest was in international law, and Shearman had offices as far-flung as Hong Kong. Surely the Mandarin Chinese he had studied would set him apart.

In October 1987, just as Bob began his white-shoe law-firm job with a new office and a secretary, the stock market took a heavy hit. The rage for mergers and acquisitions that had fueled the investment world for the past few years came to a screeching halt. This meant that law firms that had served the investment banks with phalanxes of associates doing diligence and poring over documents now lost this lucrative stake.

The Far Eastern deals that Bob had imagined, together with exotic Chinese junks in Hong Kong harbor, evaporated overnight. Day after day in his midtown office there was little to do other than read *The Wall Street Journal* cover to cover. He was bored. And a bored Bob Woodruff was never a good thing.

Bob had made a number of mainland Chinese friends in law school and one of them, Ye Ning, had connections in Beijing that might be useful. After less than a year in his law office, Bob needed a change. He was intrigued by a potential teaching position in China. It would allow him to improve his Chinese and satisfy his thirst for travel, experience, and adventure. Slowly he began to explore his options. Unsure of what this meant for us, I rarely broached the topic. I had been promoted to vice president at my firm, and my own future looked bright.

My next assignment was to spend a year on the Sports Car Club of America (SCCA) racing circuit, promoting the winning record and attributes of the new all-wheel-drive Audi Quattro. All at once, my life ebbed and flowed around the race schedule, crisscrossing the country from Sonoma, California, to Lime Rock, Connecticut, the only female on the team of a very testosterone-filled sport. The distinctive smell of the fuel, the heat of the rubber on the black asphalt, and the octane-charged super-hum of the cars zooming around the track became my home for eight months. Occasionally, when Bob could, he would join me at various races.

In early May we had a race in Napa Valley. The rolling hills around the track were a verdant green with wildflowers sprinkled everywhere. After the race, Bob and I took a walk, and talk turned to the future. He had received offers to teach American law at two Chinese universities, one near Shanghai and the other in Beijing.

The subject of Bob's leaving made me nervous. I knew I couldn't push for a commitment; that wasn't my style, and ultimatums in relationships were not my specialty. However, as a full-fledged New Yorker, I was not about to give up my apartment in the city without some inkling about my future.

At twenty-eight, I was beginning to feel as if I had accomplished many things in my career at a fast and furious pace. The concept of settling down was becoming more appealing. And although I had no immediate thoughts of starting a family, I was aware of the call of the ovaries. I wanted kids at some point, and I wanted some years as a young married woman before having them. Bob Woodruff was, for me, the perfect mate. If I married him, my life would never be dull, never predictable or routine. As a girl who grew up in the same Albany suburban house for sixteen years, there was something attractive about his gypsy feet. He was smart, fearless, ambitious, loving, interesting, kind— and best of all he shared my sense of humor.

This last attribute, almost more than any other, was to see us through the peaks and valleys in our marriage. It was the shared ability to laugh at ourselves and our situation, even when tensions were at their highest, that enabled us to survive as individuals, as a couple, and ultimately as a family. We couldn't possibly have imagined then, with our adult lives rolling out in front of us like a red carpet, how much we would be tested—and how much we would need to laugh in order not to cry.

Lee

Landstuhl, Germany, January 30, 2006

We landed in Frankfurt at 11 A.M. on January 30, and all five of us buzzed through customs as if on wheels. We piled into a giant van with our suitcases, half of mine packed with Bob's things in what would prove to be an act of extreme hopefulness and naïveté about his condition. On the long flight from JFK, protected in the darkness of the airborne capsule, I'd had a brief interlude to reflect on what had happened in the previous twelve hours, regain some composure, and set my jaw. Now, hurtling down the autobahn, we couldn't get there fast enough. I wanted to see him, to touch him, to understand exactly what we were dealing with.

Melanie was on a cell phone talking to NBC, where her late husband, David, had worked. They wanted her to go on the *Today* show and talk about how she was accompanying me. It was a big story. Bob was the only anchor to have been injured in a war, and as such he had put a public face on the hideous casualties men and women in Iraq were suffering every day.

Tom Brokaw had called a number of times and I needed to call him back. He and his wife, Meredith, had become good friends after David Bloom's death in Iraq. I respected Tom's quiet mentoring of Bob and his counsel throughout the past three years of Bob's career. When I heard Tom's comforting distinctive voice, I wanted to cry. He was concerned and yet, at the same time, incredibly reassuring. I told him what I knew, which still wasn't much, and said we were on our way to see Bob. He echoed what many would tell me in the weeks and months to come: "Whatever we can do . . ."

What happened next would drive home for me how different and how public my world had become. My husband was a face of ABC News and, as one of its anchors, he was a franchise. Once ABC heard that NBC wanted Melanie Bloom to go on the air, *Good Morning America* and *Today,* fierce morning competitors, began a complicated dance to figure out how to best cover the story. News was, after all, still a business, and injured anchors made for good copy. The spat between the morning programs would play itself out in New York at many different levels, some of which I wouldn't learn about for months.

Landstuhl was a typical German village with American highlights. I noticed the golden arches of McDonald's among local German shops. We climbed a steep hill to the military base, where we entered the back way. Apparently, camera crews and reporters were massed at the front of the base, broadcasting live and looking for scraps of information.

Bob and Doug had arrived at the Regional Medical Center hospital about five hours earlier. Jumping out of the van, I was desperate to see him. My husband was here, somewhere in this building! We were led down long corridors, teeming with people in uniform, toward the family waiting area in the hospital. It felt odd to be thrust as a civilian into a military environment. I wondered about the men and women I saw. They were so young.

As we turned the last corner, I saw Vinnie in the hallway. He was talking to Tina Barbarovic, a producer from London who had worked with Bob for years. Tina was a close family friend and had left her new baby, Alex, in London to be with Bob, meet our crew, and smooth the way.

When I saw them both I ran down the corridor, sobbing, in my Josie-and-the-Pussycats pants and boots, my giant backpack flopping. I must have cut a disturbing figure. I fell into Vinnie's arms, crying softly. "Oh, Vinnie," I moaned. "I want to see him!" The rest of our group filed in and began to make introductions. Tina and Vinnie had new information and shared bits and pieces of the story and the events leading up to the attack. For the most part I tuned out. I would learn the full story later. I had so many questions. What had Bob been doing there that day? Had he taken an unnecessary risk for a story? Most important, what did the doctors think about his prognosis?

Before long, Chief of Surgery Guillermo Tellez came into the waiting room in his sand-colored military uniform with ribbons, stripes, and a name tag on his chest. Dr. Tellez was joined by neurosurgeon Major Peter Sorini, still in his green scrubs. They both struck me as kind men with truthful eyes that, I was certain, had seen too much on CCATT, the Critical Care Air Transport Team planes that flew between their base and Iraq three times a week. The realities of war, the cold hard outcome of conflict, was on full display in these corridors.

The disorientation of being suddenly jetted into a military world struck me again. So many other wives had walked in my shoes over the past three years of this war. For the military wives, there was community, understanding, and comradeship. For me, the wife of a journalist, whose only mission had been to get the story, there was no such structure.

The doctors gave us a quick briefing and tried to answer our questions. Bob was stable, he was in the intensive care unit, and they'd already performed a number of operations, especially on his shoulder and back to remove shrapnel. He had taken the full impact of the blast and they had performed a hemicraniectomy, the removal of half of his skull, to save brain function and let the brain swell. They were hopeful for Bob's full recovery. Bob was a young strong man in terrific shape, and that would help him battle back physically. I felt a measure of calm at the news, but I had so many questions. I needed to see Bob first before I could begin to know what to ask.

The military was still in the process of determining where Bob would go next, but it looked like it would be either Walter Reed or Bethesda Naval, both military hospitals in the Washington, D.C., area. He would undergo more surgeries there, they explained. But as he and Doug were stable, they were hoping to get them out on the next CCATT plane the following evening. If Bob remained in stable condition, he would be cleared to fly.

While it was far too early to tell what the end result would be, the injury to Bob's brain seemed focal, according to Dr. Tellez. There was no shrapnel in his brain, just a few shards of bone from when the skull had shattered upon the blast impact. One larger shard had been removed in Balad. These were not deep wounds, the doctor explained. The point of injury was located in the left temporal lobe, the area of the brain that typically controls speech and language in a right-handed person. It was what they called Bob's dominant side. His sinus was off midline but would be okay. There were pieces of shrapnel—rocks, in fact—embedded all around the left side of Bob's face, in the eye area, mouth, and neck. The surgeons had removed dozens of rocks already, but more would need to come out in Washington.

The concussive effects of a bomb blast, car accident, or any other violent head trauma disturb and shear neurons throughout the brain. The cognitive injuries a person could suffer were impossible to predict at this stage. Each brain injury is highly individual, and recovery still remains somewhat of a mystery to medical science. But the more faculties a person has going into an injury—intelligence, motivation, engagement in life, even support from family and friends—the better the prospects for recovery. Bob was a smart man, at the top of his game. He had the tools to give him the best chance.

I could feel the General in me already applying the filter and moving me into the zone—a bubble of optimism where I could choose to hear only positive information, to think only positive thoughts.

"One final thing," said Dr. Tellez, addressing the group again, the fingers on both his hands touching at the tips. "This kind of injury . . . it is complicated. It takes a long time for the brain to heal; it's about patience. Always remember that this is a marathon, not a sprint. Healing from brain injuries can easily take up to eighteen months, even two years." My own brain was brimming with so much information, it could not hold that important nugget at the time. Over and over we would hear the marathon analogy until it made our spines shiver. It made us want to bargain with the devil, to trade this for any other insult, anything but a head wound. I would have preferred so many other traumas, so many other problems for Bob, almost anything at all.

"Would you like to see your husband now?" Dr. Tellez asked kindly, turning to me. "You can go in two at a time." It was midafternoon in Germany. It felt as if we'd been waiting for days.

I'd both anticipated and dreaded this moment ever since I'd gotten the phone call. I wanted to walk into that room in every combination possible with the people around me. Part of me wanted to be alone with Bob, to face him for the first time by myself. But I also wanted to walk in with Mel, dear sweet Mel, my doppelgänger in so many ways; I remembered the day, three years before, when we had stared together at her husband's unnaturally serene face in the coffin. I wanted to walk in the room with David, Bob's brother and flesh and blood, who had fallen to his knees and called out when he heard the news. And I wanted to see Bob first with Shawn, my sister's husband and one of Bob's closest friends and confidants. These people were the bones that were propping me up on the journey.

"You and David should go," said Shawn softly.

David and I looked at each other and I jumped up. My legs were stiff and my back ached. I began to feel nauseated, frightened, apprehensive.

I knew the person I was about to see would look vastly different from the man who had blithely kissed me goodbye two weeks earlier.

"Let's go, Lee." Dave grabbed my arm.

As we rounded a corridor, we were met by a nurse whose tag read ANN SHULL. "You'll need to gown up before you go in," she told us. There was something knowledgeable, maternal, and comforting about her. I would have wanted her as my nurse and was instantly glad that she was caring for Bob. "There is a vicious bacterium found in the soil of Iraq named Acinetobacter," she went on matter-of-factly. "The soldiers carry it back with them. We don't want it to infect anyone else."

David and I traded quick looks, but Ann was on to the full-body demonstration with lightning speed.

"Here is how we do it: sterile gown ties in the back, tie both top and bottom strings of the mask, and put on the gloves last." She pointed to the pile of neatly folded paper gowns and demonstrated on herself.

Ann wasn't finished. There were things she wanted us to know to be prepared for Bob's condition. "His head is shaved and very misshapen, as his brain is swollen right now. The opening in the cranium is allowing the brain some room to swell, but it doesn't look pretty. There are a lot of tubes running out of his body. Each one of these lines serves a function, from his catheter to his feeding tube and the lines for antibiotics. I'm going to take you to his feet first so you can get your bearings and then I'm going to take you over to his good side. Please let me know if you feel queasy," she said, with a sympathetic look. "We don't need more head injuries."

Ann led us into a room. "You'll notice the room is very cold and your husband is naked except for a sheet. That temperature is to keep the body's swelling down." Before I could register all that information, there was Bob.

My first thought was how great he looked, tan and Adonis-like, with a sheet arranged scantily over his groin. He looked like a statue or wax model of himself, lying there completely still. The upper part of his chest was shaved where multiple EKG leads had been stuck to the skin and attached to monitors by wires. His body was perfect, swollen from the fluids they had pumped into him but simply bigger, not a scratch I could see from the front. He looked muscular and incredibly strong. Then my eyes moved up to his head. From the neck up, my beautiful husband had been transformed into some kind of freakish human experiment.

Bob's head was grossly swollen to the size of a rugby ball, misshapen at the top where his brain pushed out of the missing skull flap. His head was shaved except for a strip of hair down the back, a sort of shoddy Mohawk, giving him the appearance of an Indian brave, especially with the makeshift loincloth.

A clear tube filled with garish pink liquid protruded from the top of Bob's head, with a bulb at the end to collect the fluid. A ventilator had been shoved in his mouth and down his throat, forcing his battered and swollen lips into a crude oval shape and breathing for him as his chest rose and fell in an exaggerated, pulsed motion. There was dried brownish blood around some of his fingertips and under his nails. Mixed with that, I knew, were bits of the Iraqi soil from the ground where he had lain, bleeding and thrashing. I wanted desperately to wash that blood off. Other tubes ran from his body, hooked to monitors around his bed that beeped in the rhythmic hum of the ICU that would become so familiar to my ears in the weeks to come.

Around his neck a cervical collar held his head in place, and from the right side, in profile, I could see the beauty of his features, swollen but intact. Circling to the left of his bed was like landing on the far side of the moon. It was the left side of Bob's face and head that had taken the blast, and I sucked in my breath as I examined what remained of his face. There were cuts and stitches all over his cheeks, forehead, and neck and around his eyes. His lips were swollen with stitches running vertically from his top lip to his bottom. Contusions and stitches ran across the bridge of his nose, which was also swollen and slightly off-center. His left eye ballooned like a goldfish with a deep purple color, and I noticed some blood caked around the inside. There was no way that eye could have survived the blast, I thought. His ear was misshapen, like a cauliflower, and stitched where it had split. Blood and clear fluid leaked slowly from somewhere deep inside.

A giant incision, stitched with black thread, ran down the left side of his neck. I learned later that they had made this exploratory cut in the Balad hospital to make sure the artery wasn't damaged and cutting off blood flow to the brain—a routine procedure for any blast injury.

There were giant wounds on Bob's back where shrapnel had ripped into the armhole of his flak jacket from the ground on an upward trajectory. Three large rocks and many smaller ones had blasted holes the size of a fist into his scapula and shattered it, but none of us would even see this wound for weeks. It would have to heal while he lay on it. The priority was to keep his head in as stable a position as possible.

It occurred to me that when Bob recovered he would want to see a picture of what he looked like now. The reporter in him would never be satisfied with our descriptions and stories. He would want to see how little he resembled his former self. Now he was a giant Elephant Man likeness that lay like a corpse before me. But pictures were a chance we could not take. The Internet had opened up a realm of possibilities for disseminating information and photos. Countless careers had been ruined, launched, or revitalized when bootleg pictures "anonymously" appeared on the Web. Photographic images of Bob's gruesome face were something we couldn't risk. (Months later I would be proved right about Bob's dismay, when he would remark ruefully, over and over, how he wished we had documented that portion of his journey.)

After this initial inspection my eyes came to rest on his dark eyebrows. The four Woodruff boys have distinctive eyes and brows, inherited from their mother, Frannie. Untamed, they would revert to a Cro-Magnon unibrow. But with a little careful grooming, those brows were strong and definitive. They had always been a part of Bob's familiar look to me.

It was his eyebrows I focused on in the cold cramped room of the ICU to blunt the shock of the rest of his face. His left brow had been sliced vertically by shrapnel and a series of stitches ran through it. But his right brow was perfect, more perfect than I'd ever seen it. As a co-anchor of *World News Tonight* he had had his own makeup person, and in all his travels in the last month I had never noticed just how perfectly she had tamed them. This silly detail seemed to cheer me.

It was the only thing on his face that resembled anything normal and familiar.

"It's not as bad as I thought it would be," I said, looking up at Dave, who was performing his own silent inspection. In hindsight, this was a ridiculous understatement, a reaction born of shock. But in reality, as awful as Bob looked, I had imagined so much worse. I had imagined body parts blown off, a whole side of his head gone. He was in horrible, horrible shape and we didn't know what the outcome would be, but he was here. Physically he was here, in the same room with me. Right now that counted for a lot.

"Hi, honey, it's Lee," I said tentatively from the foot of his bed, touching his feet. "I'm here, and I love you so much. Dave is here too."

"Hi, Bob, it's Dave," he boomed. "Your big brother." We both began to speak very loudly, as if he were deaf instead of sedated. We'd all read the National Enquirer stories about people who woke up from comas after ten years and claimed to have heard every word that was spoken at their bedsides.

"You're in Germany, honey," I said. Ann had explained that we should reassure him and tell him everything was okay and talk to him about where he was. "You've had an accident, but you're going to be okay." I was trying to put some power behind my words and sound as if I meant it. I moved to his right side and kissed his swollen face through the hospital mask. I felt as if he must hear me somewhere inside, but nothing moved.

People respond to tragedy in so many different ways. For those of us gathered in Landstuhl, gallows humor would become a way of coping, of sweeping the playing field of the horror and tragedy that had exploded into our lives. I would lead the charge with my offbeat sense of humor and somehow, by doing that, give everyone else permission to laugh. Laughter would keep us sane, it would provide relief. Even laughter was a tiny way to take action.

"What's with the forty-year-old-virgin look with the shaved chest?" I asked Bob jokingly, referring to a scene from the movie in which the man tries to wax his hairy chest to appeal to women. In the end it is so painful he can't continue and leaves the job half finished. I rubbed his shaved chest and yanked at the hair further down. No reaction.

"You look beautiful, baby," I said, through tears. "So beautiful. A few cuts here and there, a little roughed up maybe. Look at it this way: They won't be able to call you a 'pretty-boy android' anymore." I began to cry. I was referring to a comment a reporter had made in a newspaper column after Bob and Elizabeth were named co-anchors of *World News Tonight*. Dismissing Bob's ten years of network reporting, much of it in overseas hot spots, they had gone for the easy sixth-grade groin kick.

The moniker became an ongoing joke between us at home whenever Bob grumbled about taking out the garbage or sorting the recycling. I'd pull out that old chestnut to get him moving. This time it didn't elicit a smile.

I continued a running monologue in Bob's right ear about who was here and who had come to Germany. Dave took over when I flagged. All the while I kept my hands on his cold body, looking for contact and connection. In the zone in my head, I could see only positive things. This would all be all right, the voice in my head told me. It would be the hardest thing I had ever done, but it would be okay in the end.

Ann came back in, ready to catch either one of us if it looked necessary. "Maybe you want to take a break and rotate out," she suggested wisely.

"He's so cold," I said lamely.

"I know he feels cold, but I promise you he is not uncomfortable. The temperature is keeping his brain from swelling further and helping to stabilize him," she said, gently steering me ever so slightly toward the door.

"We just need to check a few things on Bob now and the room is so small. . . ." She trailed off. It was clear that she wanted us to leave. Dave and I peeled off the gloves and gowns and backed out of the room. I let out a deep breath and Dave put his arm around me.

"How are you doing?" he asked. His face was white.

"I'm okay," I answered. "I thought he looked good, all things considered. I could see *him* in there."

It was easy to hear the word *injury* and assume that meant it would be a matter of weeks before things knitted themselves back together. A broken collarbone, a snapped ankle, some dislocated fingers. These were easy to repair. Bob would have some recovery time and be back on the air. A sane person, a person whose mind was not in the zone, would have taken one look at Bob and wondered if he would survive, let alone ever function again. Bob's injuries were foreign to me. They were for the victims of car accidents, traumatic violence, or war.

When David and I reentered the family waiting room, the next couple had paired up. Shawn and Melanie were ready to take their first look at Bob. "It was okay," I said, falling into Mel's arms and hugging Shawn. "He looks okay. He's *there*." Dave nodded. Either he was going along with my game or he really believed Bob looked all right.

Mel and Shawn returned ashen. Mel was crying and Shawn was supporting her, visibly shaken. Clearly they were not wearing my rose-colored prescription glasses.

"Lee," said Shawn, "Jesus. You told us he looked good. He looks terrible. My God, he's so swollen, and his head—" Shawn broke off suddenly, as if realizing for the first time he was talking to the wife.

"Oh, Lee." Mel sighed. Her eyes were red-rimmed and her voice barely a whisper. She didn't need to say anything else.

We had to get out of the little room. We were starving. Shawn and Mel pried me from the waiting room and found a kind of commissary, a cross between an inexpensive-looking European coffee bar and a bad American fast-food place. The only thing I could imagine swallowing was a muffin and coffee. The muffin turned to virtual sawdust in my mouth and I spat it out. (I couldn't eat for the rest of the day, despite everyone's admonishment to keep my stamina up.)

"Well," I said, unsure of where to begin. "What do we think?"

"You heard the surgeon, Dr. Tellez," said David. "I liked him, and he said Bob could make a full recovery."

Shawn piped up, eager to raise my spirits, as Mel rubbed my back in a sisterly way. "He's going to be okay. Just look at the guy. He's a fighter; he's going to drive this comeback. You two have been through so much together, do you honestly believe he is going to bail on you now? You just have to believe."

And the funny thing was, despite the horrible scene—the bloated head, my husband's disfigured face—at my very core, I honestly did.

Bob

New York, Spring 1988

Six months after joining the law firm of Shearman & Sterling in 1988, I walked into a partner's office and announced that I wanted a leave of absence. I was going to China.

"Why are you choosing to leave us, Mr. Woodruff?" the partner wanted to know.

"I have decided to take a one-year position in Beijing," I told him, "teaching American law to Chinese lawyers at the Beijing University of Politics and Law."

The partner fumbled with his bifocals and pulled a file from a drawer in his expansive wooden desk. "Well, you have a decent record. I see that you speak Chinese. But Mr. Woodruff, you've only been here eight months. That's a little unusual, isn't it?" The man glanced over the top of his glasses to get a better look at me, this young punk who had accepted a fat salary and then had the audacity to walk away for something else.

"I understand if you can't accommodate the request for leave," I said, moving forward in my chair. "I plan to go. It's a great opportunity for me to strengthen my Chinese, and I believe that China will play a pivotal role economically, sooner than anyone thinks."

The partner looked at me with renewed interest. He fumbled in another drawer for a file. "I—uh, need to have a conversation with a few people, but coincidentally, Shearman & Sterling has been debating about opening a satellite office in Beijing. We've been toying with sending an associate over there to help grow our relationship with the state oil company. It might be nice to have someone on the ground."

"Really?" I said eagerly.

"We might be able to use someone else there who didn't need to be on an expat package." The partner put his fingers to his temple as he perused the contents of the new file. "This might actually be a decent thing for us," he said in a softer voice, rising to shake my hand. "I'll get back to you."

Lee

New York, Spring 1988

It was April 1988, closing in on May. Bob's teaching job in China would start in September, and the weight of our future hung between us. Every once in a while, one of us would dance up to the line and then do-si-do back. As independent and up-front as I was, I was not going to be the one to bring up marriage first. And I knew from our discussions that Bob was wrestling with the fact that a wife didn't quite fit into his life vision for himself at this juncture.

Months earlier, Bob had put in for a three-week spring vacation to mountain-climb in Peru. An accomplished climber, he was excited to head to South America, shuck off the suit and tie for a few weeks, and get back to the wilderness. He would return in mid-May, and with his September departure to teach in China looming I held firm to my decision that I would not follow him there without some kind of commitment. But if we were to get married, time was running out to pull off a decent bash.

Our discussions had begun to zero in a bit more on the future, and it seemed we agreed we'd like to be married to go. But he left for Peru without popping the question. Unable to speak to him during the entire three weeks, I spent each agonizing day wondering if I should be making plans or not. This noncommittal behavior on Bob's part didn't do too much to earn my family's favor either.

The day Bob returned from Peru, he called from the airport to say he wanted me to meet him in the Sheep Meadow in Central Park. He had a beard and was wearing a felt Peruvian cowboy hat. There was a picnic blanket over one shoulder and a big bag from a nearby take-out restaurant in his hand. He dropped it all and ran toward me with a look that told me he had missed me as much as I'd missed him. Bob was tanned from the sun's glare on the snow, muscled and gorgeous. I thought he was the most alive person I had ever met.

After a giant hug, a long kiss, and a *Sound of Music*–style mountaintop reunion, Bob laid out some cheese and a bottle of wine. "Lee McConaughy, will you marry me and be my wife?" he blurted out, before the cork was out of the bottle.

I'm not proud of my answer. But it was the first thing that came to my mind, looking at this unshowered unshaven boyfriend, unwrapping Cracker Barrel cheese on a paper plate. "Are you freaking kidding?" I said. Could this guy, who'd been on a mountaintop with only men for three weeks, just off the plane, with no engagement ring, really be proposing to me in this way? It had to be a joke, and I thought it was a very cruel one.

His hurt look told me what I needed to know.

"You're serious," I said. "Right?"

"I'm more serious than I've ever been. I had a lot of time to think on this trip, and what I realized is that I've never met anyone quite like you. You're the person I want to go through time with."

"Yes," I said. "I say yes. I will." No one would ever be able to say I didn't know exactly *who* I was marrying. I was more sure than ever that our life together would be filled with adventure and uncertainty.

Our wedding, on September 11, 1988, was an entire weekend affair. My mother and I pulled it off in three short months, with only a few minor disagreements.

Despite the chaos of a "quickie wedding" as Bob and I called it, I had no hesitation or doubts about Bob as my mate. I knew we looked at the world the same way and would never be one of those couples chewing slowly at Denny's toward the end of our lives with nothing to say. *Soul mate* is overused, but it was the best term I had to describe how I felt about my new husband. He was the person with whom I wanted to face whatever life threw at us. Of course, at twenty-eight, with the toughest thing I'd weathered in my life having been a bad boyfriend breakup, I couldn't possibly imagine what life would have in store.

Just before the wedding, my gynecologist found a small benign lump in my breast. We had gone through a round of doctor's visits, knowing we wouldn't have U.S. medical care for a year. The decision was made to remove the lump, since there would be no chance for the doctor to wait and watch it. Time was running out. There was only a week or so before the ceremony.

Bob stuck by my side for every doctor's appointment, the surgery, and through the recovery period, worried and doting. My mother, I could tell, was especially pleased. No parents could be thrilled about a new son-in-law dragging their little girl around the world, but watching Bob's loving care of me must have eased their own concerns.

By the wedding weekend I sported a bandage on my chest that was barely covered by my wedding dress. I look at pictures of that weekend now, me very thin from the wedding and moving stress, an oversized flesh-colored Band-Aid right above my bikini top, standing confidently, on the wooden dock, ready to take on the world.

I see those two young people now. I remember my dress and the pride with which my father walked me up to the steps of the stone chapel and down the aisle. I still hear my friends tell me they will never forget the look on Bob's face as he saw me in that dress for the first time. "It was rapture, pure undistilled love," my roommate, Nora, had said later. "It's the way every woman would love for a man to look at her."

I think of that young couple now—us—running out of the dark stone church and into the bright sunlight, rice raining down, bursting with happiness and anticipation for our adventure to China and beyond. Our life would be, like anyone else's, impossible to script. But as we sat on the train the next day, snaking our way along the banks of the Hudson River back to New York and then to JFK for our flight, we felt like the luckiest couple in the world. Together, we believed, the power of two could make anything possible.

Bob

New York, Summer 1986

On my first date with Lee, in the summer of 1986, I laughed so hard my stomach hurt. I was still a month shy of turning twenty-six, and falling in love was the furthest thing from my mind.

I'd never met anyone quite like Lee before. She was a study in contrasts: a tomboy, independent, confident, and bold, yet giving, sweet, and feminine. She was intellectual, curious, and quick witted, a dedicated and loyal friend. Lee was a fascinating combination of the Ivory girl mingled with the best of *Saturday Night Live.*

I don't think Lee was ever fully aware of it, but she had a kind of gravitational pull with humanity. People just wanted to be around her. Not only did she make them laugh and feel at ease, but she was genuinely interested in everyone, from the waitress to the corporate CEO. She was the girl every woman wanted to befriend and confide in and yet she was also one of the boys. Lee was asked by men if she had a sister more than any other woman I know.

Very early on in our relationship I would get a sensation in my heart when Lee walked into the room, and I still feel it to this day. I call it a "pang," and it's the feeling of my heart turning over, a little flip, the physical manifestation of love.

When I decided to pursue a job in China, Lee and I were at a crossroads in our relationship, after dating for almost two years. She'd wanted some kind of commitment before chucking her Manhattan life and taking off across the globe with me. The thought of marriage at age twenty-seven was still something I had never considered for myself, but I knew that if we parted ways I might always regret it. I had met my perfect woman at a time when I had not been searching at all. And I was smart enough to recognize it.

During an arduous climbing trip in the Western Andes of Peru, I realized I missed this woman more than I could have imagined. I'd had three weeks to think about our relationship, but one incident in particular crystalized my decision.

Our climbing team was 16,000 feet up the side of Pisco Mountain when one of the men began having trouble breathing. We were there with a team of doctors measuring the effects of oxygen deprivation for a medical study. As the air got thinner, we were all experiencing labored breathing, but this one climber was clearly in trouble. There was real concern about whether or not he would make it if he didn't get to a lower altitude.

As darkness fell, his condition worsened. At 9 P.M., four of us tied ropes around our waists and attached the ropes to him. Slowly, deliberately, we walked him down the mountain to about 5,000 feet. It took six hours in total darkness on the icy, rocky terrain, and it was one of the hardest things I had ever done.

When we completed our descent, exhausted but exhilarated, I thought about what it meant to rely on another human being like that: to be tied to someone and have absolute faith that they will get you down the mountain. It was what I imagined a good marriage should be. All at once it seemed important to be connected to someone like that. I wanted to be the kind of person someone could rely on and, in turn, rely on them.

A week later, on the top of our second high peak, Huascarán in Peru, we were at more than 22,000 feet. Somehow, it all became clear to me. The air was cold and thin, my breathing was labored, and the wind chapped my cheeks as I looked out across the other mountaintops in the range. The possibility of death seemed closer there on the roof of the world. One fall, one slip; it could happen in an instant. And if you didn't take the chance to marry the person you loved, to be with the person you belonged with, you could lose it. I felt my mortality in that moment more keenly than ever.

After I got home I called Lee immediately. I had no ring, I hadn't even paused to shower or shave. Worst of all, and it would haunt me for years as a family joke, I had not asked her father for her hand in marriage. But all of a sudden, the most important thing in my life was asking this woman to marry me.

Part of me was glad there had been no phones on our climb. If we'd been talking to each other every day, if I'd been able to relay every little activity of our trip, I might not have been able to pull back and examine my life so clearly. Our enforced silence for those three weeks had given me the chance to step away from our relationship and see it for what it really was.

When Lee said yes, I was ecstatic. She supported my decision to take an enormous pay cut and make almost nothing teaching overseas for a year. I realized I would have a wife who wasn't afraid to take a risk or a chance. She had worked for years in the same company, and now she was going to roll the dice and do something completely new. What's more, she seemed genuinely excited by the idea. We would head to China and start our married life with a big adventure. Neither one of us could have imagined how deeply our year there would affect the course of our lives and my future career.

Lee

Landstuhl, Germany, January 30, 2006

Gallows humor has its roots in the quest for sanity. When the situation is so black, so dark, that grief or fear threatens to overwhelm, there is nothing like a good joke or two to resuscitate hope.

The Landstuhl Survivors nickname had stuck. Inspired by the popular TV show about teams who compete for survival under harsh environmental conditions, we each continued to find opportunities over the days and weeks that followed to "vote people off the island." First there was Shawn, getting his luggage stuck in a revolving door at Frankfurt, and then David and Shawn sharing twin beds that were dollhouse size and fighting for sleep between loud snores. Every hurdle and event, small or large, became fodder for our fun.

We would add to the Landstuhl Survivors team and broaden it once others joined us, but for now the jokes kept us smiling. They reminded each of us that we were tethered to one another, so the person who slipped would feel the strength of the rope attached to the one ahead.

The day after Bob's injury there was more television morning-show madness. We'd decided that Melanie needed to lay low and Tom Brokaw was going on *Today* to talk about Bob and his friend David Bloom, two journalists cut down at the top of their careers.

ABC had lined up President David Westin to go on the air, but it was evident we also needed a family spokesperson. After a quick powwow, we decided that big brother David would be the perfect person to throw in front of the press corps feeding frenzy. Not only did he look remarkably like his brother, he was articulate and comfortable in front of the camera.

The Landstuhl doctors who had worked on Bob had already strolled in front of the cameras to give a stock statement about how well Bob and Doug were doing. As we watched the news piece later that night, we were stunned but comforted by Dr. Tellez's pronouncement that they expected a full recovery.

It was the surprise of the briefing, without our direct consent, that would galvanize us to forge the veil of secrecy we would drop over Bob. We needed to control what was said about his condition, partly because it was our personal business but also because the situation was so grave and so volatile. Moreover, I had not had a chance to talk to my children further about the extent of their father's injuries. I desperately wanted to do that in person.

Bob's outcome would be unknown until he could wake up and we could begin some rudimentary assessments. Anyone who saw ABC's co-anchor lying immobile, his head grossly swollen and his face blasted by shrapnel, would never have believed this was a man who might one day return to work. We needed to protect Bob's future until he could show us what remained of the person we loved. We needed to give him time to heal before anyone, especially the press, could rush to judgment about his ultimate recovery.

Once Dave Woodruff had been elected to trot out in front of the cameras and give updates, he would be interviewed by ABC's Jim Sciutto and then would go live on *Good Morning America* as the family spokesperson.

I felt bone tired. Mel and I needed to find our belongings, take a shower if possible, and try to nap. I had to lie down and keep up my strength. As we walked out the back way to avoid the throngs of press, I saw Jim Sciutto, who'd been allowed inside the base.

"Jim Sciutto!" I yelled. "It's Lee Woodruff, Bob's wife." He looked tall and handsome in a tailored winter coat. He was dark-haired, with intense but friendly eyes. If I squinted only slightly I could see my Bob of ten years ago.

A few different emotions rolled over Jim's face. Pain for Bob, pain for me, happiness, I assumed, to see me, confusion as to why I was yelling to him gaily when my husband lay in critical condition inside. And, of course, disorientation over why a forty-five-year-old woman was wearing yoga clothing at a military hospital.

We embraced and Jim's kind hug, which symbolized for me the concern and support of all of Bob's ABC colleagues at that moment, broke my composure. I began to sob in his arms, as my nose ran onto the shoulder of his charcoal gray wool coat.

Later, talking to Jim, out of the corner of my eye, I saw two figures approach, and froze for a second. I knew that the van had been dispatched to get Doug's wife from the Frankfurt airport and that she was accompanied by ABC's deputy bureau chief from London, Robin Wiener. I ran toward them, picking up steam as I got closer. I could see my breath in the freezing January air, and the ground was cold and hard. The sky was a bright sapphire blue, a welcome sight after the fluorescent lights of the waiting room.

"I'm Lee, Bob's wife," I said simply, focusing on Doug's wife for the moment. Robin instinctively hung back, suitcase in hand. She and I knew each other from living in London, and I mouthed her a big hello as I focused on her companion.

"I'm Vivianne," she said, with a delightful, unplaceable accent I would later learn was Brazilian.

She was slightly shorter than I, with beautiful round eyes and a ready smile. Her face was open and friendly, set off by warm auburn hair. I knew that she and Doug had three daughters and lived in Aix-en-Provence, France. Looking closely, I thought I recognized the fissures of stress and grief etched just below her eyes. To the casual observer she might have appeared simply tired. I knew better.

"Oh, Lee," she said, dropping her bag. We embraced, and I had a vague sense of time freezing just for a second, everyone around us uncomfortably watching our grief as we both burst into tears.

"I'm so sorry," I whispered. "I'm so sorry for both of us, for them, for everything." Part of me had irrationally assumed all along that somehow this was partially Bob's fault. As the anchor and the person in charge of the story on the ground, Bob was the boss, and part of me felt a displaced sense of responsibility and guilt, not dissimilar to what the ABC executives who had originally conceived of Bob's trip must have felt. But that kind of guilt made no sense. It certainly didn't change what had happened.

Vivianne looked me hard in the face. We had both had a lot of time to think on our respective flights about the "other wife." Our two men lay in the same military hospital. We were civilian wives, without special recovery groups on the base to surround us and help us cope. We would have to rely on each other and on our families.

Neither of us would ever really feel that we belonged in this world. To Vivi, it was completely foreign. To me, less so, as I had watched the military embrace David Bloom after his death and watched their display of respect and honor for his family. But it was different. We were not military families. We would live in a netherworld between two lives, with our noses pressed up to the glass of that other understanding tribe, with its unspoken knowledge and welcoming arms. That camaraderie of shared experience would be just out of reach in our hometowns, isolated as we were from other families whose lives had been blown up by war. We would ultimately choose to fend for ourselves emotionally in our houses back home, nursing terror and grief in our hearts, curling into fetal positions to gather the strength required to get children out the door, and pasting smiles on our faces for breakfast. Vivi and I would learn the temporary healing powers of e-mailing each other when hope was in low reserve or calling to buck each other up when we despaired on the slow road to recovery.

Vivi and Robin were desperate to see Doug, of course. We knew we would meet up later. Melanie and I finally retreated to our room on the base at Fisher House to catch some sleep before heading back for more doctor briefings and another chance to see and touch Bob.

"Oh, Mel." I sighed, flopping on the bed. "Why us? First David, and now Bob. What does all this mean? How do we handle it with our kids?"

"I don't know, Lee," Mel answered. "I don't have the answers right now, but you have to find hope in the fact that Bob is alive." She would tell me later that she was still reeling at how horrific Bob looked, how critical his condition was. Already the people around me were at work, asking the tough questions, looking for extra information, buffering me against the horribly bad possibilities to allow me to stay somewhat in the zone.

"I'm so scared, Mel," I said, shivering in the cold room. The little heater against the wall was cranked on full, and it was beginning to warm the room with a noisy ticking sound. Already the sleeping aid I had taken was seeping into my brain. In the early days, before I came to rely on pills to sleep and to take away any dreams, the medication would hit me like a hammer after about ten minutes. It was blessed black and dreamless sleep—bottomless—a nothingness that would last for hours until I would awake suddenly, feeling oddly refreshed and yet not refreshed at all.

In that first brief span of wakefulness, I would learn to cherish the few seconds before consciousness returned. In those golden moments, time hung suspended, much like the elevator in the Tower of Terror but without the fear. In those first waking seconds I could trick myself into believing that everything was just as it had been before Bob's injury. My husband was on assignment somewhere, my children were snuggled in their beds unaware of life's cruelty, and I'd be rising to make that first cup of coffee alone in the kitchen, warming my hands around the mug.

And then, before I could hold on for just a minute longer, I would fully awaken into my new fresh hell.

Bob

Beijing, September 1988

When I first saw the school that we would call home for the next year I was shocked by the primitive conditions and how run-down it was. I could see Lee's reaction; she wasn't taking it well. I felt instantly guilty. Some honeymoon. As much as I felt otherwise, outwardly I needed to stay positive to cheer Lee up. I began to talk about all of the interesting things we would do, from backpacking around Asia to learning about our new city.

Looking back at our marriage, I realize how many times

we each filled that void for the other. When one person was down, the other one would pull them out of it, like a teeter-totter. Even if I didn't feel energized about the Chinese University of Politics and Law campus, there was much about China that excited me, and I drew on that enthusiasm to raise Lee's spirits.

As a foreign teacher, I earned the equivalent of $150 a week, which was four times what the average teacher at the school made. Half of my salary would be paid in Foreign Exchange Certificates (FECs), the money that foreigners used in China, directly convertible into dollars and other foreign currencies. The other half would be paid in Renminbi (RMB), the people's currency, which was not transferable outside the country but was useful for food and other local items. As foreigners we were technically expected to use only FECs, and all of the shopkeepers and taxi drivers would demand it. But as teachers we carried special cards that allowed us to use the people's money legally. There was a brisk black-market trade in exchanging U.S. dollars for RMB, and once a month or more I would bike down to the heart of the old city and find the budding entrepreneurs chanting "Chanja munney?" in a low voice.

My students were Chinese lawyers of all ages who had been slated by the Chinese government to deal with foreigners. Therefore, they were brought for a two-year period to the Chinese University of Politics and Law in Beijing, essentially to study American contract law. Use the foreigner to teach the Chinese how to bargain with the foreigner was the basic formula.

The university had asked me to teach what they called American Economic Law. Since there is no such legal discipline in the United States or Europe, I taught a mélange of contract, commercial, business and finance, and antitrust law, all of which concerned the economy or economics.

Speaking in front of thirty-five people for twelve hours a

week was a new experience, but one made easier by the nature of my students. I lectured in English, without an interpreter, so if I didn't know the exact answer to a legal
question, I could just speak very quickly or use relatively
complex words to confuse the students to the point where
they were too embarrassed to ask further questions.

"That's a really good question, Ma Qing," I would say pro-
fessorially, "but, as you certainly know by now, the UCC, in
light of its convoluted travaux preparatoires is silent on the
issue. Any other questions?" Silence. Teaching law was a
piece of cake.

The 1988 U.S. presidential election was well-timed to coin-
cide with an introduction to the American political process.
The students' first written assignment was to vote for either
George H. W. Bush or Michael Dukakis and explain their reasoning. Out of 65 students, 58 voted for Bush. The most
common answer was, "George Bush is a friend of China and
knows China well." Bush had been the chief of the U.S. Liaison Office in the People's Republic of China under President
Gerald Ford, living in Beijing from 1974 to 1976. (At that time
there was no official ambassador, as the United States recognized Taiwan as the "official China.")

One of my students, a young woman, told me she had
picked Bush in our class election because "his wife looks like
she could be his mother and a man needs a mother to take
care of him so he may concentrate on affairs of state." The
few who liked Michael Dukakis reflected a general fear in
China that would prove prophetic. "Dukakis is younger than
Bush. When a leader gets older, he becomes crazy like Mao
Zedong."

China's Cultural Revolution, from 1966 to 1976, had made
it difficult to talk about politics or politicians with most Chinese, especially in public. However, over the course of the
year, the ice slowly began to melt. By the New Year in 1989, it

had been less than two years since the last political movement, the antibourgeois liberalization campaign of 1987, but
the government was giving every indication that such liberalization was necessary if China was to move ahead.

Mikhail Gorbachev, the leader of the Soviet Union, would
be coming to Beijing to make peace after a thirty-year chill.
The year's Asian Development Bank meeting would be held
in Beijing, and for the first time since the civil war a Tai-
wanese government representative would make official contact with the mainland government, a huge political step
forward. Even the military, which had seen its power emascu-
lated by Deng Xiaoping's reforms, was slowly learning the
ways of the West. The People's Liberation Army, as it was
known, had become a 51-percent equity partner in some of
Beijing's newest and nicest joint-venture hotels.

The resultant relaxed atmosphere emboldened even the
most wary Chinese. When martial law was imposed in Tibet
in March, several of my students openly agreed with my crit-
icisms of the government. One woman even went so far as to
make an antigovernment presentation in class. "The misin-
formation campaign carried out by the government should
not prevent us from looking critically at their policy. Do you
think Tibetans really tear the skin off live people as a reli-
gious ritual?" she asked the class. "Did they really invite us to
'liberate' them from such cruelty? To say that Tibet is histor-
ically Chinese sovereign territory is to say that Vietnam,
Mongolia, and part of Southeast Asia are also ours," she continued. The rest of the class listened intently. Although about
half of my students were Communist Party members and
several were official "monitors," or watchdogs, the student
was never reprimanded for this remarkable speech.

But despite such flashes of political bravery, most students
I spoke with felt helpless and hopeless about their future in
China. Increased exposure to the West and improved political

conditions in the Soviet Union and in Eastern Europe had made many of the Chinese particularly depressed about their own condition and future.

I would become very close to many of my students, who were interested in the law and in American freedoms, but even more fascinated by our conversations. Often, I would purposely push the envelope a bit, eager to get inside their minds, which had been so brainwashed, or at least limited, by the constricted world they lived in. Almost without exception, each of my students was eager, hungry to understand the world outside of their borders. And I was hungry and eager to absorb as much of China as I could.

Lee

Beijing, September 1988

The truth of the matter is, after a fairy-tale wedding and an indulgent but brief Hong Kong honeymoon, I spent the next three days of my marriage crying my eyes out and considering divorce.

We landed in Communist China with a thud. It was the fall of 1988 and, in contrast to the lushness of Hong Kong with its vital and rich pulse and its exotic smells and sounds that echoed old China, Beijing felt like a dry, dusty, leafless place. The airport was stark and concrete, soldiers toted machine guns, and the planes scattered around the unused runways looked as if they were unchanged from Mao's era.

The "campus" of the Chinese University of Politics and Law, or Zheng Fa, was bleak and impoverished-looking. The interior roads were dirt, and I couldn't see plants, trees, or grass anywhere. Random piles of yellowish soil sat as if someone had decided to begin construction and then abruptly stopped. When a slight wind kicked up, the dirt would blow off the tops of the piles and set itself into little swirls. There were only a few buildings, pasted into a patch of land on the side of one of the city's main roads.

As we walked up the concrete stairs of Building Number 2 to our room for the first time, our luggage thumped against the steps. People stopped and stared openly at us, two *da bizis* (the Chinese term for foreigner, meaning *big nose*), one of them very blond from the summer sun. Dozens of bicycles were pulled inside the first-floor hall and chained like a herd of metal animals. On the stairs leading to the second floor, a pile of burned papers and some garbage had been swept into a corner. Just smelling the scent of the concrete building's cooking oils, garlic, the ever-pervasive thick blue smoke of the cheap Chinese cigarette tobacco, and the odor of human beings living closely together, my mind became numb.

I could read the shock on Bob's face as well. The conditions were much worse than they had described. I quickly tried to absorb the reality of where I would be living for the next year. An older woman was out in the hall, chopping a fresh chicken whose neck she had just snapped. There was a pervasive scent of urine in the building. I watched a young man with tousled wet hair hawk up a huge wad of spit with a guttural sound and shoot it out on the concrete floor of the hall. I think I flinched visibly. A long plastic sign outside the dorm had said, in Chinese and English, NO SPITTING PLEASE.

The jungle toilets, or "hygiene rooms," were located at the other end of our hall, stalls each with a hole in the concrete floor that would once again make me grateful for my mother's gas-station-restroom squat technique. Pity the poor soul who was constipated in China; you'd have to have thighs like Arnold Schwarzenegger to survive.

Two long concrete troughs with ten faucets each were located across from the stalls, for bathing, washing vegetables, and doing dishes. The water was not potable. Owing to their multipurpose use, the hygiene rooms reeked of sewage and rotting food. Dirty dishes were often stacked in the long filthy farmhouse-style sinks. Much to my horror, dotted around the doorless stalls of almost every hole in the ground were used sanitary napkins. I learned later that the toilets were emptied and used as night soil for the crops. God forbid anything unsanitary should go down the holes.

Our room was the biggest shock—a small cinder-block area about 15 by 20 feet, the size of a double prison cell, with one window facing east. We had two metal-framed twin beds pushed together with a kind of poor man's futon. Our pillows were stuffed with grain and covered with pink towels, which served as pillowcases. There was a small desk and one little closet. As a professor, Bob was entitled to a mini refrigerator and a television, on which we could get CCTV and reruns of the American action-cop show *Hunter*. Wherever we went, when people found out we were American, they would routinely ask if we knew *Hunta*.

Every morning, right on cue, an old loudspeaker system strung across the campus on rickety poles and sagging wires would come to life at 6:30 A.M. A scratchy record would play the national anthem, and then a screechy voice would shout out repetitive numbers as a form of enforced exercise for the students. We never saw any organized group participating, but the loudspeaker system remained, to wake us every morning. We soon learned to roll over and go back to sleep. Only once, on an otherwise unremarkable morning that held no obvious significance, the barely audible anthem was replaced by Madonna's "Like a Prayer," which blared with a defiance that lifted our spirits and then was abruptly shut off. In the entire time we were there, it never happened again.

This was Peace Corps living at best. When all the introductions had been made and the tours completed, the clothes unpacked and the giant map of China rolled out and taped to the wall, I sat down on the bed, close to tears.

"Babe, what's the matter?" Bob asked, concerned and solicitous.

"Well, I miss everyone and this is . . . well, not what I expected." So much had happened in the last week, a marriage and a honeymoon, and now I felt instantly beamed into this very foreign land.

I realized that, as I was completely absorbed in organizing our wedding and the details of moving, Bob had been preparing for actual *life* in China. Far better than I, he understood what it would require. Whereas Bob had traveled and backpacked in the Third World, I had never focused on the particulars of living in a developing country. The closest my sheltered suburban upbringing had brought me was a family vacation to rural Mexico. While Bob was energized by the adventure he saw all around him, I just wanted a bath with lots of bubbles and a soft pillow. No one would ever accuse me of being a princess, but a little creature comfort didn't seem too much to ask for at this stage of the game.

"This is going to be great," Bob said, holding me. "You'll see. I know the setting here is a little rough, and now I know why no one sent me pictures even after I asked for them." He grinned at me hopefully, working hard for a smile in return. He too was feeling hugely disappointed by the school but could see he had to buck me up first.

My lip began to quiver and the tip of my nose started to turn red, sure signs I was about to cry.

"We're a team," he said gently. "And we are going to travel and see the country and backpack through Asia. We will have had this special time together for the rest of our lives," he added, brushing a piece of hair out of my eyes.

For the next two days I cried on and off. In hindsight, I know some of it had to be simple exhaustion. I had just been through a wedding, my family and friends were halfway around the world, I didn't speak the language, and I wasn't sure I ever could. The sounds were guttural and I seemed to have a tin ear. Would I ever be able to function independently, as I had hoped?

On day two, sitting in our room as Bob attended an orientation with his new students, a few more tears ran down my cheek as I composed a letter home. I wondered glumly how many other new American brides had to kick homemade maxi pads out of the way every day in order to urinate. And then it hit me.

Indentured slavery had been abolished after the Civil War. If I really *really* hated this experience, nothing said I had to stay, just because I had married Bob. It sounds foolish now, I know, and my parents had certainly raised me to honor my commitments, but merely contemplating the fact that I had an exit strategy let some of the air out. I could always just leave.

As I tried to explain my revelation to Bob later that afternoon, he looked confused and hurt. However, he was not about to give up. He lay on the bed next to me as I cried, hugging me and holding me, telling me he loved me over and over again. He promised that if I remained unhappy, we could simply go home. "You are the most important thing in my life," he exclaimed softly, kissing the top of my head.

As we lay on the bed together surveying the situation, arms around each other, I was finally ready to accept that this was our new adventure. And little by little, I just plain felt better. "Never mind," I said, eventually smiling. "The only thing that matters is that I love you."

After that conversation, I just looked ahead. Those months were some of the sweetest in our married life. I would come to love China and feel a great affinity for so many of the people we befriended. It was an experience, I realized later, that could have gone two different ways. It was all about how we chose to define it. Here we were, two young people with our union completely pared down to nothing; no possessions, no trappings, no money. It was just Bob and me and our relationship to each other. We could have resented the close quarters, wanted more, discovered that our love didn't thrive away from the energized, glitzy distractions of New York. We could have sunk, instead of choosing to swim. But we'd both ultimately chosen more wisely than that.

Our time in China was forged from a common experience, stripped down to raw love and what truly matters between two people. This time created a solid foundation of bedrock on the floor of our union.

Before I left New York, a colleague had made some phone calls. The firm of Hill & Knowlton had a Hong Kong branch and, at the time, was the only large Western public relations company to have an office in the People's Republic of China. Although I did not speak Chinese, I was a find for an American company in Beijing. A vice president with Western marketing skills who did not need an expensive expatriate package? I was hired practically on the spot.

The doors of the PRC were creaking open under Deng Xiaoping. American businesspeople smelled opportunity. Lee Iacocca would be coming through Beijing for high-level government meetings and a big banquet. His firm, Chrysler, would be buying Beijing Jeep Company in a landmark joint venture, and there was work to be done. American giant General Electric had operations here. Bausch & Lomb, Allied Signal, and Mobil Oil: the list of clients was growing as U.S. businesses decided to get in on the act. It wouldn't hurt for Hill & Knowlton to have a Western face out in front in Beijing to meet with advance people and dignitaries.

Moreover, there was an entire fleet of foreign journalists from the United States, Great Britain, France, and Germany living in Beijing. It was beneficial to have a Westerner to deal with them, write the press releases, and develop relationships. That person would be me. Little by little, I came to view China and our time together there as an adventure. I rose to the challenge. From a distance, as I joined the stream of bicyclists heading to work under the giant portrait of Chairman Mao on the Forbidden City wall, I blended right in.

Lee

Landstuhl, Germany, January 30, 2006

Back in our waiting room, Vinnie Malhotra solemnly handed me a Ziploc bag of Bob's effects that the military had given him in Balad. He looked guilty and sad, as if carrying the bag had been both a tremendous honor and a burden. It reminded me of those World War II films in which the wife breaks down when given the remains of her soldier's life. In the bag I found Bob's reporter's notebook, open to his last page of notes. It was covered with bloodstains. There was a pen, his wedding ring, an Iraqi press pass, his passport, and his wallet. In the front of the wallet was his ABC News ID. He looked bright and clean and handsome in that tiny picture, so different from the hulking shell of a man lying sedated down the corridor. When I opened the wallet, a little shower of sand fell from the compartments. Iraqi soil. That stunned me for a minute. I jammed the whole plastic bag in my purse. It was, for the moment, too much information. I had purposely avoided asking specific questions about "the incident." I wasn't ready to hear about it or picture it or even feel potential anger at whatever Bob had or hadn't done in the process of chasing his story.

The doctors invited us to look at Bob's CT scans. I declined, but Shawn and Dave went back to view the black-and-white images and returned incredulous, shaken. There were shrapnel bits peppered throughout his head and neck. A few tiny white shards of his skull, embedded in the outer folds of his brain, glowed bright white against the black contrast of the films. My husband had cheated death by a whisper. It was a miracle that he was alive, even barely, in the room next door.

I didn't want to see the realities of what was going on in Bob's brain. I would also choose never to fully learn how to read the heart monitor screen or any of the other devices that beeped and glowed around him. I didn't want to walk in and see a number that read lower or higher; I didn't want to follow his progress so minutely. I needed to keep my eye on the big picture.

It had been decided that, even as civilians, Bob and Doug would be allowed to fly from Landstuhl to Andrews Air Force Base on a Critical Care Air Transport Team flight with injured service members. Bob was in critical but stable condition.

The CCATT planes had been stripped of their seats and outfitted to transport patients with all their medical equipment plus one-on-one nursing and doctor care. They were a brand-new approach, developed to diminish the time between a battlefield injury and treatment in a specialized trauma facility like Landstuhl. As soon as the patients were stable, they were transported to the United States. Landstuhl Survivor member Bob Murphy of ABC would later whip out his company credit card and charge Bob and Doug's passage in the flight on his corporate card, a first for him.

With Vivi with us now, it seemed appropriate to visit Doug with her. I had never met him. Although I'd heard tales about the field and some of the names, Bob kept that part of his life fairly separate. Like most journalists who live an intense life on the road, when he was home he wanted to focus on family life and the realities of bills and schedules. It was a way of reentering family life and of keeping two very different worlds apart.

I followed Vivi into the ICU where Doug was lying. Almost immediately I found myself fighting a stab of jealousy at his level of alertness. He'd been chatting with his nurse and with some of the ABC folks. I was, of course, grateful and relieved that Doug seemed so well. He had a giant scar across the top of his head where they had opened his skull to check for swelling, but Doug's injuries were much less severe than Bob's. Doctors had sewn his head back up, after removing some debris and replacing Doug's shattered skull with a titanium plate.

I felt a bond with Doug right away, much as I had with Vivi. His face was warm and open, his eyes kind. There was obvious love between the couple, and I envied her the fact that she was able to talk to him and be comforted by the sound of his voice.

Doug asked about Bob, and Vivi and I gave him the update.

"But there's bad news, Doug," I said. "Vivi and I have been talking and we've decided that you and Bob aren't going to do this for a living anymore." Doug looked confused; it even took Vivi a moment to understand that I was kidding. "We're going to be opening a bakery and brew pub in Aix-en-Provence, right where you live. You boys will be the bakers, you'll have regular hours, and Vivi and I will be the cocktail waitresses."

Vivi and Doug broke into big grins. "What will we call it?" asked Vivi, giggling. She had one of the most infectious from-the-gut laughs I had ever heard.

"Hmmm," I responded. "We'll call it the Flying Dough. How about that?"

Another visit to Bob and more updates from the medical team, and it was time to find food and get some sleep. Shawn, David, Mel, and I gathered in the community room at Fisher House, where we were staying on the base. There was no dinner, and as the others scrounged in the communal kitchen for some dry food, all I could stomach was tea. I knew I needed to eat, but nothing appealed to me.

Shawn had turned on the TV. Footage of Bob had run on all the U.S. stations. Pictures of our family, taken the past summer, were being flashed on screens around the world. News stories were speculating about Bob's condition and what his head injuries might mean. There were blow-by-blow accounts of what we were all doing in Landstuhl and computer-drawn reenactments of the attack, showing where the military vehicles had been positioned. Film clips were dredged up of what an IED looked like in real time, in real life.

I turned away from the screen. I needed to stay in the zone. The zone would provide the armor I would need to be a warrior wife, to stand vigilant by Bob's bed, understand the doctors' multiple recommendations, question his medications, check after nursing-shift changes that the right directions had been followed, go to battle for my husband's care, and stay on top of every little detail. I would join the legions of spouses who have sat by bedsides through countless diseases, accidents, cancers, and wartime injuries, nursing their loved ones, learning new vocabularies, and making decisions as daylight evaporated and time took on its own meaning by a loved one's bedside.

Lee

Westchester County, New York, January 30, 2006

Back at our house in suburban New York state, life was moving at warp speed. Answering the phone and staying in touch with friends was a full-time job. Bob and I had moved nine times in over seventeen years of marriage. We'd made friends in cities around the world. With so little information being released to the public, many of them took this opportunity to check in. Letters and packages were showing up at our door. Wonderful women in my town and beyond were making meals and bringing them over. A boomerang even arrived from Australia, signed by one of Bob's cameramen.

Thousands of dedicated viewers who had watched Bob for years scribbled letters, wrote out mass cards, added our family to their prayers, and began posting messages and thoughts on the ABC Web site. People wanted to thank Bob for his service to the country. They were grateful that there were reporters willing to put their lives on the line to bring home the story. To some, Bob was a patriot. One headline in the January 30 edition of *The New York Times*, however, called Bob's presence in Iraq a "ratings strategy," implying he was an anchor seeking publicity for the newly relaunched *World News Tonight*. Looking at Bob's track record of foreign reporting and war coverage, it was hard to defend that position. As a reporter, Bob always wanted to be in the midst of the action, never content to sit in a studio, reading the news. Many at ABC News, infuriated at this cheap shot, fired back in Bob's defense, including an angry Barbara Walters on *The View*. David Westin responded in a letter to the editor:

> I must object to *The New York Times* characterizing as a mere "ratings strategy" Bob Woodruff's and Doug Vogt's reporting when they were seriously wounded in Iraq. It demeans what two brave men did for the right reasons. Bob and Doug sought nothing more than to inform our audience. They represent the many other news organizations, the *Times* included, whose people put their very lives on the line to report things that are important for the American people to know.

Focused on Bob, I was oblivious to all of this. My two sisters, Nancy and Megan, had arrived at our home to run the household and decipher the kids' jam-packed lives and after-school schedules, which mostly resided in my head. Picking up the threads of my life, right down to the milk delivery schedule and the recycling, would not be an easy task. But with the help of my friends Nora and Alicia, and our babysitter Diana, they would all somehow patch it together.

Parents offered the children rides to everything, picking up the slack and making the job easier. Meal schedules were made and days assigned. Neighborhood grocery runs always included items for our household. Two dads on Bob's weekend soccer team organized our garage. Our amazing sitter, Diana, whom we'd known since we moved back from London three years earlier, filled in many of the blanks, locating necessary objects and sleeping on the floor in the twins' room each night in my absence, pulling long extra hours and overnights with love.

Bob's folks had also arrived at our house, to wait for us to return from Germany. Bob's father, hard of hearing for years, had televisions blaring in different rooms, waiting for news of his son, weeping openly on and off. My sisters were constantly shooing him out of the room. Cathryn would walk by and see a news clip about her father, freeze like a doe as she watched it, and then ask a million questions with a panicked look in her eyes. Finally, exasperated, someone yelled for Mr. Woodruff to simply shut the TVs off.

My parents cycled in after the Woodruffs left for Bethesda, where Bob and Doug would be taken. Like the rest of the family, they provided a stable extended set of arms for my children, who had essentially been abandoned by me in the wake of the tragedy. Time and time again, people would remark on the amazing dedication of our two families, the Woodruffs and the McConaughys, in providing an extended net of care and love and support. Some of our siblings hadn't seen one another since our wedding. It was incredible to watch Bob's three brothers, my two sisters, and all their spouses knit themselves into formidable teams in various combinations.

Reporters were also calling the house, some using cagey means to get a family member on the phone by pretending to know us. An *Entertainment Tonight* crew showed up at the door and was politely asked to leave. For the most part, the press was incredibly respectful. After all, this was not a pregnant pop star walking into a Mobil restroom with bare feet. This was a colleague, one of their own.

Thousands of e-mails poured into ABC News and into our personal e-mail. Bob's injury had been reported on a Sunday, as people were heading out the door to worship. His name had been on the lips of

many in congregations across America that morning. Prayers were offered in churches, temples, and mosques and at bedsides around the
world. The Choctaw Indian nation, to which Bob's dad claimed lineage,
held a prayer ceremony. Of course, I knew nothing of this at the time.
That kind of surreal public display of my family life was totally foreign
to me.

Looking back, I am thankful for my ignorance of all that was taking
place. Cocooned on a military base in Germany, I remained focused on
Bob and what we had to do next. The minutiae of my household and
the needs of my children would have overwhelmed me if I'd had to concentrate on them in those early days.

The first step was to get some sleep before the flight back. It was already past midnight when we turned in. Mel and I climbed the stairs to
our room at Fisher House, changed into pajamas, and pulled the thin
blanket up to our chins. Sleep came with the help of a little pill, and
again it was deep as a canyon and velvety black. If I did dream, I had no
memory of it at all.

The next morning, as we had hoped, Bob and Doug were deemed
stable enough to fly. Our bags were packed and we all prepared to head
to the airport. The two planes would be in the air at roughly the same
time, and there was something comforting about that thought. As we
entered the hospital to say our goodbyes, a nurse put a quilt in my hand
and one in Vivi's. It had been sewn by volunteers, the Heirloom Quilters
Guild in West Jefferson, Ohio: women, I imagined, who had learned
how to keep their hands busy while their husbands and sons were in
harm's way.

The quilt was red, white, and blue, with cloth squares that carried a
flag motif. On the back it had been signed by everyone who had cared
for Bob in the ICU. The nurse explained that Bob was an honorary soldier to them, one of their own. The quilt would travel with him on the
C-17 to Andrews Air Force Base, draped over his legs at the bottom of
his hospital bed, a tangible reminder in the months to come of just how
far we had traveled.

Bob

Ramstein Air Force Base, January 31, 2006

After only a few hours in Landstuhl, Doug's apparent improvement in the short time since he had been transported from Balad was remarkable. In sharp contrast, I remained unconscious, grossly swollen and intubated, and with a breathing tube down my throat. The family and friends who came to visit me in the ICU told me I was unrecognizable.

We were loaded onto the large medical transport plane from the yawning mouth of the plane in the rear. As two of the most seriously injured, Doug and I were put toward the back.

Kevin Cullen and Michele McDonald, *Boston Globe* reporters, were also on our CCATT flight from Ramstein Air Force Base back to the States. They were doing a story on the medical evacuation of soldiers. Extraordinary progress has been made in the field hospitals of Iraq and with the Critical Care Transportation Teams. The goal is to get the patient to the U.S. within forty-eight to seventy-two hours; it is a highly coordinated effort involving all four branches of the military. As with Doug and me, the injured from the battlefield are usually stabilized quickly and then airlifted to Germany on cargo planes outfitted to transport each patient on a gurney with their medical equipment and one-on-one nursing and doctor care. Once in Germany, patients are evaluated and stabilized further and then quickly put on a plane to the U.S. Michele told Kevin that she had ethical concerns about taking photos of us. She worried that my family might see a photo of me before they could see me in person. I will always be grateful that she and Kevin put Lee and the children above getting a picture of me for her story. That's a tough balance to achieve, especially with bosses back at headquarters demanding the story. She put herself in my shoes that night as a parent.

Doug and I were again each assigned a doctor, ICU nurse, and respiratory therapist. Dr. Jonathan Lohrbach, a major out of Nellis Air Force Base, was overseeing my care in flight with respiratory therapist Jeffrey Wahler.

"Bob woke up and moved his extremities after the blast," Lohrbach, a surgeon in Las Vegas in civilian life, reported to Kevin on the flight. "That's typically a good sign. But he isn't out of the woods yet." He told Kevin I had shrapnel in my brain and a broken scapula. The dried blood that had covered my head in Balad had been cleaned up in Germany, so the entry wounds on the side of my neck and face were more obvious than the day before.

"It's a terrible thing to say, but Bob is the typical patient we take. It's IEDs," Captain Vannecca Phelps, my ICU nurse, told Kevin. "The brain is a big hurdle. There is no way to say how much will come back. But he moved today, so that's encouraging."

Early in the insurgency, improvised explosive devices had been crude weapons, more likely to maim than kill. They had evolved to where they now could take out the most heavily armored vehicles in the U.S. arsenal. The bombs were larger and more sophisticated, often causing multiple deaths and leaving those who survived with traumatic injuries. At the time of my injury, IEDs accounted for more than half of the American military casualties in Iraq.

With the ever-larger and more powerful IEDs have come more horrific and debilitating injuries. Early in the war, IEDs posed a threat primarily to arms and legs; now, they are causing brain injuries, even when shrapnel does not penetrate soldiers' heads. Doctors in Balad and at Landstuhl have also seen an increase in multiple burns to the skin, a result of incendiaries—chemicals designed to catch fire after the explosion, hurling shrapnel into the air like a fire-ball. Fortunately, our IED was packed only with rocks. This in itself would be a concern, as doctors know that metal shrapnel is heated to such a high temperature in a blast that it is effectively sterilized before entering the body. With rocks, my doctors would be unsure about the level of potential infection from the Iraqi bacteria.

Some of the soldiers on the flight came to the back of the plane to see Doug and me. They stood over my motionless body and asked the journalists why Doug and I were there. "Why would people who didn't have to be there risk their lives like that?" one of the grunts asked Kevin.

"Because they're journalists," Kevin answered simply, having weighed the risks many times himself. "That's what they do."

After a nine-hour flight, the plane touched down at Andrews Air Force Base, and again the precision of the military teams kicked into gear. Together with the soldiers, Doug and I were moved quickly off the plane on our gurneys, dwarfed by machines, lines, and IVs.

A crowd of photographers and reporters were waiting in a knot. A sign was posted just above my head to alert those transporting me of the special precautions they would need to take because of my missing skull piece. Not everyone exercised the discretion Kevin and Michele had shown in not taking my picture on the flight. The wires had carried my photo when I had arrived from Balad and was being moved from the C-17 to an ambulance on the tarmac at Ramstein. The NO BONE FLAP sign was prominent above my head. My twelve-year-old daughter, Cathryn, would see this photo in *People* magazine that week and burst into tears when she learned the specifics of my head injury. As one accustomed to covering an unfolding story, I had suddenly become the subject of one. It was not the first time I would be thankful for my sedated state.

Lee

Bethesda Naval Hospital, January 31, 2006

Our Landstuhl Survivors numbers had grown. Heading back with us were Robin Wiener, Vivi Vogt, and Vinnie Malhotra, still visibly shaken—gutted—from the events he had witnessed over the last seventy-two hours. Slowly, the laughter and the camaraderie began to work on him, but it would be weeks before his and Magnus's eyes totally lost their haunted, even guilty look when they spoke to me or Vivi.

Our first-class cabin took on something of a party atmosphere. Food, wine, jokes, and stories flowed. Our experiences had bonded us, but somehow Vivi and I stood apart. There was a haunted look in our eyes. Everyone else would, at some point, be able to walk away and go back to their lives and their spouses, no matter how horrid their dreams or how intense their moments of profound sadness. But ultimately only Vivi and I would truly understand the small and large differences this war would etch on our men. Like so many military wives before us, we would bear the day-to-day twenty-four-hour burden of caring for husbands with an uncertain future. Long after they appeared to have recovered, we would see the subtle scars of what this story had cost.

When we landed, I was one of the first people off the plane and in line for passport inspection. Numbly, I handed over my passport and looked blankly at the agent. It was disorienting to be back on U.S. soil so soon.

"Did you have a nice trip?" she asked brightly.

"Uhhh." I looked up, dazed, like a drunken woman, unsure of how to answer her. We had been in Germany for a little over sixty hours.

She looked closely at my passport, and instantly her brow furrowed and the smile faded. Here we go, I thought. I had grabbed my passport so quickly. Perhaps it had expired or there was some technicality that would throw me out of line and under some harsh klieg lights with a German shepherd nearby.

As she handed it back to me under the Plexiglas window, her face softened and she gently squeezed my hand, catching me completely off guard. "The nation's thoughts and prayers are with you, Mrs. Woodruff," she said.

The passport official's words were the first taste I would have of the magnitude of the story and how our family's experience would touch a chord, not only with military families but with countless others who had suffered grave injuries or illnesses and fought hard to recover. Bob and I were the temporary faces for what so many others had been through before us. The support and backing we had from ABC and from friends and family made us luckier than most. Yet we would also be uncomfortable with the attention Bob's injuries received. To us, what we were going through was no different from all the military families who had walked in our shoes. I thought of those families every single day, and I still do.

Bob's profession made me proud. I wanted my children to understand how competent their father was, how capable, how human, and how loved. I would never forget the lessons learned in China about the freedom of the press. For all the criticism media people continually get about being bleeding-heart liberals, most of the journalists I know put a huge premium on striving for objectivity. No matter what you want to say about our government, the First Amendment is a right we should never take for granted as a people. Freedom of expression, no matter how misguided that expression may be, is like oxygen to Americans. We wouldn't miss it until it was gone.

Upon arriving at Bethesda Naval Hospital, we were led upstairs to a room where the doctors would meet with us. Our numbers had grown. In the briefing room, our contingent now included the original Landstuhl Survivors, Bob's brothers and parents, and David Westin and others from ABC News. In addition, we had added Susan Baker, one of our dearest friends in D.C. and a pediatric anesthesiologist. Her husband, Robin, was a renowned neonatologist. They were both extremely smart and dedicated, had known Bob and me for years, and proved invaluable in helping us navigate the medical waters, research information, interpret terms and procedures, and spend time with Bob's parents, patiently explaining what was happening as the rapid-fire decisions and conversations often required us to move on in the interest of time.

Susan gave me a tight hug. She quickly pressed a gold chain into my palm, something I had requested so that I could wear Bob's wedding ring around my neck until he awoke. The necklace became my equivalent of a set of worry beads. I would find myself fondling the band, slipping the ring over my finger, or bringing it to my lips throughout each day and night. Now I felt for the inscription inside the band, which said simply 9·11·88 Love, Lee. The ring was my way of touching Bob and being next to him when I was not physically close.

Once, on a story, Bob had gone up in a navy fighter jet off an aircraft carrier, and he had been instructed to remove his ring. He slipped it in a pocket of the flight suit but after the ride, it wasn't there. Bob was so upset that the pilot took the plane back up in the air and turned it upside down to see if the ring would fall out of a crack. Nothing. In true Bob fashion, when he checked the suit one more time, he had found it, much to his relief, in another pocket. He had been so upset relaying that story to me that I was touched. That gold band had survived crazy story assignments, volcano walks, rock climbs, and undersea dives. Now, I thought, it needed to survive this too.

One by one we filed into the briefing room, and then the doctors came in, a seemingly endless line of white coats, green scrubs, and military dress. Each person introduced himself or herself. They appeared to come from every branch of medicine: trauma and critical care; oral and maxillofacial surgery, neurosurgery, orthopedic surgery, and ENT (ear, nose, and throat) surgery; anesthesiology; and general surgery, including a host of residents. How would I ever keep their names straight? I was dimly aware that Bob's public face made this a high-profile case for them. If anyone needed a reminder, all they needed to do was gaze out the window to the phalanx of live-TV trucks parked along Wisconsin Avenue.

I pulled a pad of paper from my oversized purse to organize some thoughts and try to keep a record of what they were saying, but when I looked down at my pad later it was mostly blank. It all felt like a giant circus, with different rings, acts, and sideshows. My head swiveled to a different corner of the room each time someone spoke. As each team gave their presentation about Bob's status, I looked around the room to try to catch a reaction from Dave, Shawn, Susan, or Mel. It was as if I needed to gauge my own response against theirs. My core was still amazingly steely. I would not let the bad information touch me. I would remain positive and listen for nuggets of hope in what they said.

One significant nugget came from this initial briefing. Bob was critically ill, Dr. Rocco Armonda, the neurosurgeon, explained, but he did *not* have a penetrating brain injury. Despite the rock shrapnel, the important parts of his brain were still intact. Moreover, the rocks had not appeared to cause permanent maiming damage to his face, although there were multiple contusions. We would not know what kind of internal damage the shrapnel had wreaked on his throat, neck, and facial nerves until Bob woke up and tried to speak.

His intercranial pressure, the pressure on his brain, had remained normal, but it was clear that there had been a discrete injury to the speech and language part of his brain, located in his left temporal lobe, his dominant lobe as a right-handed person. Additionally, as we'd learned in Germany, the blast had a concussive effect, shaking the whole brain. It would be impossible to know the effects of that until Bob awoke and they could begin to assess his cognitive ability.

The tube in the ventricles of Bob's brain, draining fluid off of the swollen organ, would remain for the time being, Dr. Armonda told us. The cerebral angiogram seemed to indicate that blood flow to his brain was good, and there was no evidence of damage to the blood vessels.

Bob's Glasgow Coma Scale, an evaluation that rates a patient's neurologic response on a scale of 3 to 15, was 3 to 4 when he arrived in Germany. (Three is the number you get just for being alive, totally unresponsive.) While in Germany, his scale had risen to 8. This was a good sign, they explained. The doctors believed that his jaw was fractured, and there were possible injuries to the esophagus. A large rock was lodged in the right side of his neck, his "good side," and they would need to explore that surgically as well. It potentially had caused major damage as it ripped through Bob's throat from the left side of his face, crossing all the way through to the right side of his neck. There was concern that cerebral spinal fluid was dripping out of his ear; if so, there might also be a fracture at the base of the skull.

Bob's scapula had been shattered by three big rocks, the orthopedic surgeon explained. There was a lot of dirt, gravel, and even pieces of his black nylon shirt in the wounds, and they would need to continue to clean them before ultimately sewing them up. Right now the wounds had been left open and were packed with antiseptic gauze, but they wanted to operate and close them soon.

Like so many of the soldiers, Bob had been contaminated with Acinetobacter. He had tested positive for this tenacious genus of bacteria that live in the Iraqi soil. So far he had not had an infection, but, as in Germany, we would all need to wear gowns, gloves, and masks to see him in the ICU.

It would be four to six months before they would replace the opening in Bob's skull with an acrylic composite, Dr. Armonda explained. With some soldiers, they were able to save the original skull and implant it in the fat of the abdominal wall until it was time to replace it. In Bob's case, the force of the blast, all 155 millimeters of the bomb, had shattered the skull on the left side, injuring the speech and language area of his brain, the very part that worked for a living.

I tried to hold on to as much of this information as I could, but I would have to ask others to repeat it later. However, I raised my hand after the initial presentation ended. "But Bob spoke after he was injured. Isn't that a good sign?"

Phil Perdue stepped forward, the physician in charge of Bob's overall care. "It *is* a good sign that Bob spoke right after the injury," he began, very carefully. "But it is pretty common for that to happen and it may not be an indicator of the outcome. Also, we don't know what was damaged in the subsequent surgeries to save his life in the field hospital."

"There are a lot of important nerves in that area and in the face," chimed in one of the ENTs. "It's some high-priced real estate."

"Is he blind? Deaf?" I asked, with a forcefulness and calm I didn't feel.

"We don't know yet, ma'am," said another doctor softly.

"Think of it this way," Dr. Armonda said later, when I asked what he thought about Bob's future. "If you are a person who sharpens pencils for a living and you have a brain injury, you will probably not have as many neurons from your former life to help rehabilitate yourself.

"But if you are a person like Bob Woodruff, who is forty-four and has made great use of his brain in his life, speaks multiple languages, has an intellectual curiosity and abundant life experiences, you have a better shot at how well those neurons are going to reconnect. Think of those neurons as a road—I-Ninety-five, for example. If the only way your brain knows how to get from New York to Washington is along I-Ninety-five, and a giant jackknifed truck closes all lanes of the highway, you are in trouble.

"But if you are Bob Woodruff and you know alternate routes, you can take back roads or board Amtrak or hop on the shuttle flight at Reagan National. If you are a person who can come up with other solutions, who has really used your brainpower, you have more chance to develop alternate pathways for cognitive function and reasoning and putting all those neurons back together again."

It seemed a small thing to hang on to—Bob's brilliance—but the analogy gave me comfort. If ever there was a brain that knew how to navigate and use its neurons, I thought, it was my husband's. Perhaps brainpower and sheer will to live would drive his recovery. With Bob, I knew, anything was possible.

There were pat phrases that the Bethesda medical staff employed often: "It's a long road" . . . "The brain is like a computer rebooting, waiting to come online" . . . "It's a marathon, not a sprint." We would often cringe at these lines, but they reminded us that recovery from a brain injury would seem eternal. Improvement would occur at a snail's pace. If anyone believed this would be a simple healing, like breaking a leg, they needed to think again. It would take a while for this information to sink in, but eventually it did. And the phrases helped us understand.

"We'll need you to sign some consents, Mrs. Woodruff. For surgery, ma'am. We'll need your permission to operate, we need to read you the risks of anesthesia." One of the doctors pushed a pile of papers under my nose and it occurred to me suddenly that this all came down to me because I was Bob's legal guardian; he was solely my legal responsibility. I hadn't considered this before. Even though his parents and three brothers were sitting around the table, he was mine. I was no longer the daughter-in-law, I was now the adult. They had no say. There was something scary and shocking about that simple revelation. Bob was incapable of making decisions for himself.

I looked at Bob's parents. They seemed stunned and overwhelmed. I'd known them for twenty years, and the last few days had been extraordinarily difficult. Bob's mom was a striking blonde with long legs who had kept her svelte figure for life. It was her eyes, those deep-set clear Norwegian eyes with dark brows, that had been passed to the boys. She was one of the most upbeat people I knew and had more friends than almost anyone.

Her signature saying, "It only takes a minute," applied to baking chocolate chip cookies for sick friends, driving to visit her boys at college, or unpacking us after every one of our moves around the country. She loved her four sons fiercely, with the pride of a lioness, and she would defend them to the death. They never had any flaws in her eyes and could do no wrong. For a daughter-in-law this was as admirable as it could be maddening.

Much like my parents, Frannie had been born into a family and at a time when people didn't dwell outwardly on feelings and emotions. Like my own mother, she thought the tabloid craze to tell all was undignified. There were certain things you didn't say out loud. There was a lot to admire in that generation, real heroes and defined villains, manners, morals, and ethics in a black-and-white code. But the world had moved on, and this world was confusing. It was a world where sons got blown up while doing their job. The possibility of burying one of her strapping boys defied the natural order of things in a normally ordered life.

Bob's dad, "Big Bob" as the boys called him, was an old softie. He was quick with a joke and the boys loved to tease him back. It was from their father that the four Woodruff sons learned the demonstrative aspects of love: hugs, tears, sentimentality, and I love you's. They would all grow to be men comfortable, in familiar circles, with revealing their emotions. For that, the Woodruff wives would be eternally grateful.

As I watched Bob's parents tentatively prepare to visit him for the first time, their precious son with part of his skull missing, I ached for them. They'd known and loved Bob for a quarter century before I'd come on the scene. While their day-to-day life no longer revolved around Bobby, as they called him, these two people had brought him into the world. The thought of seeing one of my own children helpless in an ICU was unimaginable. I rested my face in the open palms of my hands as they left the room.

Bob

Beijing, April 1989

By spring in China there was a change in the air that no one could have anticipated. National politics were in a state of unrest and economic reforms had overheated the nation. Inflation was high, and the average Chinese worker was having a harder time buying everyday goods like food and clothing. Rumors persisted about corrupt party members, graft, bribes, and scandal. The leaders were not practicing what they preached.

On April 15, the death of former secretary-general Hu Yaobang fell like an ember into dry brush. Friday night after his death, 200,000 students came out to Tiananmen Square to mourn him. The mourning became a veiled means of supporting democracy and democratic reforms, for Hu had been a champion of free speech and a free press, making him a hero among the students. His death had become a flashpoint for anger at the perceived nepotism of the government.

As the days passed, the movement continued to gain strength, changing from mourning Hu's death and extolling his accomplishments to the beginning of democratic protests. The students became bolder, chanting slogans about democracy and freedom. Released from their prison of expression, the students were speaking out in favor of reforms. Soon they were occupying the square and boycotting school, setting up tents and food services and creating a large-scale protest directly across from the massive concrete Communist Party buildings.

Life on our campus took on a slightly different tone. The students were excited, and there was a crackling energy in the air that had not been there before. Students also told me that their mail was being opened at school and there were reports of people listening in on phone conversations.

My students were actually lawyers who had already graduated but were studying in a special program established by the Ministry of Justice. They were under strict orders from their bosses not to participate in the student demonstrations on pain of losing their bonuses, which constituted a large portion of their meager pay. But on May 17, for the first time in Communist China, lawyers marched against the government. Now, like every other university teacher in town, I had a de facto vacation while Lee continued toiling away, putting the finishing touches on Canada-China Month, a PR project that had taken many hours and much coordination between the Chinese government and the Canadian embassy.

I tried to study Chinese in the extra hours, when the routine of my teaching days came to a screeching halt, but I would often find myself drawn to the square, biking down to visit with some of my students or just see what was happening that day.

One night Lee and I visited Zhong Nan Hai, the Chinese White House, where the students were camped out on a hunger strike. One of the Zheng Fa teachers was there, and because I was a teacher they let us through the security lines that the students had so carefully erected so I could talk to her. We told her how proud we were of what she was doing and that we were thinking of her. She was painfully thin and was supported by two or three of her students, her summer dress so flimsy in the heat. Behind her in the tent was an amazing scene: students draped everywhere, many of them looking completely exhausted. The days had grown incredibly warm and mounds of garbage and trash littered the square. Sitting cross-legged in a totally rigid formation, People's Liberation Army soldiers in drab olive uniforms were lined up by the entrance to the compound.

In the weeks before the demonstrations, I had met with one of the partners at my law firm, Shearman & Sterling. They had been considering opening an official Beijing office, and there was a chance that Lee and I could stay. There was an even greater possibility that we could be sent to Hong Kong next. Lee's firm, Hill & Knowlton, had talked to her about a potential position there.

But on May 20, martial law was declared in the city of Beijing. The students had refused to move from the square, despite the government's repeated requests. All at once, military helicopters were flying low down the major boulevards in the city, buzzing almost at the height of the few office towers that dotted the skyline at the time.

May 21 was the date that the Shearman & Sterling law partners had picked to come back and make a final decision about the office. The meeting was an about-face. As the partners talked to me, a bizarre sight happened, something directly out of a movie. All at once four army helicopters swooped out of the sky, giant blaring loudspeaker systems squawking unintelligibly about martial law. The helicopters flew so low we could see them each buzz by the third-floor balcony at the Jiango Hotel window, following the path of Chang An, the Boulevard of Peace, that led to Tiananmen Square. The students on the square rose up in a show of solidarity to convince the helicopters not to drop tear gas while students with megaphones were preaching nonviolence and telling people how to react if gas was dropped.

I could not imagine a more bizarre scene for these lawyers to be witnessing on one of their infrequent visits to the capital. It was a grim sign that the People's Republic was not yet the most stable place in which to open an office. They were concerned about Lee's and my safety and urged us to check into the hotel for that night at least.

To no one's surprise, the partner in charge of the Pacific Rim announced that he had made an immediate decision. There would be no Beijing office. Furthermore, they would not be moving people to Hong Kong at this time. I was stunned. I had thought that at least we would be able to stay in Asia. As I walked around the square after the meeting, I felt dejected and uncertain about our future for the first time.

The white plaster Goddess of Democracy Statue, a Chinese version of the Statue of Liberty, was raised in the square on May 29. It was the ultimate expression of defiance to the government; she stood staring straight at the portrait of Chairman Mao on the Forbidden City wall. More than six feet tall, she was clutching a torch with two hands, sort of like a baseball bat. As an American I couldn't help feeling enormous pride at how these students looked toward our Constitution as a kind of model.

I thought of Lady Liberty standing in New York Harbor and what that image meant to so many people around the world. I was proud and also somewhat uncomfortable that I held a passport to a country where we had so many freedoms, and yet there was so little appreciation by many Americans of exactly what that meant in the greater world. It was easy to get greedy as well as complacent about your liberties when you lived in a democracy. It was a luxury to sweat the small stuff.

Looking at China now, and at some of the economic and social freedoms that have been accorded to the people in the last twenty years, it is hard to imagine the power and the magic with which that time was imbued. The students were taking an enormous risk. There was a feeling of intense excitement and pride, and a sense in those early days too of possibility. This gamble might actually work. Perhaps the old men of the Chinese government might blink.

With Lee's relationship to the foreign journalists, she got a call at Hill & Knowlton from CBS. They knew I was a teacher and they wanted to interview an American teacher about the striking students. They liked the fact that I was teaching law and not English, as it gave me more credibility to discuss the political angle. In addition, the Zheng Fa students and teachers had been at the forefront of the original mourning that sparked the demonstrations. Would I be interested? the producer from CBS wanted to know.

I didn't hesitate. Without classes I was becoming bored. And I had also spent a great deal of time on the square and could talk knowledgeably about what the students were thinking and feeling. A time was arranged, and I biked down to the makeshift CBS offices at the Shangri-La Hotel to meet with the producer.

Dan Rather was there and people were all around him trying to get him to sign things. There were still many tourists staying in the hotel, and the atmosphere had the aura of a carnival. The square full of students had itself become a tourist attraction. Dan was doing his live broadcast in front of a pretty prefab pagoda at the back of the hotel. If someone had told me then not only that Dan and I would share a house in Afghanistan twelve years later but that he would also become a friend, I would never have believed it. If someone had told me that I would eventually occupy an anchor seat at one of the networks, I would have laughed even harder. Back then, the lure of journalism was only a seed beginning to germinate in my mind.

I spent over an hour that day being interviewed by veteran reporter Jack Sheahan for the Sunday evening news, anchored at the time by Connie Chung. I was fascinated by the process and all the equipment, and hung around to watch as they edited the news piece and to meet some of the crew.

One of those people, Susan Zirinsky, a producer for the show, would play a pivotal role in our lives.

Susan, fondly known as Z, had more energy and intelligence packed into her little pinkie than most people expend in a day. The Holly Hunter character in *Broadcast News* had been modeled after her, and she was equally lovably neurotic, accomplished, and in control as befit our crazy industry. There was no one better.

After my on-camera interview, I managed to meet Z. With school out of session due to the demonstrations, I wanted to make myself useful, but I could also smell the adrenaline of a business that was so foreign to the legal world that I had come from. I could physically feel the excitement of being in the middle of something so vital. News was immediate. It caused you to act and react; there was kinetic energy as events unfolded. Decisions could be made in a split second.

"I'd like to ask you about a job as a fixer," I said to Z. For any news-gathering operation on foreign soil, especially non-English-speaking countries, a critical part of the equation is someone called *the fixer,* usually a local person who can speak the language and who knows how to get things done and how to get around locally. They facilitate things for the news crews and reporters, translate, and keep their ears to the ground for news or rumors that might be part of a larger story.

"How good is your Chinese?" she said, cocking her head and really noticing me for the first time.

"I'm okay," I said. I knew my Mandarin still needed a lot of improvement, but it seemed about on a par with the American students CBS had already hired.

"Well, we need better than okay, we need really good," said Z, in a friendly but firm way. "We're expanding the operation here and we need translators that can really get us around the city and help us understand what's going on."

I shook her hand, thanked her, and moved to the elevator bank to push the DOWN button. But our conversation was bothering me. This was my chance. At that moment an American student walked by and said something in Chinese to one of the hotel employees. I can do that, I thought. I speak better than that.

In that instant I made a decision that shaped the rest of my life. I turned on my heel and marched back. Z was poring over a script, glasses on top of her head, chewing absent-mindedly on a fingernail. "Give me a shot," I said confidently. "My Chinese is really pretty good, as good as anyone you have here, and I can do this job. If you don't agree, fire me after a week." I stood my ground, but my heart was beating faster.

Z broke into a grin. Z loved chutzpah, and this was red-blooded American chutzpah right in front of her. "Okay," she said. "That's fair. Can you start tomorrow?"

Being bitten by the journalism bug was as simple as that. Reviewing documents at a law firm would never feel the same after the excitement and energy of watching one of the world's epic events of the decade unfold. But I would have much to learn. Talking to the producer at CBS after I saw the final cut of the news piece with my interview, I was appalled and dismayed.

"Wow, I must really have stunk when you interviewed me," I said to the editor. "I talked to you guys for about an hour, and you only used ten seconds."

"Yeah," the man said. "That's pretty standard, about all the time we have in this business. Even ten seconds is a lot." Making my case in TV news was going to be a lot different from doing it in a court of law.

Spring gave way to summer heat as the students became more bold. We interviewed peasants and members of the army, we talked to students and intellectuals, and we combed the square. It was exhilarating work, and I was in awe of everyone: the correspondents and camera people, the soundmen, and the producers, whose job it was to distill the story for the day, check the facts, and get it on the air. Those Beijing days were heady for everyone in the news media, but I knew that I was seeing journalism at its apex.

I had been pulling fourteen-hour days or longer with the CBS crews, and I would return to our dorm room at the university at odd hours, exhausted and exhilarated, full of stories, which I would eagerly relay to Lee. The student movement and the story appeared to be losing steam. A malaise had set in on the square. But like so many things in China, it would soon prove to be deceptive.

Lee

Beijing, June 3, 1989

On the late afternoon of June 3, I had been washing clothes and drying them on a line that Bob had rigged in our room over the bed. "You're doing laundry while Rome burns?" Bob had said to me incredulously, from a CBS satellite phone that the reporters had lent him on the square. It was stuffy in the room, and very little air was moving outside.

He called me again to report that troops were moving into the square on foot en masse. "The shit has hit the fan," he said to me, excited and distracted. He could hear gunfire in the distance and the rumble of tanks. There were people everywhere, he reported. The citizens appeared to be talking the soldiers down from the tanks and he said it was getting wild. Random fighting was breaking out.

"Stay where you are," I cautioned him. "Please don't get in the middle of everything," I pleaded.

He assured me that he wouldn't. "I probably won't be home

tonight," he said. "There's too much going on here. Don't come down now," he warned me. "It's chaos." The school dorm, on the other hand, was quiet as a tomb for the first night in a long time. All the students were either on the square or on their way down. I was exhausted. The constant noise in the hallways and the ever-present loudspeaker system, now taken over by the students, had meant fitful sleep for weeks. I lay down with the thought of just closing my eyes for a second. Over my head, the clothesline full of shirts and socks waved gently in the warm breeze from our open window as I drifted off.

The next thing I knew, the phone in our room was ringing loudly. It was 4 A.M. A million miles away I heard the voice of my sister Nancy. "Lee, are you watching TV?" she asked nervously, not understanding that the only news we could get was from CCTV, a government-controlled station.

"No, why?" I answered, immediately on alert.

"They just reported that the army began firing at the students on the square. Many are dead. It looks like chaos there."

"God, Nancy, Bob may be out there somewhere. I don't know. I have to find out what's going on." I hung up and immediately dialed the CBS News local number. A young person with a flat American accent answered the phone.

"I'm looking for my husband, Bob Woodruff," I said. "He's a fixer for you guys. He said he would be at the bureau tonight?" There was the sound of a muffled phone, as if someone was covering the receiver or passing it over to someone else.

"Um," said the voice of the desk assistant, "uh—we don't exactly know where he is. Do you think you could call back? We're waiting for the crews to check in."

The answer was not sufficient. "That's my husband out there working for you guys. Surely you must know where they are; I know they carry radios," I said, more insistently. I might have been born with the eldest child's need to please but I was no pushover. Living in New York had taught me that.

"Hold one second," said the voice. Her stall tactics had run out. All at once I heard Z's authoritative voice on the phone. We'd met once or twice in the hotel when I'd biked over to visit Bob after work. There was something so capable about her demeanor I liked her instantly. She was Jewish mother and big sister all rolled into one.

"Lee," said Z, "the truth is that we *don't* exactly know where Bob is. He was on the square with Bob Simon and his crew when the lights were shot out. We're trying to get in radio contact with them but there's no answer right now. Their phone is out of batteries, that's the God's honest truth. But they are going to be okay." She reassured me, in a voice that didn't sound entirely reassuring. "We're sending another crew out now to find them."

"I'm coming down," I said, without hesitation. "I'll be there as soon as I can." I hung up. If something had happened to Bob, I wanted to be where the information would come in.

I grabbed a backpack and shoved some clothes in and a few toiletries. As I closed the door I could not have known it would be the last time I would see our room for almost two weeks. We would return to the school once, hiding, to pack our things quickly, no longer welcome in China. Our university would be identified by the government as one of the "black nests" of democracy. Someone would report that Bob used the book *Animal Farm* to teach his students.

Quickly I flung the pack on my back and as I biked away from the school I started crying softly. How many of our students would return? My heart was pounding. Where exactly was Bob, and why didn't they know? He certainly wasn't risk averse. If there was something they had needed him to do, he would have done it eagerly. He had quickly become one of the fixers that Z trusted most. And Bob Simon was one of CBS's best and most fearless reporters. If the two men were together, they would be somewhere in the midst of the crackdown.

Beijing was eerily quiet. The wind whistled through my ears and I realized that, nervous as I was, there was a clarity of thought in my head that would guide me. Though terrified that I might learn tragic news when I got to the CBS bureau, another part of me was steeled against it. This was the first time I would discover how I responded in a real crisis.

My life had been simple and fairly trouble-free thus far. Two parents still alive and together, and no tragedies up close, only a high school friend killed in a drunk-driving accident while I was at college.

Clearheaded, rational, adrenaline fueled, I would not understand the true importance of the zone until years later with Bob's injury. But I marveled during this bike ride that I was not falling apart, sobbing, giving in to fainting spells, or hunched over the toilet bowl vomiting.

As I biked along the ring road I saw groups of people huddled under the streetlights around radios. Under martial law, the city was declaring a new set of rules about congregating and curfews. I felt a solidarity with all of them but was aware that my status had changed. As a foreigner, consorting with me was now potentially dangerous. At the very least my status was unclear. Tentatively I raised my hand to wave to a group of older people I was passing. One woman in a Mao suit had the bound feet of the pre-Communist era; next to her was a younger man.

"Be careful, La Wei," he called out in English. "It is very dangerous out there now. You should not be on the street." Over my head I heard a chirping sound, and when I looked up I saw two bats swooping and then more, a whole swarm. The bat is a symbol of good luck in China. What could their appearance possibly mean now?

I raised my hand again to thank him, not wanting to yell out in the velvety darkness. I had a few more miles to go and my legs felt exhausted despite all of my months of biking. I was pedaling as fast as I could, keeping an eye out for the potholes and rocks in the road that were a trademark of the outer streets. I passed another neighborhood group and their sentry, who I assumed was posted to look out for the army. Farther up ahead toward the hotel, some people had stopped two army trucks with supplies. Some of them were sitting in the road, blocking the trucks.

Bob

Beijing, late afternoon, June 3, 1989

There is a Chinese adage that is resurrected whenever there is a political movement, and it was on many Chinese minds during the days of martial law immediately leading up to the crackdown: "After the autumn harvest, accounts will be reckoned."

The afternoon of June 3 was just another sunny lazy day for us as we waited and watched the square from the vantage point of the Monument to the People's Heroes. The monument had become familiar ground to every news crew and journalist covering the demonstrations. Student guards surrounded the area, allowing only the foreign press and certain ranks of student leaders to enter. ABC, CNN, CBS, and NBC cameras were continually panning the square as bored news crews drank beer and told jokes. NBC was even taking orders for T-shirts that would read TIANANMEN BEACH 1989 and on the back SERFS UP.

At 2 P.M., one of the producers with us asked me to follow a couple of U.S. embassy personnel who had just been filmed on the monument in order to get their names. Apparently he thought it inappropriate for our government to be behind the lines during the demonstration, since it could be interpreted as foreign interference. I trailed the two as they strolled to the Great Hall of the People. Pushing through the crowd, I caught the first glimpse of the soldiers. Filling the street was a sea of about five thousand green helmets, surrounded on all sides by the people of Beijing. An additional blockade, a public bus, was placed sideways across the road, a common sight ever since martial law was declared. There were no television cameras in sight, so I radioed the CBS headquarters at the Shangri-La Hotel to request a crew immediately.

The crowd cheered as I climbed a tree next to the soldiers, helping me up and practically ordering me to take pictures. They were angry and outraged at the soldiers. It was clear that the army had appeared from inside the Great Hall of the People with no warning.

Suddenly, three, maybe four, distant explosions rattled the air from the west as several clouds of smoke floated up in the sky. We later learned that this was tear gas. In order to get a better camera angle, several of us climbed up on top of the bus, blocking the soldiers. They were angrily ordering us to get down, when a rock the size of a billiard ball hit me on the inner thigh. I couldn't tell if it was thrown by a soldier or a civilian.

Eventually, the troops went back into the Great Hall and I returned to the square. Over the next two hours, at least three students, bloodied by leather belts, clubs, or helmets wielded by the frightened PLA, displayed their wounds to the crowd and to the press. Some held their bloodstained shirts above their heads; others gripped helmets ripped from their assailants. Finally, at eight-thirty, the sun set in the west. I was ordered back to CBS.

As darkness fell on Beijing that night, we began hearing reports, from our own crews and outside sources, that armed troops were descending on the square. I began to map their movements, trying to keep up with rapid-fire updates from the city center. At 10 P.M., correspondent Richard Roth radioed in to report hundreds of troops, marching seven abreast, past the Beijing Hotel, just 150 yards east of Tiananmen Square. Ten minutes later, Lisa Weaver, the fixer who had relieved me at the monument, reported that soldiers who had come up from the south had withdrawn behind the Kentucky Fried Chicken restaurant southwest of the square.

At 10:50, Jack Sheahan, the CBS Beijing bureau chief, received a report that a large "fireball" was burning somewhere near the Military Museum, about a mile west of the square. Immediately two camera crews rushed to the scene, just as Reuters reported a rumor of gunfire in the general area.

Cameraman John Liu was the first to arrive, met by hundreds of locals beseeching him to get to Muxidi, where they said up to twenty people had been killed. As one wounded man was carried past them, they followed him quickly to Fuxingmen Hospital. "There are a lot, maybe five or six wounded right next to me, and they are carrying them in about one a minute," screamed Kenny Geraghty, a young South African soundman, from the radio.

"Are they gunshot wounds? Can you see?" asked the producer back at the base.

"Looks like bullet wounds to me. I've seen about five more wounded come by me.

"We're hearin' a lot of gunfire comin' from just north of here." We could hear the noise of a crowd in the background; then the soundman came back on. "We're gettin' out of here, people are really emotional."

"Okay, do whatever you think is safe."

The shooting at Muxidi continued, seemingly unabated. At 12:16 A.M., the first armored personnel carrier rolled into the square from the south, and at 1:09 A.M. Fuxingmen Hospital reported more than eighty people seriously wounded. They said they had no time to count the dead. ABC reported more than a hundred wounded or dead. Throughout the night I kept track of reports of troops, gunfire, and the death toll, spurred on by one of the most intense adrenaline rushes I had ever experienced.

At 2:49, Richard Roth called from the southwest side of the square and spoke to one of the producers, Bruce Dunning, who had been one of the last people out of Da Nang in 1975. "Are you getting out of there? Is everyone okay?" we heard him ask before hanging up. He turned and reported to us. "There's an APC rolling into the square. Roth says every-one is okay but his batteries are running low."

John Liu, producer Peter Schweitzer, and I headed for the square by jeep with a new phone, three bottles of water, and a bottle of Johnnie Walker Red for Derek Williams, a Viet-nam-era cameraman from New Zealand. Using only back alleys, we snaked our way down the square from the south-west. Having practically lived there for the past two weeks, we knew the area well. But things were different tonight.

The residents of the hu-tongs, or alleys, were all awake, grouped outside their doors, discussing the tragedy unfold-ing, yielding to our jeep as we passed. Fifty yards from the square we were driving along the south side of the Great Hall of the People when a clip of automatic weapons fire rang out immediately to our left. John stepped on the gas and we turned sharply into an alley. We hadn't even noticed the thou-sand or so soldiers sitting on the steps of the Great Hall as they fired over our heads.

Roth and his crew were not where we agreed to meet, so we moved north along the west side of the square, keeping close to the line of brightly burning lampposts. Suddenly, the line of lights running east to west across the square went out, followed by the line just north. As we walked, darkness fol-lowed us as the government blackened the square.

We contacted the CBS base and got Roth's new location, but Williams was in no mood for scotch. Once we dropped off the batteries, they refused to leave with us despite the fact that a new column of troops was marching into the square from the southwest corner. All of sudden, it seemed, gunfire was everywhere.

As we hopped in the jeep to get back to the base, we heard that Roth, Williams, and possibly several other CBS people had been taken captive and probably beaten by the PLA while Roth was reporting live to New York. We had left him only minutes earlier.

Lee

Beijing, June 4, 1989

The CBS temporary bureau in the Shangri-La Hotel was humming with activity, but there was a noticeable pause when I walked in. Z looked tense.

"He's in the square," said Z, not missing a beat when she saw me. "He wanted to go." My heart sank. It was 5 A.M. and my hands were trembling. Z explained that Bob had come back as he had promised me, but then two crew members, a fixer and a correspondent, had had their base radios lose power, and Bob and cameraman John Liu had volunteered to take a new radio to them on the square.

What I was seeing on the monitor above my head made me sick. The injured were rushed on bike rickshaws to hospitals and students held up blood-soaked clothes. There were so many troops and so many scared people on the square. The city seemed to be on fire, buses and trucks were burning, there was mass confusion, and the helicopter was back overhead.

A phone call came in from the fixer Lisa Weaver. She had been separated from the crew and was alone with the radio, terrified and trying to avoid getting hit by stray shots. One of the producers radioed to Bob and John, who were looking for her unsuccessfully in the crush of people. Just then New York called and Richard Roth, only able to talk to New York and not the Beijing bureau, gave his coordinates on the southwest corner of the square. Bob and John were going to try to find him with the new battery. We learned later the lights were being shot out on that section of the square first, and Lisa called back to say the crew had been taken by the troops. We didn't know exactly who, other than Richard, they had taken.

Just then soundman Brad Simpson showed up with his leg cut and swelling from being pushed into a barrier by the troops as they wrestled with his camera.

"Brad, can you please get on the radio and tell me if you can get Bob and John to answer?" I pleaded. Something about my look of panic must have moved him because, instead of cleaning himself up, he immediately began trying to reach the two men on the radio again. For five minutes, no one came on the air. Z looked over tensely. She had heard the sounds of troops kicking Richard and smashing the camera before the radio was confiscated. We would learn later that Richard had been taken to the Great Hall of the People by the troops but ultimately released.

All at once, behind Brad, I saw Bob and John walking in and I stifled a little squeal and gave him a big hug. His eyes were bloodshot and he smelled like a long night in a hot place. There was something in his eyes that made him look almost high from all he had just experienced. For a journalist, what was happening on Tiananmen Square was akin to mainlining heroin.

"I was scared when we didn't hear from you. . . ." I trailed off.

"You're not going to lose me that easily," he said, with a full-wattage smile. It was clear he was hooked on this journalism thing.

Bob

Beijing, June 5, 1989

In the days that followed the crackdown, Beijing was transformed into a completely different city from the one we had known. On June 6, Lee and I biked to the school. I had heard a rumor that some of the students there had been shot. It didn't take long to locate them where a group had assembled at the front of the campus.

In the building where I had taught all year, three bodies were lying faceup on two long tables pushed together, each atop several twenty-pound blocks of ice. The three corpses looked up to a heaven they were told didn't exist, shot by bullets we were told were never fired. In the case of the third student, his head was crushed by a tank or other vehicle the government denied had ever charged. Long drained from beneath their waxy skin, their blood had run over the edge of the table, forming small pools on the concrete floor.

Although it was morning, the warm June day was melting the big blocks of ice in steady drips that mingled with the blood. Dark dried blood was crusted around a bullet hole in one student's neck, in sharp contrast to his white face. I thought of hunting with my brothers in northern Michigan and the way my father would hang a deer upside down. These students reminded me of that, hunted and shot like animals. Caught in the crosshairs at simply the wrong place when the bullet was passing by. Jubilation and joy had turned to horror and grief. Around them students were mourning, talking softly, crying, touching their dead comrades' feet and hands.

Lee and I paid our respects and tears stung my eyes. These were not my direct students, but students of the undergraduate school. We felt out of place, older and foreign. These fallen students were theirs to mourn. Who had taken such gentle care of them, purchased the ice, combed their hair, folded their hands? Where were their parents? Our hearts broke for these young people and all the people of China. A sense of purpose and hope had been extinguished so suddenly. Elation had turned to despair.

We stayed in China for more than a week, working for CBS, and went back to the university once more only to get our things. We had to pay a driver the equivalent of almost $100 U.S. just to take us there and wait, he was so afraid to be seen with foreigners. There was apparently a rumor that an American teacher at Zheng Fa was teaching incendiary classes and had gotten people at the school all riled up. There was only one person that could have been: me. At first I was furious, then slightly nervous, and then I simply felt betrayed. I had said it wouldn't be so bad to be thrown out of the school or the country for teaching what you believed, but it still stung.

In one of the last classes I'd held, we'd had a rousing talk about the events leading up to the protests. I had expressed my views about how the government was letting the people down, and at the end of class my students gave me a standing ovation.

The situation in China had turned dramatically since then, and one of my students had betrayed me. I would try not to take it personally. For students of history, the pendulum in China had swung again. In one swift motion it had gone back to the terrifying days leading up to Mao's Cultural Revolution.

Lee

Bethesda Naval Hospital, January 31, 2006

Somehow my husband had gone from a vital, living, breathing man to a critically wounded set of organs and flesh hooked up to tubes. While his life-and-death condition had stabilized since Landstuhl, he was by no means out of the woods. There was a huge danger now of secondary infections in his weakened state.

We were still absorbing how our lives had been overturned in an instant; how a husband, son, brother, and father was clinging to life through a set of steel doors just down the hall in the ICU. We were all stunned after the first official doctors' briefing in Bethesda. There had been so much information, delivered by so many people. And this was not a bad dream or a nightmare from which I would wake up.

"Well," said Bob's mother, turning her coiffed blond head to look at her sons, "I'm not sure I understood any of that." She really did sort of sum things up.

It was late, and it was time to feed David Woodruff to the wolves. David Westin would join him in front of the crush of cameras stationed outside the hospital to answer questions directed at ABC News.

As the eldest child in our respective families, Dave Woodruff and I were a lot alike. Like me, he was the one who got the coffeepot started in the morning. He was constantly in motion. Now Dave was undergoing a trial by fire as family spokesperson, but we knew he was up to the task.

ABC issued me a new cell phone from their bureau, with a number I could give out only to those I chose. But even this second phone rang incessantly. And in that first week in Bethesda, it felt as though the anesthesiology residents called each day to read me the potential risks involved in anesthesia, as Bob underwent more surgeries to remove rocks and clean the wounds in his back.

At one point, as they ticked off the multiple risks—respiratory problems, nerve injuries, blood clots, heart attack, and loss of bodily function or life, to name just a few—I became exasperated. "Why don't you just start with death and then we don't have to go any further," I barked. It was meant to be funny, but the person on the other end of the line didn't laugh. She had probably seen her share of things that went wrong. And of course they were required to describe the risks.

"I guess you've heard this before," she said, not knowing how to answer my sarcasm.

"You have my permission," I answered. And again I thought how odd it was to be making decisions about my husband and not be able to ask him, talk to him, get his counsel when I needed it most.

In that first week, many ABC News executives came to Washington, one by one, to meet me and the family. Their shock, grief, admiration, and respect for Bob somehow included me. I felt as if I'd known them for a long time. There was an obvious deep sorrow among this group of

ABC brass. There was also a palpable guilt that Bob's assignment had put him in harm's way. Each of these men and women had families of their own, and each must have been putting themselves in my shoes, if only momentarily.

Bob's colleagues and co-workers all reached out as part of a tight net to surround our family with concern and love. There cannot possibly be that many businesses where people travel together for weeks at a time, sleeping on dirt floors, borrowing razor blades, crossing borders in rattling Land Cruisers, and bellying up to bars in Third World countries where the drinking glasses need a good rinse. Being a foreign correspondent breeds a particular loyalty and closeness that is hard to imagine. Bob spoke about this occasionally to me, and after his injury I understood what he had described. It made me even prouder of him and his work.

After a few days in Bethesda, Melanie Bloom went back to her girls. My sisters flip-flopped to be with me one at a time, Bob's brothers took turns visiting, and his parents stayed. Magnus, the soundman who had been in the tank with Vinnie when the bomb exploded, arrived from London. He was instantly embraced by Vinnie and by Jimmy Woodruff, and they would retreat to the bar at night and pour out the details of how the attack had gone down and what had happened. It was a story I would not be ready to hear for a long time.

In those first few days I would take a walk with my sister Megan very early, as people were rising. Heading out along an old trail that passed behind neighborhoods, we would look in the windows and see mothers laying out breakfast and lighted upstairs bathrooms where people were climbing into the showers. I would think how absolutely normal it was, all those years when our life had looked equally ordinary. All those mornings I had woken up, reluctant to leave our warm bed. If I had only known then how wonderful it was, that simplicity of life's everyday routine: a cup of coffee by the computer, the cool of the kitchen floor before I put on my slippers, the warmth of my children's skin as I nuzzled them awake after a night of dreams.

As we walked outside, Bob was trapped in an airless ICU cubicle, moving in different ways. He lay on the hospital bed, almost dwarfing it, strong as an ox. When we visited, he seemed in constant motion, kicking, agitated, trying to get out of bed. Sometimes his eyes would open with a glassy faraway look. They had pulled the breathing tube from his mouth and intubated him instead. The long blue tube was now snaking out of a hole in his throat. His chest rose and fell as the machine breathed for him.

Bob was strong, the doctors said. That he had been in such good physical shape when the bomb exploded had probably saved his life. We had yet to see the gaping shrapnel wound on his back. It was some sort of a miracle, his surgeon Dr. Dan Valaik said, that the blasted rocks had stopped just a millimeter before the chest wall. They could have so easily punctured a lung or an artery.

The skin had been ripped open in five areas from the blast, right next to the lining of the lung. In the first few days after Bob arrived in Bethesda, they would clean the open wound three times, each time pulling out more dirt, gravel, and tiny pieces of Bob's black nylon shirt, packing it open to clean again. Finally, after the third surgery, they stitched it up. If it hadn't been for Bob's head, this injury would have been the major wound and he would have been lying in a different position. But a brain injury of Bob's magnitude meant that he had to lie still. His back could close and heal, even with him lying on it for the entire duration, which was not optimal. It was not the first time I would be glad he was sedated.

Bob began to look like the Michelin Man as the fluids filled his tissues. His hands and arms were like a giant's and his skin was taut, as if it would burst. His brain was still swollen out of his head like a giant tumor and the cuts on his face were turning to bruises. His left ear continued to leak a clear liquid, and the doctors were trying to determine if it was spinal fluid. I would position myself on his "good" right side, although the doctors suggested we keep talking to him from both sides, to retrain his brain to listen bilaterally.

Repeatedly, in his sedated state, he would throw his legs over the bed as if he had somewhere to go. The nurses and corpsmen would push him back down and hold him. Eventually they would have to place restraints on his arms, as if he were a patient in a mental hospital, to keep him from pulling out his tubes. We learned to stagger our visits so that someone could be with him during the day, to hold him down without the cruel wrist bands that made me feel they were treating him like an animal.

In his sedated state, day and night held no meaning for Bob. I could feel his awareness of me, though. I would whisper that I loved him, that he had been hurt and he was going to be okay, but that he needed to lie quietly. He couldn't answer or even respond with purposeful movement, but his restlessness would lessen.

Each day I would walk in at 6:30 A.M. and check on his overall condition and the night's behavior with the ICU nurse. Then, in that overly cheery voice that a mother uses with her baby, I would begin to coo and babble at Bob. I would talk about anything that came into my mind, a place we'd visited, a story about one of the kids, a silly nickname. Somewhere inside there his brain was healing, the doctors said. It would need to make those connections again and this time was as vital as any, even though outwardly it appeared he wasn't registering a thing. The brain is mysterious and, as with a newborn baby, stimulation is critically important.

We began gathering music, buying a boom box and copying our home movies to DVDs for Bob to watch. Bruce Springsteen, Miles Davis, Don Henley, Johann Sebastian Bach—they were all enlisted to become Bob's healers. We would try anything to stimulate his mind. Friends blew up giant photos of each kid and the family and we mounted them on the walls for when Bob woke up.

A family photo album that Sherrie Westin had put together for Bob was probably overly optimistic in those early days, but when I would see his eyes open blankly, I would hold it up and repeat the names of our children one by one. Perhaps it was wishful thinking but he seemed calmer at those times, and the sound of my voice seemed to bring him to a different kind of attention. I would touch his feet and stroke his hands, but I was terrified to touch him anywhere on his face, with its blank, vegetative stare looking back at me. Where were my husband's vibrant eyes?

In one of our few moments alone together in those early days, I had a bizarre thought. I imagined all the couples who had been in this situation: the car accident, the war, the factory injury, the sudden fall off a roof, the head injury skiing. How many of those husbands had decided maybe they didn't really love their wives long before the moment that their lives changed forever? How many couples were simply going through the motions?

It occurred to me that while some of those wives might never envy me, per se, maybe some of them could have used a little brain injury to jolt their husbands back to reality. Maybe there was a husband straying, or one who was just a little too fond of the Barcalounger and the remote control. A little brush with death might help remind them exactly what they did mean to each other and get those old priorities straightened out. Tragedy had the potential for real opportunity in a floundering marriage.

But here was the baffling thing. I couldn't for the life of me figure out why this had happened to Bob and me. We had had our share of big bumps in the road, but for the most part we were a couple who appreciated what we had. I wondered many times what it would be like to sit out a lonely vigil at your husband's bed, all the while infuriated over his transgressions with the little trollop he'd met at the office. I was grateful to feel only love, the pure white heat of emotion that cleanly burns out other feelings, be they anger, guilt, or even rage.

That first week was a blur. Each day passed with doctors, decisions, communicating with ABC about the information we were giving out, and strategizing about what to say. Sometimes I would take a nap for an hour to recharge my batteries, as I could never seem to make it past 5 A.M., even with a sleeping aid. That was when I involuntarily played the images of the attack over and over in my mind and made deals with God about taking back that one instant.

Then it was time to think about my children's need to see their father. This was a horrific thought on many levels. Their image of their dad was vital and loving. I wasn't sure they had even seen him sick before. How would they react to his shaved head, almost unrecognizable face, and swollen brain? What damage would be done by seeing their dad, unable to communicate with them, as he writhed naked under a bedsheet, attached to tubes that kept him alive?

One of the people who entered our life in those early days was the neuropsychologist Dr. Maria Mouratidis. As head of the Traumatic Stress and Brain Injury Program at Bethesda Naval Hospital, she treated the wounded and their families every day and assessed patients' cognitive abilities.

Dr. M, as we called her, was a font of information. She told me that even being near a blast had a concussive effect on the brain and could permanently affect things like executive function or the decision-making process. Cognitive therapy and other interventions were critical in helping people get back on their feet and heal. Dr. M explained all this and then the topic moved to my children.

It was bizarre to be living apart from them in a hotel, and I knew eventually we would need to get the family together. As much energy as it would take to be a single parent under the strains of grief, my children were also the source of my strength.

We decided that the kids would come down that first weekend. Mack would head to the Super Bowl with his uncles Shawn McLoughlin and Dave Woodruff. He'd been originally scheduled to go with Bob and sit in the announcers' booth for a stint. After the attack, David Westin had made it possible for Mack to have the experience with other family members.

The three girls and I would stay at Susan and Robin Baker's house, so that it would feel as normal and comfortable as possible. Although it was important that this not feel like a vacation, I wanted familiarity. We had met the Bakers when we lived in Washington, and their three girls had grown up with my kids through the years. Seeing them again all together would be a welcome distraction.

Dr. M helped me with some phrases to use with the kids and we decided to gauge their emotions as the weekend progressed. There should be no promises of seeing their father at this point. There was no way around the fact that it would be traumatic for each of them. And it didn't make it any easier that there were no definitive answers as to what their dad would be like and how he might be changed.

The most important thing—common sense, really—was to be honest with the kids. If there was an answer I didn't know, I needed to say so. If they were worried about something, I needed to let them know I was worried about it too. My children had to feel that they could trust the adults around them. More than anything else, consistency would be important.

We decided that one quick hospital visit for Cathryn would be the way to go for the first weekend. Mack would see his dad the following weekend. The twins would wait until later. They were so young, and the sight of their dad would be too grim at this juncture. It would be best to buy more time and hope that Bob would wake up and they could see him functioning at a higher level.

The kids arrived at the Bakers' and we fell into one another's arms. It had been only a week, and yet the children looked so big to me, so changed. I didn't even remember having said goodbye at home before I took the flight to Landstuhl.

They were anxious like puppies, looking at me with eyes that sought to read every emotion. I knew that how I appeared to them would set the tone. They had to trust me. Like meeting a prospective client, this first impression would be critical.

"Mom, you look skinny," Cathryn said. She touched the hollows in my cheeks, and I batted her hand away playfully. The Baker girls folded in around them and the twins ran to play with Otis, the puppy. We would have the upstairs guest room in their spacious Washington home. It would become our home away from home, a place where we Landstuhl Survivors could go night after night for dinner, wine, and a fire. It was our respite from hospital and hotel, the antiseptic smells, the institutional environment.

With input from Dr. M, we decided that Cathryn would see Bob that Saturday morning. At the hospital she began shaking like a leaf. As we walked through the metal doors of the ICU, she grabbed my hand so tightly I felt she would break a bone. I put my arms around her. I wished

I could have transferred my strength to her by some kind of mental transfusion.

"Mom, I'm scared," she said. Cathryn seemed so tall. She had her dad's coloring and his expressive eyes. Her hair was long and dark like his, often pulled back in a ponytail. Her smile can throw sunshine on an entire room. And when she was little, her grin took up so much of her face that we nicknamed her the Joker. You simply couldn't see Cath smile and not want to smile yourself. Now, as we closed in on Bob's room, her knees locked up. Her brows were furrowed and her whole body went rigid.

"Honey, you don't have to do this right now," I soothed. "It's okay. Maybe it's just enough to be near Daddy. Maybe you aren't quite ready to see him." On Dr. M's advice I had tried to prepare her for what she was about to see. I could not know whether I had undersold or oversold the image.

"No," she said adamantly, drawing reserves of strength from somewhere down in her toes. "Let's go." We parted the curtain and walked in together.

As her eyes came to rest on Bob, I heard a sharp intake of breath and saw her eyes well up in tears. There is simply no way to prepare a child for seeing her dad as a human slab.

I squeezed her hand harder and began babbling at Bob in my cheery caregiver voice. "Hey, honey, guess who's here?" I began my familiar monologue, pushing Cathryn around to Bob's good side. "Your Cackie is here, honey. She's right here with you."

At the sound of my voice and the mention of Cathryn's nickname, Bob began moving more rapidly. His eyes were open, like a blind man, seeing but unseeing. His body became more agitated.

I watched Cathryn watching Bob, taking in all the tubes and the beeping machines sending signals across a monitor. She seemed to want to ask me a question, but then she approached her father, taking his hand with its IVs and pulse oxygen monitor into her own. Bob's swollen hand dwarfed her little one.

She sidled up next to his good ear and cleared her throat. "Hi, Daddy," she said, in a voice growing more powerful with each word.

The summer of 1986, when we started dating in New York.
Babes in the woods!

The studious lawyer shows
an early passion for news.

Our wedding day, September 1988.

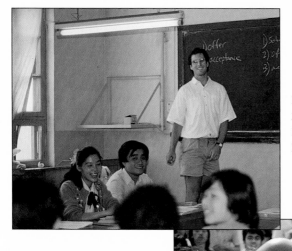

Bob in the classroom at Zheng Fa University in Beijing, teaching American law to Chinese lawyers, 1988.

A photo Bob took of unidentified students on Tiananmen Square after the crackdown. "Tell the world!" they cried.

Lee on the streets of Beijing picking up packages mailed from home, 1989.

On the balcony of our
spectacular North Beach
apartment in San Francisco, 1990.
Definitely pre-kids!

Camping in Michigan's
upper peninsula.

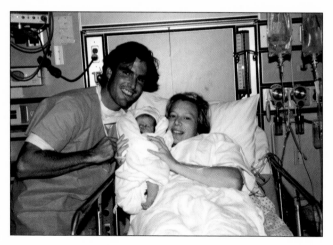

Macklin Robert Woodruff, our first child,
is born in San Francisco in July 1991.

April 2000: Lee with Nora and Claire,
the millennium babies—two
miraculous bundles of joy
and sleeplessness.

Cathryn and Mack hold
their new sisters.

Our family with Robert and Frannie Woodruff on the left,
Terry and Dave McConaughy on the right.

The Woodruff brothers:
Jim, Mike, Bob, and Dave.

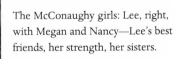

The McConaughy girls: Lee, right,
with Megan and Nancy—Lee's best
friends, her strength, her sisters.

David Bloom beats Bob once again and the winner gets to pose
in the victorious "big game" position.

Melanie Bloom and Lee.

Bob in Afghanistan, 2001, with a local team of assistants,
covering the Taliban's retreat into hiding.

The top: Elizabeth Vargas and Bob in the promotional shots for the new
World News Tonight format, 2006. A major advertising campaign was
scheduled to run the week he was injured.

During the initial Iraq invasion, in 2003, James Brolan and Bob were embedded with the marines. They lived through some horrific sandstorms, in which the sky turned an eerie color. James was killed by an IED in Iraq in May 2006.

Bob with U.S. and Iraqi troops, an hour before the IED (improvised explosive device) exploded.

Producer Vinnie Malhotra in the APC (armored personnel carrier) with an Iraqi soldier and the interpreter.

January 29, 2006: Seconds before the IED went off, Doug took this picture as he and Bob prepared to shoot their stand-up. The Iraqi soldier pictured reportedly lost his hand in the attack.

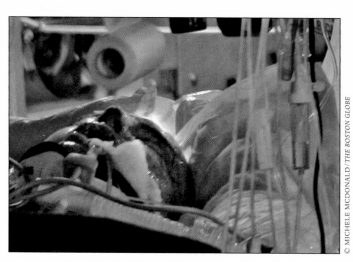

A close-up of Bob during the CCATT flight. Reporters from *The Boston Globe* snapped this shot, but did not share it with anyone, respecting the family's privacy.

The inside of our Critical Care Air Transport Team (CCATT) flight. The C-17 cargo planes are outfitted with all the medical equipment each patient needs, including one-to-one nursing care and doctors. This ability to provide continuous care has dramatically reduced the time it takes to get the injured back to the States. Medevac flights take priority even over the movements of Air Force One.

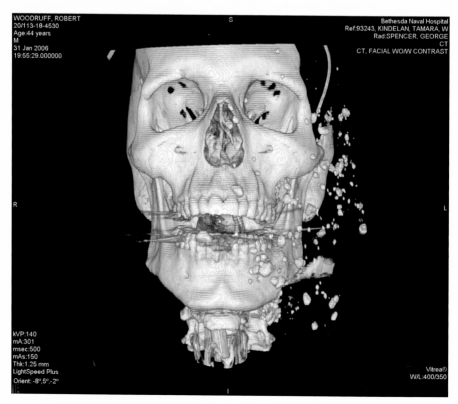

The 3-D CT scan of Bob's skull, showing all the rocks that were shot into his face, neck, and around his eyes. Not visible is the big rock that passed through his throat and came to rest against the carotid artery on the right side of his neck.

March 8, 2006: Two days after Bob first woke up, Mack and Cathryn
flew down to see him up and around for the first time.

Melanie Bloom visiting Bob at Columbia Presbyterian. He wore the
white helmet for almost four months, anytime he was on his feet.

Doug Vogt (the cameraman also injured with Bob) and his wife, Vivi, came back to
the States for Doug's first checkup in Bethesda. It was the first time
Doug had seen Bob awake since the incident.

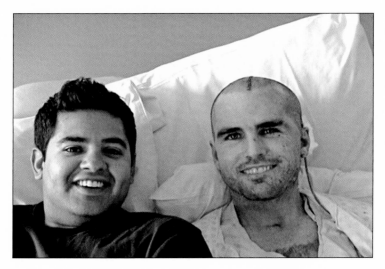

After the surgery to repair Bob's skull in May 2006,
Vinnie came to visit to cheer Bob up.

June 13, 2006: Walking back into the *World News Tonight* newsroom for the first time,
with ABC News president David Westin, was an emotional moment.
Bob still tired easily, but was excited to see his ABC family.

Back home on the beach in their own town. This picture says it all.

"It's Cackie. I love you so much. I know you are going to get better. You have to get better because we all need you to come home. Mack and Nora and Claire are all missing you too, so you have to get better. . . ." She trailed off and looked at me. I nodded approval.

"Tell him about school, honey," I urged her. And she began a commentary about her friends and classes, ending with how difficult math homework had been without him.

We love our children for so many complex reasons, the first of which is that most basic of human connections. Our selfless acts of service continue through the years; late-night feedings, flu bugs, and teenage moods be damned, they are hewn to us through bonds that defy words. Bob had an indelible connection to his children, and Cathryn, his eldest daughter, resided firmly in every chamber of his heart.

Bob's first daughter was a wonder to him from the moment she was born. Every ounce of wily manipulation that is genetically coded into the female was pure fascination for him. To me, it was strategic. I could see the same sly eye-batting tactics I had employed on my own father, to extend my curfew or cajole a little extra allowance for the blouse I wanted desperately to buy.

But Bob was bamboozled. Cathryn had his heart from the moment he first held her and looked into her honey-brown eyes. She was simply born happy. And she spent most of her days as a fairly contented kid. She and her father had all kinds of little rituals, especially when he was on the road and they would talk by phone. No matter what country he was in or what deadline he was on, she would call with math questions, taking the phone in her room and shutting the door to work it out from Gaza or Serbia or Baton Rouge.

"Daddy, let's do a kissing contest," Cath said now into Bob's ear. Her expression brightened as she looked at him. She was on familiar territory and was relaxing, getting used to her father's new face. It had been one of their bedtime rituals on the phone, when Bob was out of town. Both parties would kiss into the receiver as long as they could, and the first one to give up was the loser.

Cathryn lifted her head up to Bob's cheek and began to kiss it. I noticed with gratitude that one of the nurses had recently shaved him, leaving his face smooth and white on the right side. Looking at the two of them, so close, I felt the reverberation of our daughter's heart. I saw strength and sorrow and so much uncertainty. As her mother, I wanted to have all the answers for as long as time would permit. I wanted to be able to hang the moon in that way parents do before kids realize their fallibility. But right now there was nothing I could tell my daughter about her father with any certainty at all. I felt not omnipotent but impotent, vulnerable and small.

But then, as I looked at Bob, I saw the most incredible thing. It was a sight that provided a jolt of hope to last for the next few weeks. A small tear was running down from the corner of his eye, his good eye, on the side where Cathryn was kissing him.

"He's crying!" I yelled, to no one in particular. "He hears Cathryn's voice and he's crying." The nurse came around, roused by my calls. It was, to this point, my only living proof that Bob was *there*, inside that Frankenstein head and swollen body. The nurse would back me up later, when I told the doctors. Cathryn and I had seen it. And it was enough for the two of us.

"There is a connection there of blood and bones and DNA," Dr. M had told me the day before. "He may love you as his wife, but his children are a physical part of him. They share his genes and cells and genetic makeup." Maybe that would have the power to heal him, I thought. Perhaps that kind of love would be strong enough to bring Bob back to us.

Back at the Bakers' that night, while the twins played with the dog, I was hit by a volley of questions from Cathryn. "Why can't Dad breathe on his own? Will he be the same? Can he hear us? Will he be ugly like that?" I just wanted to sleep. Deep dreamless sleep without ministering to my daughters' needs, but that was impossible, of course. The next day and they'd be gone. I needed to focus all my energies on them, to give them enough love and attention to last until I would see them again. So I sat and carefully answered everything I could. I snuggled and told stories and rubbed backs. I comforted them and explained things, and when the last girl fell asleep I snuck into my own bed and pulled my knees up into a ball. How will we live? I thought. Braces, college tuition, medical bills; what loomed in the future for us? Running a household without support from Bob—emotionally, physically, and financially— was a sobering thought.

I wondered what Bob would think if someone could have shown him a film loop of his little family at this moment. It had been blown up like his skull, broken into pieces and thrown instantly, like the gear of a car, into reverse. His heart would ache, I thought, if he could see us now.

The next day I kissed my kids goodbye, with tears in all our eyes. They flew back to New York with Bob's brother Mike, who would stay for a few days and provide a much-needed male influence. "Why aren't you coming home with us?" Nora had asked me the night before. "Why are you always so nervous?" Claire had chimed in, with that laser beam troubleshooting kids always have.

Later Mike told me he had sat next to Nora on the plane. "Uncle Mike, do you miss your brother?" she had asked, far wiser than I would have guessed.

"I do miss my brother, a lot," Mike answered. "And I miss my dog too. I've been away from her now for a while and she's a new puppy."

"Do you miss your dog more than your brother?"

"No," said Mike. "No way."

"I miss my daddy too," said Nora, snuggling closer to Mike.

Lee

San Francisco, Spring 1991

Our apartment in San Francisco had one of the most magnificent and romantic views I had ever seen. Perched under the Coit Tower in North Beach, its floor-to-ceiling windows and sliding glass doors and deck displayed the scene from the Golden Gate Bridge to the Bay Bridge. Early in the morning when fog coated the bay, the foghorns sounded far out into the water and reverberated off the Marin hills. As the sun rose, we had the perfect perch from which to continually fall in love with our favorite city.

As the baby in my belly got bigger, it became harder for me to sleep in. I would spend a lot of early morning time leaning over the balcony, a cup of decaf in my hand, wondering how this child would inevitably change our lives.

Since returning to San Francisco the fall after Tiananmen Square, we'd settled into a nice life. Both of us could walk to work, Bob to the downtown offices of Shearman & Sterling and me to Porter Novelli, where they'd shoehorned a place for me in the office after we returned.

Bob's law firm had been happy to offer him a job back in New York or in San Francisco, as job opportunities in Hong Kong and even Japan had dried up after the Tiananmen Square crackdown. I had convinced Bob that he had invested three years in law school and he should give it a shot in another city; perhaps it might feel different from the confines of the giant New York office.

But despite the great California outdoors, the mountain biking over the Golden Gate Bridge, the beautiful apartment, amazing friends, the six-figure salary, and his impending parenthood, Bob Woodruff was miserable inside.

My first clue about how our lives might change came on October 17, 1989, when a giant earthquake, registering 6.9 on the Richter scale, hit the greater Bay Area. After calling me to make sure I was safe, Bob's first instinct was to grab our video camera and rush out to try to get shots of the fires and other catastrophes happening around the city. Of course it didn't matter that every major media outlet was there at that very moment for the World Series or that local crews were already on the scene. Journalism had gotten into Bob's blood during the events in Tiananmen Square. He instinctively wanted to be where the story was unfolding. We joked about it later, how he'd gone to the ABC affiliate to try to sell his footage. At that point, one might as well have been bringing coals to Newcastle.

If I'd looked hard enough I would have seen my entire future in Bob's actions in the hour after he arrived home following the earthquake. His drive, desire, determination, and confidence as he grabbed his video camera, kissed me, and ran out the door foreshadowed everything to come. He was out looking for the action, adrenaline-charged and single-minded. I was home, minding the nest in a capable fashion, wishing he'd return so we could be a family. The San Francisco earthquake proved to be a microcosm of our life.

Bob was unhappy, and I knew that an unhappy husband would in turn be an unhappy father. He was spending long hours as an associate at the law firm, working on a tedious involved bankruptcy case, often coming home close to midnight. With a child on the way he wondered how much time he'd ever be able to spend with us. This was not a guy who was going to take fatherhood lightly. I had to set my husband free.

Bob

San Francisco, 1991

"Do you understand it's not going to be like Tiananmen Square?" Lee asked me. "That was the apex. That was about as big and exciting as it gets for a journalist. You are going to have to spend years going to school board meetings and covering recycling programs in small towns." I just smiled at her.

For me, journalism seemed the perfect career. You could learn about a new subject or story every day and then try to boil it down in an understandable way. There were hard and fast deadlines, and I loved the idea of marrying pictures with words.

I began volunteering at KTVU-TV, an independent television station across the bay in Oakland. I worked on the early-morning shift, driving to work at 4:30 A.M. in my lawyer's suit and ripping interesting stories off the news wires for the morning show writers. After this shift, I would head to my job at the law firm.

Since our days in China, I had kept in touch with Susan Zirinsky from CBS. I gave her a call while considering my career change. But there was very little she could do to help a total novice from her perch at the network level.

"Go out there and get experience at a local station," she'd urged me, after initially trying to talk me out of this craziness. "Then, if you still want to do this, we'll talk."

At the station I met some of the cameramen and editors who would help me make my first "demo tape," an essential part of getting a job in the news business. At the same time, I decided to apply to journalism school at UC Berkeley. Lee had worked out a part-time job with her PR firm for after the baby was born, and we would live on some savings we had socked away and Lee's part-time salary.

A graphic-designer friend had recommended Lee to write a franchise brochure for a pizza company, and she'd made a few thousand dollars staying up late nights and writing. She hoped to find some more freelance jobs to help bolster our income.

I was in awe of Lee for what she was willing to do for me with our first child on the way. And I felt somewhat guilty. Although I would have supported any decision of hers to work or not work, she deserved stability as a new mother. She deserved the luxury of choice about whether or not to stay home full-time with our child.

Throughout our marriage, I would urge her to follow her heart every time she moaned about her workload or her clients. "If you don't want to work, you quit tomorrow," was my familiar refrain. "We will survive. I always want you to do whatever you want." Although it sounded like lip service, I truly meant it.

Lee

San Francisco, June 1991

Most of our friends thought we were crazy. Or they told me how admirable it was that I was "letting" Bob pursue his dream. Many of the women I knew confided in me that they didn't think they'd ever be able to do that. I joked with Bob that this was his first, last, and only midlife crisis at age thirty. There would be no hot young blondes, red sports cars, or any other spoils in his future. This was it. He had my blessing.

Our college and law school friends were rapidly moving onward and upward, banking large salaries, buying houses, and getting promotions in years that were fat with investment banking money and Wall Street bonuses. We were backtracking, giving up the potential for partnership and guaranteed money. Turning our backs on Bob's $130,000-a-year salary for a possible career in journalism was both frightening and exhilarating. It was like stepping off a cliff and praying your parachute would hold. With a newborn.

No amount of babysitting in high school could have possibly prepared me for the enormousness of motherhood. In those first few weeks it was like having a goiter attached to my body. A wonderful attachment, to be sure, but a full-time weight as well. I found myself in pajamas until well after noon most days. Brushing my teeth seemed a major triumph and showering could only be managed during Mack's catnaps. Day and night passed without any meaning to my infant son. When it was time to eat, it was time for me to wake, and I grew accustomed to reading a book and watching the lights of the giant cargo ships below in the bay as he nursed in the wee hours of the morning. Bob, born without functioning mammary glands, would wake in the morning, stretch his arms out to their full height, and ask me innocently how my night was.

Sometimes, exhausted and looking for companionship in misery, I'd elbow Bob awake just to ask him to bring the baby to me. It was at these moments I thought of an African etching someone had given us before Mack was born. The tribal ritual was for a rock to be tied to the husband's testicles while the wife was in labor. Every time the wife had a contraction she could yank on the string—thereby causing the husband to feel his own sympathetic pains. I liked the way this tribe thought.

Mack's July birth meant my maternity leave was coinciding with summer and the chance to be at Lake George with my family. Bob had gotten into the highly competitive Berkeley School of Journalism program. We had decided he would be a full-time student in the fall. In the meantime, he had put together a videotape of news stories that he had slightly rewritten from other stories and then inserted his stand-up. That way he could use the existing footage from the original news piece.

The tape was pretty grim. I'd pay a lot of money to find it now. The quality was horrible, dubbed over from a copy, Bob's voice was strained and unnaturally high, his cadence was stilted, and his body language was about as uptight as a WASP from the Detroit suburbs can be. I'd spent enough time media-training clients on camera to know what he should and shouldn't do, but I was careful not to be too critical. The raw material was there, and I knew Bob well enough to understand that when he put his mind to something he could accomplish a great deal.

Despite applying to journalism graduate school, he still sent his demo tape to TV news directors in smaller local markets around the country. He was hedging his bets. We'd done the research on the stations with my PR media books and spent nights slapping labels on padded envelopes.

As I hand-addressed labels to far-flung news directors, I tried to imagine life in a small town in South Dakota or being a new mother in Tallahassee, Florida. Who would be my friend in Oregon or Maine? How would I survive summers in New Mexico? There were some towns I sincerely hoped would consider him and others that I silently prayed would pass him by.

At the end of the summer Bob left me at Lake George with Mack to head back to San Francisco to start journalism school at Berkeley. The phone rang that first afternoon and I took it out to the porch, handing the baby over to my mother so I could get an uninterrupted report about Bob's first day.

"I've got good news and bad news," Bob said breathlessly. "Which one do you want first?"

"Give me the good news," I said tentatively.

"Well, I got back from my first day in graduate school, which I'll tell you about in a minute, and when I got home there was a message on the machine. One of the stations in Northern California wants to hire me as a reporter."

"Wow," I responded, thinking silently that this was a real fly in the ointment. We'd had our plan all set. "So what's the bad news?" I was afraid to ask.

"Uh—well, the salary is twelve thousand a year."

"Oh."

"So what do you think I should do?" Bob chattered on. "I talked to the professors at school and they urged me to stay. They talked to me about all the courses and what a great education it is. It's a prestigious program. But then I spoke to one of the deans, and off the record he said he was supposed to convince me to stay but that I should go for the experience and take the job. It's exactly the position I'd be in when I got out of graduate school. I'm confused."

"I'm not," I said. "This one is easy. Take the job."

Bob

Redding, California, Fall 1991

Less than a month after I accepted my first job in TV as a re-porter, we drove all our worldly possessions in a giant U-Haul up to Redding, California, a town in the mountains almost four hours north of San Francisco. Out of about 200 broad-cast markets in the country, KCPM-TV was number 130.

I would become what was known in television as a "one-man band." This was a euphemism for the fact that the station was so small you did everything yourself. You drove your own car, set up the camera on a tripod, turned it on, walked around to the front, and set up a monitor facing yourself so you could see how you were framed in the shot. If it was a live shot, you communicated to the station with a walkie-talkie so they could tell you if you were too low or too high on the monitor.

On my first day on the job, I had no idea how to work the equipment. There were only three reporters in the bureau and it was housed in a kind of office park. The NBC affiliate's slogan was MAKING A DIFFERENCE IN THE NORTH VALLEY, and to think now that the North Valley was getting its news from someone as inexperienced as myself was frightening.

I remember my first live shot most vividly. In that first week of my new career, a train had crashed out near the mountains. It was a chemical spill, and there was concern that residents could be affected. My pager went off and I rushed to the scene to interview police and firemen. As this was an unfolding event, Channel 24 wanted to go live. I had a chance to call Lee and make sure she'd be stationed right in front of the TV to see my "live" debut.

As the anchor introduced me "live from the scene," I began speaking into the stick microphone, describing what had been happening when I'd arrived. All at once I began to gesture to the train behind me for extra emphasis. I was so nervous I didn't think about the fact that I was using my microphone to point. Back at home, as she told me later, hovering around the TV with Mack in his baby seat, Lee watched my live shot through her fingers. Her hands were covering her eyes.

Each time I pointed with the mike, my voice would disappear. You could see my lips moving but you couldn't hear a word. Finally, mercifully, it was time for the studio to roll the video on the taped part of the story. This meant I would have to voice-over the narration parts and stop talking when the people on the tape were being interviewed. The problem was that with no monitor I couldn't see what was happening. I'd have to rely on a voice coming from the walkie-talkie to cue me when to talk.

Somehow, I missed a cue and began talking into the mike at the same time the police chief was talking on the tape. "Stop talking!" a voice screamed out of the walkie-talkie clipped to the tripod. I stopped. "Talk now, *talk!*" the voice screamed again when it was time for me to read more of my script. But the damage was done; the timing was off. Defeated and freaked out, I came back on at the end to sign off.

"Hey, buddy," Lee said softly to Mack back home, sitting in his baby seat with the plastic toy bar in front. "I think we'd better go pack some things. I'm not sure Dad's going to make it in this career."

"Did you see me on TV tonight?" I asked the landlady hopefully as I pulled in the driveway later that night.

"Worst damned thing I ever saw on TV," she said, and I laughed out loud. What else was there to do? I couldn't possibly get any worse. I had nowhere to go but up.

Lee

Richmond, Virginia, 1992

After that first year in Redding, our next stop was Richmond, Virginia. Bob had attended a Radio and Television News Directors' Association conference at his own expense. It was a chance to rub shoulders with some news directors from around the country. He had even gotten himself an agent in New York, Henry Reisch. A news director named Elliot Wiser had spotted Bob doing a presentation on one-man bands and shortly afterward offered Bob the chance for his next rung on the ladder at a CBS affiliate. The salary would be a slight jump at $18,000 a year.

Our little family was expanding. After two early miscarriages, I had a baby girl we named Cathryn. Somehow we made room and found time for this new little person in our lives.

In his own newsroom and at other stations in the city, Bob was catching people's eye. When he walked into a TV station for the first time, someone would size him up and immediately assume that, because he was good-looking, he was not very bright or talented. And each time, Bob would put his head down, ignore gossip and interoffice dirt, and focus on the task at hand. Eventually, the work would win every time.

The competitive station, WRIC-TV, had seen Bob's work too. They were putting together a new morning show, and the director approached Bob about being a morning anchor and asked him to submit a tape. Word was that Bob's tape won out over more than a hundred competitors, even though he had never anchored a program.

There was one problem. Bob's contract had a no-compete clause, which meant he couldn't go as on-air talent to another station in the same market without sitting out for six months.

After a tough contract dispute, a judge ultimately found in favor of Bob's employer. Although I am a huge believer that things happen for a reason, we couldn't help feeling glum. We'd poured so much energy into fighting this battle. There is no way to know what twists and turns Bob's career might have taken if he'd become the morning anchor in Richmond. We can only see in hindsight that the path he did take brought him success, happiness, and challenges too.

Lee

Bethesda Naval Hospital, February 12, 2006

In the immediate aftermath of Bob's injury, I was so focused on his potential brain damage that his other injuries seemed less significant. But one particular injury was impossible to ignore, now that they'd done as much as they could surgically for Bob's brain.

It was one rock, that marble-sized piece of shrapnel that had entered the left side of Bob's throat. As it blasted through the flesh it had sheared off the lower part of his jawbone, cracked two teeth, and traveled all the way across his neck to rest less than a millimeter from his carotid artery on the right side. His good side.

That the rock had stopped, like the shrapnel in his chest wall, resting against an artery that, if pierced, would have surely killed him, was a miracle in itself. If was as if the unseen hand of God had stopped those rocks from going a whisper farther. Every doctor told me he would have "bled out" before they could have saved his life.

Not only was this rock a potential source of infection, in its precarious location it could shift and move at any time and cause untold damage. Until Bob woke, there would be no way of knowing what damage the rock had already done. And there was high-priced real estate in that part of the head: the throat, vocal cords, nerves of the tongue, esophagus, and voice box. The rock seemed to have cut directly through that area, and there was a good chance Bob would be unable to speak or use his tongue, even if his brain function was intact. There was no way to examine that area with the ventilator tube down his throat. The rock would have to come out.

Dr. Armonda explained that they were making a 3-D computer-assisted model of Bob's skull, an action reserved for patients with the most dangerous and complex injuries or illnesses. The acrylic model would also include the rock. In this way the surgeons could determine the best approach. It would be a tricky procedure, and there were significant risks. The rock sat under Bob's ear on the right side. They would need to cut into the "good side" of Bob's face to retrieve it, and it would be invasive. There was the potential that nerves would be cut and they would have to remove part of the bone on that side to gain access to the rock. The surgery could affect his ability to speak.

I was still very much in the zone at this point, which involved action-oriented thinking. I thought about the fact that we were in great hands with the military doctors and that so many things up to this point had been done to save Bob's life. Without a moment's hesitation, the surgeons, doctors, and nurses who had all played such a vital role in Bob's care had known exactly what to do, after three years of war and IED blasts. Now we had the luxury of time, a chance to reflect and consider the options. I knew that if our roles were reversed, Bob would be doing everything to make sure I had the best team, the doctors with the most experience. It was time to step back from crisis mode and get the best advice we could. It wasn't about faith in my medical team at Bethesda; they had my complete confidence. It was about ensuring we did the absolute best thing for Bob.

Throughout the past week of my hideous nightmare, I had kept in contact with Dr. Peter Costantino. He had been one of the first to call my cell phone in Disney World when the news broke. And if you believe in fate, the story of our meeting Pete and his wife, Laurie, only makes sense when you look at it in hindsight.

Three months earlier, Bob and I had been attending a baby shower for one of our friends in New York City. As we walked toward the building's elevator, the door was closing and a man inside thrust his arm out to hold it for us. We stumbled in, thanking him, and pushed the button for our host's floor. For a moment the four of us stood there awkwardly and then we both laughed, gesturing to the presents we were carrying.

"I think we are going to the same place," said Bob, and we struck up a conversation and somehow ended up talking to Pete and Laurie for a good part of the night. Pete was warm and his eyes sparkled with a dry sense of humor. He was a highly regarded surgeon who operated on hundreds of brain tumors a year and did reconstructive surgery.

We marvel now, the four of us, at the hand of fate, chance or divine intervention. One minute more and the elevator door would have closed. One extra car ahead of us in the parking lot, a few slowpokes at the toll booth, and we would have missed them completely. We would have gravitated toward familiar people at the party and seen the Costantinos as just another pair of faces as the toasts were made.

From the start, Pete had assured me that Bob was in the best hands possible with the military doctors. With a blast injury, it all came down to experience and numbers. And the people who were treating the most patients with this injury, and in great numbers, were the military doctors. They knew not to hesitate for a second.

"We all love Bob's doctors," I said. "Dr. Rocco Armonda and Dr. Phil Perdue are formulating a plan and assembling the team to remove the rock. Is it okay if I ask them to call you so you can discuss Bob's case?"

And so began a terrific relationship between the private sector and the military that would ultimately have positive implications for all soldiers with traumatic brain injuries. If there can ever be silver linings in something so horrible and tragic as your husband being blown up by a bomb, the potential to combine forces for the good of the men and women injured in Iraq might just be one.

The next day I caught Dr. Armonda in the hall. There was something comforting about his trim military posture, his close-cropped hair, and the intelligence that beamed from his eyes. I liked him immensely and he instilled confidence in us all. I could usually get him to crack a smile if I worked on it a bit. He was confused at first by my jokes with the family and about Bob, but he soon grew comfortable with my brand of humor.

"We have a family friend," I said. "He is a neurosurgeon in New York. He is very concerned about Bob, and I've told him about the rock. I would love it if you would call him, just to talk to him. Is that okay?"

"Absolutely," said Dr. Armonda. "I'd be happy to talk to him."

One of life's fulcrum events was about to take place the week after the kids left Bethesda: the annual kindergarten play. The twins had been working on it for weeks and had been humming their songs excitedly. Although I'd signed up for set design, I'd been a no-show once Bob was injured. I cringed at the thought of going back to my town, of facing people and their sympathy. I dreaded walking into my house and seeing my life as I'd left it, life now going on without Mommy or Daddy at the helm. I'd built a cocoon from the world in Bethesda. Other people were answering my cell phone; I had no computer for e-mail; I had shrunk my world down to a pinprick of light that contained only the day-to-day status of my husband's condition.

I'd lost the communal language of the suburbs, yet I longed for the mundane carpooling, the routine of grocery shopping, and the familiarity of chatting on the sidelines of my kid's soccer game. But I no longer had any idea how to begin those conversations. How do you engage in small talk when you have vanished from your life and your husband is lying in a coma in an ICU? An enormous chasm had opened up between myself and the person I used to be.

Showing up for the play would send the biggest message to my kids that I was there for them. The play was a heartbreaker, including the slide montage at the end, of all the kindergartners in candid shots set to Carole King's "You've Got a Friend." The play had been on Bob's calendar; we'd discussed how he would do everything he could to be there. I cried through almost the whole thing, brightening up only as my twins beamed out into the audience at me. Being there had been so important. But the house was lonely and empty without Bob. Our king-sized bed felt like a football field. I wondered if he would ever share it with me again.

Vivianne and I had had meals together and comforted each other. We had come up with a saying: "First you must touch the black and then go back up to the light." It was our way of acknowledging that you have to let the fear in, but to dwell on that fear will only cripple you. You need to move back into a world of hope. "My yoga teacher would say *breathe*," I joked with Vivianne.

We spent what seemed like hours replaying what we knew about the attack and going over the *if onlys,* something I would learn later is a common phase for people after a sudden tragedy that could have been prevented. If only they had been inside the tank. If only they had been in a different vehicle or if the convoy had only moved out in a different order. If only they had scrapped the mission; if only they had been in the other hatch. The exercise was so unproductive, so hurtful, it felt like trying to stretch from a jail cell for a set of keys just out of reach, but I couldn't shut my brain off from playing that film loop.

"Just three minutes on either side of that bomb," Vivi and I would say to each other. Three minutes would have made a difference. It was a painful game and we tired of it, trying to accept that no amount of rehashing the event could change the outcome.

Doug had been moved out of the ICU and up to the fifth floor, which felt much more like a normal hospital room, far less frantic and life-and-death than the twenty-four-hour activity of an intensive care unit. Vivi told me that Doug, at first, seemed more flat and unemotional after waking and I could see she was grieving for the man she had loved, even as he recovered. In the weeks to come she would see dramatic changes in her husband as he began to heal and piece things back together. But for the moment, Bob's and Doug's injuries were so different that I could not even compare them. Wives see things in their hearts that no one else can. It frightened me that someone so seemingly normal on the outside could have been tinkered with so badly on the inside. It terrified me that my husband might be altered forever: this intelligent soul, my loving partner, the children's father. Through the many letters and cards that colleagues sent I would learn the many ways he had touched people's lives. "Bob was one of the truly good guys in this business," one of his cameramen wrote. "Even though he was an anchor, he would always help us carry the equipment." And through a colleague's note I learned that Bob had made it a practice to draw straws among his crew for his first-class airplane seat, a new perk of his job. He wasn't comfortable flying up front while the rest of his team was in back.

While I was home for the play, my suitcases had been moved into a new hotel room, and when I unpacked I was missing my favorite face cream. Now, as ridiculous as this may seem, I liked that face cream. Using that face cream at night was one of the few things I could count on in a life devoid of control. Since I was way too thrifty to actually spend my own money on it, I usually relied on the generosity of my beauty editor friends at the magazines I worked with to supply me with a tub. Crème de la Mer, it was called, and it felt like silk on my dry, wrinkling white skin. My husband might be clinging to life by a thread, but I could still apply my expensively luxurious face cream each night like royalty.

Soon the missing face cream became an obsession. I called Bob's mother, who had packed my things up while I'd been back home with the kids, but she didn't remember exactly where it was. That was when I realized we had professionals. This was a mission for the expertise of our security team, who had been stationed around us twenty-four hours a day, getting us to and from the hospital and airport and maintaining our privacy. Larry, Darren, and Frank were itching for a higher purpose. Perhaps they could put a trace on the missing face cream.

"We're on it, ma'am," said Larry officiously, when I called.

"Good to go," said Darren.

"Roger that," said Frank.

An hour later my cell phone rang. "Lee, it's Darren," he said. "We've swept the room and come up negative."

"You've what?" I said. It took me a moment to realize what he was talking about.

"We've swept the room for the face cream," he said. Immediately I had a vision of three men kicking down the door of my former room at the Pooks Hill Marriott as a couple quivered in their beds while the men rifled through drawers and in the closet safe.

When I decided to check the suitcases that my mother-in-law had repacked for me one more time, there was the jar of face cream, zipped into an outside pocket where Bob's mom had placed it. Sheepishly, I called the security team.

"Stand down," I said, liking this new military lingo. "I am now in possession of the Crème de la Mer."

"Roger that," said Larry, with a chuckle.

Lee

Phoenix, Arizona, 1994

Our next move took us to Phoenix, Arizona, where Bob had accepted a reporting job at ABC affiliate station KNXV and we settled into life in the Southwest. I continued my freelance business, dragging my portfolio and writing samples to new prospective clients, handling PR for Benefit Cosmetics. Weekend hikes with the kids up Camelback Mountain and Squaw Peak and forays up into Flagstaff and Sedona taught us to appreciate the starkly lush beauty of the desert landscape. Working in local news, Bob was also home almost every night for dinner and to help with the kids. He also helped me with my freelance business, stuffing envelopes or printing computer labels after the kids were in bed.

I multitasked and mega-multitasked. With two young children I learned to cram everything in, rising at five-thirty to swim or run and then get on e-mails before waking the family up. I'd pack Bob's lunch, almost every day, just to make sure he didn't eat fast food but also to help save money. His original salary had almost tripled, but with two children we still counted on my income to pay bills and to enjoy life out at a restaurant or go to a movie sometimes.

For all these years my income had far outstripped Bob's, and if that ever bothered him he never admitted it. He was proud of me, proud of what I was doing for the family and proud of how successful my business was. He recognized the sacrifices I was making and understood that largely they were for his dream. Maybe that made me a patsy in the eyes of some and maybe it was farther than most women would be willing to go. But for me, it was mostly an adventure.

There was something else, a part of me that needed to know I could always take care of myself and my kids if anything ever happened to Bob. When Bob was injured, I would be grateful that I had been so driven, grateful for all of those years of keeping on with my work.

Our two years in Phoenix would have been close to idyllic, but they were marred by our first brush with grief as a couple when we lost a baby and I underwent a hysterectomy. The journey through that grief prepared me, in some way, for the grief to come. It put me on familiar terms with loss and sorrow and the fact that, as trite as it may sound, time really is the ultimate healer. No matter how black the hours, light, laughter, and feeling will slowly begin to trickle back one day.

But I also learned that the scar is always there, just below the undergarments, although the raw wound may close. And when you turn, examining yourself at the end of the day before bed, it is you who can see it best in the mirror.

The loss of our son taught me that there are no shortcuts to healing. There is no circumventing the pain. To truly heal, you must walk right through the blazing core of grief and face it head on, every agonizing day. Only then can you begin to take baby steps toward recovery. Grief is an alchemist. It will change you, morph you into someone more empathetic, more aware of what is precious, and more clearly able to see your priorities.

I bristled when, in an effort to make me feel better, people would say to me, "Things happen for a reason" or "God doesn't give you more than you can handle." It felt like greeting-card philosophy to try to package something so complex into bite-sized chunks.

As I sat on my wicker couch on the back porch staring numbly at our lone grapefruit tree for hours after my hospitalization, I played a loop in my head of what could have been. I had an image of a third and final baby in my arms, of being happily exhausted by an even busier, bustling life. Instead, I was a brittle woman, an apathetic mother, nursing an empty womb and a shriveled heart.

"At least it wasn't as if you lost a *real* child," people would say, meaning well. But I had. In my mind I had already held that son to my breast; we had named him and counted his fingers and toes. He had already filled out the little dotted outline in my mental image of our family, a family of five. Our perfect family.

"At least you have your two other children," others would say, searching for words of comfort when there were none. Yes, I did, and I was grateful. But that didn't mean I had lost the right to grieve as fully and as deeply as if I had suffered ten stillborn deaths in a row. That didn't mean the pain was diminished or that it somehow meant less.

What I learned, most of all, through my pain and my immersion in sorrow, was that I didn't want to blunt this. It hurt. This was horrible, searing pain and I needed to acknowledge it, to myself and to others.

"This sucks. This is so unfair," said my friend Leslie one morning, bringing me coffee and comfort after the kids had left for school. I liked her simplicity, telling it like it was.

The hysterectomy had made the question of future motherhood final. It was a painful way to close the book on my fertility. But when something is gone that you've taken for granted, you suddenly want it more than anything else in the world. My loss became an ache, like a phantom limb, and that ache dulled and retreated into a chamber of my heart for years to come, deadening my ability to laugh from my diaphragm, to experience the euphoria of pure joy.

I remember understanding in Phoenix that not even the love of my husband was strong or important enough in my black depression to pull me back into the light. I knew my husband would survive my absence, but my kids would be forever wounded. And in the end, it was my two children who pulled me through. It was that DNA connection, those two sets of precious eyes, anxiously watching my lethargy. It was their need for food and hugs and stories and snuggles and potty training that slowly, gradually, drew me forward, a rope tow to which I clung.

The shared experience of loss both joined Bob and me together as a couple and divided us. Men and women grieve differently. I needed to chew it over and roll it around, and Bob wanted to bury it like a bone.

Years later, lying alone in a hotel bed in Bethesda, I thought about how fortunate we'd been then to have each other. The loss of that child, the image of what could have been, was the most painful thing I had ever known. But the loss of Bob, the uncertainty of his outcome and the responsibility of caring for our children, now loomed before me like the dark mouth of a cave. I wanted him next to me to make me strong. If he could only lie with me and we could talk about it, we could tackle anything together. I was petrified. I'd never felt so alone in my entire life.

Your child or your husband, which is worse? The dark thought flashed through my mind in Bethesda like a Sophie's Choice exercise, and I struggled to force it out quickly. I had hoped that our black days in Phoenix might inoculate us against another of life's disasters. But I was savvy enough to know that the world doesn't work that way. There are no good-luck charms, no talismans or deals with the devil. Misfortune and trouble can find you at any time. The part of me that believed in the order of the world, that decent people triumph and good deeds are rewarded, was shaken hard that year in Arizona. After that, a little part of me, deep in my heart's scar tissue, would always remain watchful, like a sentinel, waiting for the other shoe to drop.

Lee

Chicago, December 1996

Another move, another job opening, took us east. ABC News had an affiliate service called News One. It sent reporters to major stories and made them available for live shots or taped pieces to the local affiliate stations around the country. Bob was now at the network.

He worked out of the Chicago office, covering the Midwest. Bob was thirty-five years old, well within his personal goal of reaching the network by that age. Once again we packed our things, sold our ranch house, and bought a four-bedroom in Winnetka, Illinois. Bob caught the train at the base of the hill to the Windy City, and I set up shop, once again, in a bedroom of our home. I liked Chicago and warmed to its blue-collar swagger, its meatpacking feel, and its glittery Miracle Mile. I loved its little neighborhoods and the blues and jazz clubs where cultures seemed to meld.

Our time in Chicago was a time of growth for Bob and a time of growing away from Bob for me. Looking back, I see it as one of the worst times in our marriage. I wanted desperately to put down some roots. I was becoming weary of moving and finding new pediatricians and friends, applying for library cards, and sending out changes of address.

Six months into our life there, on the very day that workmen were first knocking into the walls of our home for a renovation, the phone rang. It was the good news/bad news scenario all over again.

"Guess what, honey? Big news," said Bob. I couldn't possibly guess. "ABC wants me to go to the Washington bureau to work for News One there. I know it's quick, and we've only been in Chicago a short time, but I take it as a good sign."

Mmm, I mused. The simple fact was that to turn down an offer for upward mobility at the network was career suicide. I knew we were going to do this. "Well, I guess we have to go," I answered, less than enthusiastically.

We decided that I would stay with the kids in Chicago and let them finish the school year, and Bob became a weekend commuter. During his week in Washington, he lived in a four-star hotel. But when he arrived in Chicago he was just plain tired. He immediately wanted to connect physically, whereas I craved an emotional connection.

I still hadn't dealt with my sadness over losing the baby and the hysterectomy that followed in Phoenix. And I was angry at Bob's career, angry that the timing of his contracts drove everything: dictated when we would conceive and when we would be covered by insurance, kept us on the move like nomads in a desert. With Bob simply gone, what once had seemed like such an adventure began to feel more like a death march. Inside I was seething.

One weekend Bob told me he was too tired on Monday mornings to fly back to work and he would be going back on Sunday afternoons. Now we would have a mere forty-eight hours with him each week at best. And in that time he would be exhausted, interacting with the kids or catching up with bills. This new declaration felt dangerously close to a breaking point.

"I'm sorry that visiting your family is such an inconvenience," I sputtered.

I knew Bob was caught between his desire to move forward and make more money for all of us and his need to stay focused and sharp on the job. But we had needs too. The year in Chicago ended with me exhausted, frustrated, and bitter. There were moments I worried that, much like a boyfriend you'd outgrown in high school, you could never recapture lost love. I understood the damage that anger and resentment could do to a relationship, but at times I seemed powerless to harness my feelings. It is scary to learn that the heart really does have a mind of its own. No amount of intellectualizing or *should do*'s can make you love again.

Time was the best balm. I looked into my heart and realized we needed to move forward. Little by little, after the move to D.C., though it took me a while to thaw, we eventually knitted Bob back into the fabric of our family life. There was too much history, too many places we intersected: our children, our experiences together, our outlook on the world, and one big united front that would have been far too complicated and painful to tear asunder. In the end, we had chosen each other wisely. We had the stuff to go the distance, no matter how difficult some of the miles along the way would be.

Bob

Washington, D.C., May 1997

When I got the opportunity to go to Washington with News One, I was elated. Moving on to the nation's capital would mean a chance to see things from a national platform with greater intensity. I hoped to work more too, covering the federal government and the ongoing drama of politics.

On the other hand, I felt a nagging sense of guilt. I was staying at the luxurious Mayflower Hotel, right next to the ABC Washington bureau. My family was in Chicago in a house under construction, faced with an impending move. Lee was simmering, and our phone conversations got more tense. I could hear the frustration in her voice, but I assuaged my guilt by telling myself that it was only temporary.

There are moments in your life when you know you are concentrating more closely on your work than you are on your family. For me, being a journalist and a father often meant that, while I was doing what I most loved, in my heart I knew that on some level I was depriving my family. Yet I did nothing about it.

I consoled myself with the knowledge that now, at the network, I would be living in a city where many of the stories would be local. Unlike Chicago, where I found myself traveling around the Midwest in pursuit of news, most news in Washington happens at the White House, Congress, the Justice Department, the Supreme Court, and the other halls of government. I told myself I would largely be home when they all got to D.C. In fact, it would be perfect once the family came. I would simply hang on until we could all be together. This was the kind of town where we could put down roots. I wanted more than anything in the world to make it up to Lee and was confident we would grow back together.

But after about two years of being promoted to full-fledged network level as the Justice Department reporter, I began to feel restless again. In the end, this kind of beat reporting was not right for me. I always had a vision of seeing more of the world and reporting on international stories from the road. Little by little, Washington began to seem like a small town. The seeds of excitement over foreign events in exotic locales that had been sown during Tiananmen Square were beginning to sprout.

Lee

Bethesda Naval Hospital, February 13, 2006

The Bethesda Naval doctors, Dr. Costantino and his partner Dr. Chandra Sen, seemed to be getting along well. Dr. Armonda had told me they had shared CT scans and information and were formulating the best approach to get the rock out of Bob's head with the least amount of damage. The rock was in a tenuous place and, unlike a tumor, they would not be able to slice it out bit by bit.

Bob's parents and his brother Mike went with me to the small hospital waiting room on the day before the surgery. It was time for Dr. Armonda to give us a rundown on what would happen. It would be sixteen days tomorrow since the attack on Bob's convoy, sixteen days that Bob had been unconscious, and there was no telling how and when he would wake up. When I visited with him he was restless, agitated; his legs seemed always to be in motion, and it took all my strength to push him back in bed. His eyes would open and look at me blankly. Sometimes I felt as if his mind had left us and he was far, far away. Other times I swore he recognized me and knew I was there. At those times I could almost hear the sounds of the repairs going on inside his head, as he worked on some level to make those new connections.

Bob was in a sedated state, but technically he was not waking up either. His brain was not ready, Dr. Armonda had explained. The medical staff tried to achieve a difficult balance between lowering the sedation a little to see if Bob would "come out of it," but not so much that he would begin to tear at the tubes and hurt himself.

It seemed there were tubes everywhere. Tubes to remove solid waste and urine, feeding tubes that ran directly into the stomach, tubes for IVs and medication, a tube to breathe, and wires to monitor his heart and oxygen. Bob reeked like a hospital; he smelled of bodily functions, medicines, chemicals, and even death. To me, it was the smell of despair, and as I entered his room each day, dutifully pulling the curtain closed to try to preserve some dignity, I began my routine. Gowning up and putting on the gloves and mask, I would rub Bob's calves and feet, kiss his face, cut his nails, pull down his hospital gown, and pull up his tangled sheet.

Dr. Armonda steered our conversation toward a discussion of some of the characteristics common to traumatic brain injuries. He explained that many people with head injuries exhibit actions that are inappropriate: agitation, frustration, and outbursts not unlike an infant's. Bob's movements were consistent with someone who had suffered a traumatic brain injury. When many patients first wake up, and even afterward, they can be easily angered and rattle off strings of expletives. Abnormal behavior might simply become part of what Bob's therapists would teach me to call "the new normal."

With most brain injuries, the filter in our heads that we all use to get along in society slips. People lose their inhibitions in ways both shocking and painful for their loved ones. One woman I spoke with after Bob's injury confided in me that her husband masturbated continually in front of other people for months after his injury. Another's husband, once a doting and loving father, would routinely scream at his five-year-old daughter for the flimsiest reasons. Then there was the horrible story of the soldier's wife who had to be put in a safe house because her husband, her high school sweetheart, had tried to strangle her in her sleep after his head injury in Iraq.

Because Bob's injury was in his left temporal lobe, on his dominant side, Dr. Armonda warned us that he would have speech and language difficulties. There was no telling to what extent until he woke. "Bob will have to relearn things," said Dr. Armonda kindly.

"Like what?" I asked, trying to stay calm. Until then I had avoided this kind of conversation, hoping for Bob to wake up first so we could learn where his baseline was.

"Well, think of a baby. First they learn to speak and then to read and then to write. Bob will probably have these same challenges. Naming things will be difficult. They are very common with his injury," said Dr. Armonda.

Immediately I pictured a giant Baby Huey in a playpen: my handsome full-grown husband, hairy chest and all, in an oversized cloth diaper with pins, crouched in an overgrown crib. The vision was too much. I began to cry. "A baby?" I asked. "That's a frightening image."

Dr. Armonda realized that he had reached this wife's limits for need-to-know. "The brain heals in amazing ways," he added. "You can't discount that. And Bob has so many factors going for him."

"Let's just say I get my husband back in some form, do you think he will ever work again?" I asked. "Will he be able to do his job?" I had been afraid to ask this question, but I knew the doctors had seen enough to have a good idea.

"Probably not," said Dr. Armonda, averting his eyes to his folded hands. "But it doesn't mean he can't have a fulfilling life." The look of pain in his eyes was one of the few times I would see a crack in Dr. Armonda's professional reserve.

I realized then that I had been living in a fog that was all too optimistic. Doctors had been trying to tell me things, gently, and my mind had not been ready to take it all in. Would my husband be some kind of monster when he awakened? Would he be emotionally flat or blank? I had stepped out of the zone, and I felt naked. I had tried not to ask too much, to talk about timelines and behavior, the *what-if*'s and the *what-could-be*'s. I had to manage what I was hearing because I was as fragile as bone china, but there was one more question I needed to ask.

"Dr. Armonda," I said, now openly sobbing, "will he still love me?" He steeled himself for a second and collected his thoughts before grabbing my one hand in his two massive ones. His face was about a foot from mine and, as much as I understood that doctors are not gods, I wanted to believe his clear honest eyes.

"I can tell you that not one of my patients with this kind of blast injury has ever woken up and not loved the people they loved before. That just doesn't happen," he said earnestly.

We reassembled at the hospital that evening when the New York surgeons arrived, so that we could meet everyone and have one last powwow. The surgery would be first thing in the morning, and they expected it could take as long as six hours.

Dr. Peter Costantino, Dr. Chandra Sen, and Dr. Rocco Armonda barely noticed Mike, my brother-in-law Mark, and me when we first came into the small hospital meeting room. The three surgeons were intensely discussing various options for surgical approaches. (Dr. Costantino would tell me later that when he visited Bob in the ICU after our meeting he thought he had the wrong room, so unrecognizable and swollen was his face.)

Dr. Costantino turned the putty-colored model of Bob's skull around in his hands, flipping it over at the base to examine the rock. First, he studied the rock and its position and then he looked up at me, incredulous. "I cannot believe your husband is alive right now, Lee," he said. "Bob is a very, very lucky man."

This was becoming overwhelming. These men were holding a model of my husband's skull in their hands! I wanted to escape. I wanted to be any of the people around me who could simply leave all this behind, get on a plane, walk into their houses, and defrost a lasagna for dinner. I wanted *normal* back again.

Before bed that night, I stared down at the winter wonderland on the streets of Washington. The roads were well plowed, and huge piles of snow lay in drifts on either side of the walk. A few errant flakes blew down from the windowsill above. I thought about the big surgery the next morning. I would need to keep myself busy while they were operating.

I said good night to my kids on the phone and promised they could check in with me anytime the next day regarding their dad's operation. Cathryn dealt with my absence by calling me frequently. Mack had retreated. Often I would have Cathryn hunt her brother down just to talk to me, but we barely seemed to say more than good night. I understood that he was a typical fourteen-year-old boy, but his silence and seeming nonchalance on the phone worried me. With the twins, it was easier not to talk to them on the phone at all. It always dissolved into tears and "When are you coming home?" which was tantamount to someone's sticking a hot poker in my eye. There were times when I would hang up in frustration and mutter to myself, "What have you done to us, Bob? Our little family has been hit by its own IED." I desperately wanted to be there to tuck all of them in.

Waiting out the surgery in my hotel room, Mike Woodruff and I drank coffee, cracked jokes, called his brothers and my sisters, and did what we could to cheer each other up. Mike was the third of the four brothers; an artist and carpenter. He was single, a bit of a philosopher; sensitive and much loved. He knew the names of all kinds of birds and constellations and built things with his hands, intricate frames and amazing photo albums. Mike and I could talk for hours, and any topic was fair game. Mike put up a brave front to cheer me, but I knew he was hurting just as much.

My cell phone rang at 10:30 A.M.; it was Dr. Costantino and Dr. Armonda. The rock was out and the surgery was over. They were ecstatic, like a couple of teenagers. What could have been a nightmare surgery had taken only one hour and fifteen minutes. We were to get there as fast as we could. The doctors would give us a postsurgical briefing within the hour.

Mike and I jumped up, high-fiving and hugging each other. I did a little victory dance around the room. Bob had pulled through once again. I thanked God we'd had such an amazing surgical team, the best combination of doctors, nurses, and assistants, the best brains and hands in the business. I thanked God for the many prayers and good thoughts so many people had offered. I thanked God for Bob's powerful will to live.

The doctors filed in and Dr. Costantino held up the offending rock, the size of a small marble neatly sealed in a clear plastic vial. Each of us palmed it, marveling at the damage it had done.

With Bob back in the ICU, we were finally allowed to see him. He looked much smaller. The overall body swelling had gone down, and he was losing body and muscle mass. His face was still swollen and, although the drain was out of his head, he had new bandages on the right side of his neck and up to his ear where they had made the incision. The left side of his face was still swollen and red, with black specks of rocks peppering the skin.

Bob's chest rose and fell rhythmically with the ventilator. He was far away from us now, eyes closed.

"I love you, Bob," I whispered into his good ear. "I'm here for you, and I will be here always. You just had a great surgery, and now you can begin to heal. I know you feel my presence. I am right by your side every step of the way."

"Hey, Bobby," Mike called, massaging Bob's legs and trying to help keep the circulation going. "You're the man. Hang in there, bro. You're healing. Just keep healing."

"Just one thing," I said, leaning down to kiss Bob goodbye. "Next year, promise me that we will spend Valentine's Day a little differently, okay?"

After Bob's surgery, I knew I had to send out some kind of e-mail to all our friends and family to let them know that, although I couldn't possibly speak to everyone right now, I could feel their thoughts and prayers.

Communicating to our friends was going to be a challenge. We had kept the details of Bob's medical condition and the many surgeries private. At all costs I had to hide how grim the situation was with Bob from the public and from my children. It was no one's right to know yet. Until he woke up and we learned whether or not he could talk, think, read, or write, I had to choose my words very carefully. I didn't want to give glowing reports, but I couldn't afford to make it all sound like gloom and doom. Bob was being medically sedated, it was true, but it was also true that anytime they tried to lower the sedation he became agitated and restless. His head wound needed to be stable to heal, and his brain was not yet ready to wake itself up. It was still rebooting; the connections inside were not yet complete. Although he had been on a liquid diet for all of these weeks, he was still strong as an ox, even pulling out his stomach feeding tube and balloon with one tug.

An e-mail from David Westin to ABC and our list of friends on February 23, just a week after Bob's surgery to remove the rock, put the best face on the situation:

> Despite the fact that he continues to be mildly sedated . . . Bob's physical strength continues to impress his entire team. Bob's responses to Lee and the children are even more heartening—Lee told me that Bob "reacts to their voices, returns their smiles, and is initiating kisses."

The notes, DVDs, and books people were sending, on the hopeful assumption that Bob was just lying around watching movies while he healed, filled me with sadness. Would he ever understand the subtle nuances in a movie? Would he be able to read a book again?

That night, back at the hotel, Vivi had left me a package. It was a pair of pajamas with smiley faces on them. On the card she had written, *Remember, love is in the guts and the rest is in the brain.*

I was beginning to miss Bob so much. Even from my perch next to his sedated body, I was having a hard time remembering what his face looked like. It was the phenomenon that widows report, an inability to recall certain characteristics of their loved ones. My old Bob was fading like a ghost. I understood now that I might never see those same looks or hear those same tender words again. I thought about what I would do if we ever survived this and Bob came home. At least I would have family nearby, my sister Nancy and my brother-in-law Shawn.

Through it all, my sister Nan was a rock. As the mother of three and survivor of a brain tumor, Nancy understood life's uncertainties better than most. She had faced her share of challenges and kept her sense of humor. When she survived, she promised herself that she would keep fresh flowers in her house all year long. It was the kind of luxury our own mother never would have indulged in, and it had become Nancy's emblem for life: the need to be kind to yourself every single day because you simply can't know what is next.

Growing up eighteen months apart, Nancy and I had developed our

own shorthand language, which our sister Megan shared. We could finish each other's sentences and use nicknames or code words that made
no sense to outsiders. When we answered each other's phones, callers
would automatically assume we were the other sister, so similar are our
voices and manner of speaking. Sometimes, on the phone, we had even
fooled our husbands for a moment.

As the sister who lived only twenty minutes away from our Westchester County home, Nancy was in an easier position to man the front
lines than Megan. In a testament to the kind of friend that Nancy is, legions of women in *her* town cooked dinners, drove kids, and dropped
off gifts in an effort to care for her family while she was caring for mine.
If I ever want to take a close look at the inner workings of my nature,
the good parts as well as the things I'd like to tweak, all I need to do is
look at Nancy. She is the closest thing to a twin I will ever have.

Bob

Washington, D.C., Spring 1997

My stint in the ABC News Washington bureau was a time of
transition. As the low man on the bureau totem pole, I had
weekend duty when we first arrived. The new guy was always the one who drew the short straw.

One of the more interesting assignments I occasionally
got was weekend White House duty. These were the Clinton
years, and the White House was a more colorful and open
place than it would be in administrations to come. This was
before Monica Lewinsky and the press was still welcome, the
access consistently open.

In 1999, when NATO dropped bombs on Yugoslavia, intended to end Slobodan Milosevic's campaign to control the
largely Albanian population in Kosovo, I raised my hand ea-

gerly to go overseas. I have no memory of discussing this with Lee first, but she understood this was what I wanted to do. She could see I was developing itchy feet.

On that first night, as I watched the antiaircraft fire from the rooftop of the Belgrade Hyatt, I felt again the rush of witnessing history. When Milosevic finally surrendered and the Serb army agreed to pull out of Kosovo, we moved there days before NATO troops entered to take control. As Milosevic fell, Albanians who had been hiding in the mountains converged on the NATO tanks to kiss the British and American soldiers and throw flowers on their route.

After that, I was hooked on this strange endeavor of covering wars and conflicts. Being a war correspondent is probably the journalistic equivalent of a World Health Organization scientist tracking the spread of a virus around the world. War is an affliction of the human race. It's a disease, and its outcome more often than not will alter the course of history.

Wars revealed so many horrible stories about injury and death. But in the midst of that landscape, there was always powerful evidence of hope. Among the violence were people who had learned something profound about life. Places of war allow you to witness extremes, the highs and lows of life, people starving and defeated, people victorious and surfeited.

It is a strange addiction, covering war. It involves a sometimes fatal curiosity about tragedy and triumph. Fear makes one feel more deeply, rise to anger more quickly, cry more easily. It is not necessarily fun or exciting, it is simply profound. And during that time, your brain is intensely engaged. In the middle of covering Kosovo, I barely slept for days on end. In Afghanistan and Iraq, it would be the same. But in those moments, in some way, I had also never felt so alive.

Why do people choose to work in a war zone? In the words of legendary war photographer Larry Burrows, journalists who cover wars and conflicts are there "to show the interested people and to shock the uninterested." I thought there was a great deal of truth in that, and even something noble.

Naturally, being on assignment in these places was always in stark contrast to what was going on at home. One night during the war in Kosovo, I called the family to check in before bed. As I went through the litany of the day I heard gunfire outside. "Hold on a minute, Lee," I said. "I'm just going to crouch down for a minute." After a small pause and a crashing sound outside I got back on the line. "What was that?" she asked in a panicked tone.

"There was just some gunfire outside the window," I explained, as calmly as I could, and then Lee put Cathryn and Mack on the line so I could say good night.

Lee

Washington, D.C., 1999

Although Bob was still officially the Justice correspondent, other story assignments were beginning to take him out of our orbit. I could see he was energized by heading to a remote island in the South Pacific (to do a piece on Cargo Cults) and covering the war in Kosovo. I remember one night, as he called us before bed, I could hear gunshots over the phone. "I'm all right, Lee, I'm inside the hotel," he said, trying to reassure me.

I wanted to believe him. I wanted to believe that nothing could happen to a journalist, a mere witness to events. But I knew better. The brief sound of bullets was just a tiny window on the dangers Bob began to encounter on the road. He would shield me from most of it, and I was reluctant to ask. Sometimes it was easier to operate on blind faith.

From my perspective, one of the most significant things that happened for us during our time in Washington were the friends we made.

And for me, always the slightly odd peg in social gatherings, with a husband rarely in attendance, Melanie Bloom was finally the friend who could understand my life without any explanation needed. Melanie was married to NBC White House Correspondent David Bloom.

She understood the crazy hours, the apologetic phone calls to friends canceling the theater or dinner at the last minute because a pager had gone off, the inability to make solid vacation plans in advance. "You had me at *hello*," we joked with each other. Surrounded by friends who had "normal" jobs and were perplexed or slightly pitying of our upended lifestyle, we treasured our friendship like a rainstorm in a desert.

It was our banker who fixed us up as couples, as we liked to call it. There was a black-tie benefit and roast for Larry King at a downtown D.C. hotel, and the bank had bought a table. He had mentioned the Blooms to us and thought we'd all be compatible; two reporters with young kids, both of us having moved to Washington around the same time.

At the cocktail portion of the evening, Dave and Bob sized each other up, two competing reporters trading notes. While their worlds hadn't collided in the field, they knew each other by reputation. Both men looked incredibly handsome in their tuxes, and I felt like the belle of the ball.

Melanie sat a few seats away. She was a gorgeous blonde, statuesque and with fabulous taste in clothes, the kind of woman I'd always aspired to be, someone who looks effortlessly put together. In my Filene's Basement bargain dress and with no evening bag with which to reapply lipstick, I should by rights have hated her. But Mel was one of those rare gals whom both women and men gravitated toward; the type of person my mother's generation would call *lovely*. Try as you might to find some reason to dislike her, you simply couldn't. She was intelligent, articulate, giving, and poised, with a wicked sense of humor. A little girl from the plains of Kansas, she made no bones about the fact that hers was not a sophisticated upbringing, just simple midwestern fare with family sing-alongs at the piano after dinner.

One of the biggest reasons to hate Mel was her diet. She seemed to exist on chocolate chip ice cream, Snickers bars, and Cap'n Crunch cereal. Vegetables did not pass her lips, and fruit was out altogether. Occasionally I saw her eat salad, and she downed Dr Peppers, the ones with full calories. And here was the thing: she had the figure of a supermodel. Okay, so maybe I was born with a pretty decent metabolism too, but I ate beets and lima beans, loved spinach and sushi. You could usually pinch an inch somewhere around my hips.

In our dynamic duo, I was the Cagney to Mel's Lacey, the Rhoda to her Mary, the Rizzo to her doe-eyed Sandy. You can see where I'm going here. There was an innocence about Mel that made me want to protect her. And she felt the same mothering instincts toward me.

David clearly adored her, and I admired that. Marriages that stayed together were tough to come by in the journalism business. I had once heard a divorce rate of more than 50 percent mentioned among correspondents, foreign reporters in particular. Many of the older reporters I'd met seemed to be on their second wife. Mel and Dave shared a lot of the same thoughts and visions we did. They had twin girls who were Cathryn's age, and they lived about ten minutes away.

There were other similarities. Bob and Dave had been bookish sports types in high school, with no girlfriends. Each had blossomed in college. They both came from families of boys. Fierce competitors in the field, Bob and Dave both loved to argue a point, Bob with his legal background and Dave with his debater's training. The Blooms introduced us to the game of Taboo and reignited our interest in doubles tennis.

Mel and I talked so much that first night we both went home feeling oddly energized, as if we'd been drinking caffeine all evening. If someone could have told us exactly how twinned our lives would be—the addition of more daughters, the subsequent moves, and the loss of our husbands in different ways to the same war—we might have both run screaming from the room like Cinderella at the stroke of midnight. Instead, that night we felt the beginning of something precious.

Our children became fast friends, and when our husbands were out of town or working on weekends we often killed the hours together. More times than not it was sitting in one or the other's family room watching a home-produced play our girls had made up, singing songs from *Grease*, or sending the children down the cellar stairs to play, so we could talk.

Bob

Washington, D.C., 1999

David Bloom and I had two distinctly different styles but somehow, as friends, our personalities worked. Much like Lee, David was incredibly gregarious, chatting with waiters or anyone who came into his orbit. He was naturally curious about everything, which made him a good journalist, and he had a boyish enthusiasm and energy I found infectious. I can still see him bounding into the room, leading with "I have a great idea!" This usually involved an outing of some sort or a tennis match.

Dave was an avid competitor on the tennis court as well as a worthy competitor in the field. He loved his family and was very proud of his three girls, Chrissy, Nicole, and Ava.

Among the four of us, I was the foil for Dave's overzealousness, and I took great pleasure in bringing him down to earth with a zinger or two. He also provided a valuable sounding board when it came to career advice. Before the U.S. invasion of Iraq in 2003, David quietly cooked up the idea for the "Bloom Mobile," a vehicle created specially to transmit pictures from a camera mounted on a Humvee while it rolled through the desert with the troops. He went through elaborate machinations, dealing with the top brass at NBC and the Pentagon and getting everyone on board, from the tire company to the car manufacturer, to make this happen. It had been a major investment and completely his brainchild.

David confided to Mel later that it was tougher than he'd imagined to be so secretive in front of me. As excited as he was to beat out the other networks in covering the war, there was something hard about sitting on top of this giant secret when your friend came to the war zone so much less well prepared. Of course, a big part of David couldn't wait for the vehicle to be unveiled. Like anyone in his shoes, he took enormous pride in having all that hard work and planning pay off, and to watch his competitors' jaws drop at the new technological triumph.

Lee

Washington, D.C., 1998

In retrospect, our time in Washington was a wonderful interlude. The city was so accessible, green, and livable. There were press parties at the White House and black-tie dinners. We explored the Mall and the many monuments and government buildings with the kids.

But inside I still felt a blackness that blotted out any joy on some days. I still dreamed of the baby I didn't have. While I tried to stuff those feelings down and appreciate the gifts I had, a big part of me couldn't accept that all this was final. There was still an honest-to-goodness hope that someone would just drop a baby on our doorstep.

Surrogacy, having another woman carry your baby, had been something Bob and I had looked at only perfunctorily in Phoenix. As part of my need to "do" something in the wake of my grief, we had seriously investigated adoption and ordered a brochure and video on surrogacy. It seemed that the outcome of in-vitro fertilization with a gestational carrier was never certain, and it was expensive. Many states didn't allow it. We didn't give it another thought until a friend mentioned it to me one day in 1998. By then, more scientific advances had been made.

"Why not?" Bob said calmly, when I casually raised the issue one night.

"What?" I wasn't sure I'd heard him correctly.

"Why not? We both would love another child. What do we have to lose? If it doesn't work, we know we explored every available option, and we can close the door and move on with our life as a family of four."

Much as I'd never felt that the door was closed to having another child, somewhere in my heart I believed that this would work. I was thirty-eight, just over the statistical hump and into declining fertility in the average female. All those years of preventing pregnancy, I thought ironically, as so many women in infertility clinics have thought before me. And here I am begging for just one good egg.

If I'd wanted further proof that women hold up more than half of the sky, as they say in China, I only had to look at the whole fertility process. The hopeful mother spends weeks injecting herself with drugs like a junkie. There are follicle-stimulating hormones and Lupron shots, luteinizing hormones, and daily sonograms to count the number of egg follicles. There are painful cliff-hanging moments where you hold your breath and pray that the follicles are still growing, and then of course there is the procedure to retrieve the eggs. The husband, on the other hand, has about a half hour of what is really tough to call hardship. Ducking out on a lunch break, his entire job is to go into a room on a Barcalounger with a lava lamp and spend a few minutes with a *Playboy* centerfold and some lubricant. Where is the justice in that?

After many months and two failed attempts with a wonderful surrogate to whom I am forever indebted, there were only two embryos to implant on my last cycle. Bob and I agreed it would be our final roll of the dice, and I was desperate for it to work. The last failure, a miscarriage after the implant had first taken, had been particularly haunting and painful for me. Those last two embryos were to complete our family. Nora and Claire were born one month and four days shy of my fortieth birthday.

On January 1, 2000, anticipating the birth of our twins, my two children and I had watched the fireworks as they splashed in the skies over the Mall and illuminated the government buildings. Bob was, of course, at work, reporting on the arrival of the new millennium. In the chilly night I drew my two exhausted kids close to me and tried to freeze the moment in my mind. It was fitting, in a way, that Bob wasn't with us for this milestone. His absence from the family would be a hallmark of the next five years. But as the fireworks rained down red, white, and blue, shooting stars over the top of the Washington Monument, all I felt was pure hope and happiness. Two little girls would be added to our family in a few short months. The little black hole in my heart was filling in.

Lee

Bethesda Naval Hospital, February 16, 2006

I called the ICU to see if there was a surgery scheduled for the next day. We'd gotten word that the ENT surgeons wanted to operate on the rocks in Bob's left cheek and jaw. But Bob needed a rest. His white blood cell count was high, he was running a fever, and infection appeared to be setting in. I was willing to bet that the hunches of Dr. Costantino and Dr. Armonda were right. Cutting into Bob yet again at this moment seemed like a bad idea.

That night I reached both Dr. Perdue and Dr. Armonda at home. Somehow there had been a miscommunication. They were surprised to learn something had been scheduled. Whether the surgery was actually going to take place or if the other doctors had just booked an OR, we put a halt to it. I went to bed that night feeling as if I had run a half-marathon and fell asleep relieved that there would be no surgery for Bob the next day.

Twelve hours later it was painfully obvious that infection was setting in fast. Bob had full-blown pneumonia and he had also become infected with the potentially deadly Acinetobacter, which enlisted men and women routinely carried back from Iraq on their skin. Doctors employed a variety of older antibiotics from previous wars to combat this resistant strain. Bob was listless, not moving as much as before.

He had contracted something else that, if I'd heard it named at the time, would have turned my veins to icicles. He had sepsis, the deadly blood infection that can easily kill patients in a weakened state after surgery. However, the doctors used the term *blood infection* with me, and the part of my brain that was keeping me in the zone did an effective job of stopping my inquiring mind from learning more.

The ups and downs of Bob's medical ride were like bad airplane turbulence. Each time we throttled up, we were hit with fresh bad news. Pneumonia, sepsis, bacterial infection: I kept reaching for something—anything—positive to hold on to.

Bob had to keep fighting or he would die. Sepsis can so easily be fatal. It is an infection so severe that bacteria and toxins are flowing throughout the body in the veins, not just concentrated in one infected spot. How unfair, I thought, that Bob had survived the battlefield attack only to be in peril again. He had sustained so many procedures and operations. I willed myself to believe that he couldn't die at this point. He had already come through so much.

Swimming laps in the early morning at the YMCA was the only place where I could relax my mind. Cutting through the aqua-blue waters of the lap pool, I could make myself focus only on the rhythmic movements and let my thoughts release. I liked to daydream, as I moved through the water, about what would be happening at that exact moment if none of this had ever transpired.

The next day in the hospital, I was getting a quick, seemingly routine update from Dr. Perdue about Bob's pneumonia.

"The antibiotics should work to fight this, right?" I asked him naively. I saw Dr. Perdue's expression change. He paused.

"Mrs. Woodruff, your husband is still very much on the knife's edge," he said to me gently. "The sepsis and pneumonia are very serious."

Knife's edge. I froze. What this meant was that he was, for the moment, dangerously near death. My face, I am sure, fell instantly. I fingered Bob's wedding ring on the gold chain around my neck.

"Surely, Dr. Perdue," I said, "you can come up with a better analogy than that one." He gave me a weak smile.

Bob's new precarious status kicked me even further into overdrive. We needed to help him keep fighting. We needed to do everything we could to let him hear our voices and reach him inside the sedation. Again, I urged everyone to keep talking to him. We played the home videos. We told him stories. I began to understand that it wasn't so much that the doctors were keeping him sedated, but rather that his brain was simply not ready to wake up yet. It was still trying to put things back together. The fragility of Bob's life right then was frightening. This new placid sleeping Bob scared me. What if he never woke up?

I hated walking onto the ICU floor at Bethesda Naval Hospital and seeing all the curtains open; so little dignity, I thought, for these men who had sacrificed so much. Although I chose to avert my eyes, if I wanted to I could look into each room and see a microcosm of tragedy and sorrow, a life stalled, for the moment at least, in each bed. I could see tears, parents and wives hoping against hope. I could hear prayers. Sometimes I heard fighting among family members. I could witness despair and fatigue etched on the faces of the wives and mothers outside the door. I saw hospital gowns twisted up and sheets disheveled, naked bodies and violated privacy.

I closed Bob's curtain every time I was there. It was a small gesture, but it bought him a measure of respect in my eyes. It gave him back a piece of himself when so much had been stripped away.

My sister Megan was with me for a few days. Meg is the baby of the family. She is the most rational of the three of us. Whenever I pictured an alternate life for myself, I liked to picture Meg's life, with two kids and a supportive husband, home every night with a schedule flexible enough to pinch-hit for her when necessary. Meg was the essence of calm.

Wearing our yellow hospital gowns, we walked into Bob's ICU room like cheerleaders. "You're in Washington, D.C., and you've had an accident in Iraq," I said as if it were a tape recording. "But you are safe, totally safe. We are going to get through this together and I'm going to help you heal. The kids are okay and I'm okay. We're worried about you, but we know you are going to make it." It was getting harder and harder to see Bob so swollen. His fine cheekbones had disappeared in a balloonish bloat with the new medications. At that point I could go into his room for only short periods of time, before I needed to walk in the hall to breathe some air outside the ICU.

Although Bob remained under heavy sedation, he was beginning to make some kind of response when I spoke—a movement, a head turn.

Sometimes he would reach his hand toward my face. "I'm going to kiss you," I told him. "You know I can't wait to kiss you. But you are going to have to brush your teeth first."

And all at once Bob did something amazing. He stuck out his tongue as if to kiss me, and then he licked his lips.

"Whoa!" Dr. Sorenson, the ENT, yelled. "The lingual nerve must be intact!"

As I lay in bed that night, I thought about the time that had passed. It was closing in on three weeks since Bob was hit by the IED. I learned later that the longer Bob's drug-induced coma persisted, the more concern there was about the severity of damage. If Bob's career was finished, we were going to have to reinvent ourselves somehow. I had my work; I thought I could dial it up to full time. I never wanted to make our kids suffer for the bad luck that had befallen their dad. We can do this, I told myself. I was stepping out of the zone a little to think negatively this way, but perhaps my mind was letting things in incrementally. This felt healthier somehow. That night I realized I needed a backup plan.

Lee

Bethesda Naval Hospital, February 20, 2006

Hour by hour, Bob fought the infection. His body responded to the powerful medications, and the color began to return to his face. During one of my visits, his parents and Vivi came to his ICU room. At first Bob was calm but then he became agitated, opening his eyes in a purposeful manner. Vivi and I were talking to him and she was massaging his calves. Every so often I would repeat, "I love you, I am with you forever, you are safe, you are in a hospital in D.C. and you are okay. We are taking care of you, and the kids are okay."

All at once it was as if he came alive, swimming up through the medications. He became wild and opened his eyes and mouth, trying to talk to me though the trache tube. I swear, and Vivi is my witness, that he mouthed the words, "I love you, sweetie."

He tried to reach out to Vivi's face and then pulled my hand toward him. Lord, he was strong, so damned strong. I understood instinctively that he wanted to talk to me. He was desperate to communicate but the trache tube was preventing any kind of speech, if in fact he could talk at all. We still didn't know.

I held his hand, tears running down my face, and I kept talking. I told him over and over again that I knew what he was telling me. He was kicking and rolling on his side so much that his trache tube came out with a wild rush of air and I panicked, yelling for the nurse. Finally she had to administer a shot to calm him down. It was disturbing to see him so upset and anxious, as if he were reliving the trauma of the blast. But there was also something encouraging in his reaching out in that way.

The nurse told me afterward that she had known I was coming and had waited a little bit to sedate him that morning. She wanted to see how far he had progressed and how he would respond to me. Now she was extremely pleased. She also saw him mouth *I love you.* She and the other nurses were the ones who really marked his progress, sitting and watching and tending to him hour after hour. I loved these nurses.

Over coffee downstairs, Vivi and I excitedly discussed what Bob had just done. Dr. M had talked to her about Doug getting wild. It was common for blast injury victims to remember and relive the incident, the fear and terror that come in the instant of the impact. The best advice was to remind him that he was safe, Dr. M had said.

"Will he hit me?" Vivi had asked, trying to picture her gentle husband doing such a thing.

"It does happen," Dr. M answered. She never minced words. Vivi and I talked about the future, what it would be like to be married to a man we hardly knew who had had a switch flipped, leaving him haunted and tortured.

I would have a number of sessions with Dr. M to plumb the depths of information about traumatic brain injuries. In one of these conversations, when the topic moved to post-traumatic stress disorder, or PTSD, I learned something chilling.

I'd watched Bob come home after covering many a horrible story. Typically, he'd be quiet at first. It was the worst after September 11 and after the Iraq invasion. He didn't want to talk much and then slowly, hour by hour, he would begin to knit himself back into the fabric of our everyday lives: toasting frozen waffles and brushing the twins' hair before school, driving Cathryn to dancing class, dumping the laundry to be folded on the bed, quietly avoiding too many details in our talks.

"Bob has seen a lot of human misery with what he does," I explained. "He has always been able to come home and shake it off. He saw mass graves in Kosovo, death in Afghanistan and Iraq, and unfathomable sorrow in Indonesia after the tsunami. Doesn't his ability to have processed this in a healthy way mean he may escape post-traumatic stress disorder?"

"I wish I could tell you it worked that way," said Dr. M. "Actually, research shows that the more trauma a person has been through, the more they have seen, the worse the PTSD is. The cumulative effect appears to make the person much more susceptible."

All that collective human misery coalesced into one brain, I thought with a chill. There was the child's leg Bob found near a mass grave in Kosovo; the blood of Jesus Suarez del Solár, the marine in Bob's embed division who had stepped on an unexploded U.S. bomb during the 2003 invasion. There was a whole city's worth of devastation in New Orleans, and there were bodies on the beaches in Banda Aceh two weeks after the tsunami, so bloated they were pitchforked into a truck bed. Bob had a mighty good library of human misery inside his head, I thought. And now, I had learned, all that footage would be his worst enemy.

Lee

Washington, D.C., June 2000

Twins. Who thought that was a good idea at forty?

Not to put too fine a point on it, we used a "gestational carrier," which meant the twins were our biological babies, Bob's and my DNA.

I explained to my kids one night that we were simply borrowing the "oven" because Mommy didn't have one anymore, getting into more technical detail about babies than I had ever intended for children ages six and eight.

The upshot of this honesty and information overload were the phone calls I received the next day from Cathryn's kindergarten teacher and some of the class mothers. "Cathryn says her dad is having a baby with another woman," the teacher began awkwardly. We'd waited a good three months to tell the children and our families and friends that we were expecting. They had no idea we were doing any of this. We'd wanted to keep it completely quiet until we had good news to share.

I imagine more than a few parents at our school were none too pleased with the Woodruffs when their children came home asking perplexing questions about how babies are made. But for the most part, everyone we knew rejoiced with us.

As the twins' April birth date approached, Bob's ABC contract was moving toward the latest in a series of deadlines. He was committed to what he wanted to do next. Although another network was dangling their White House reporting position, his dream had always been to be a foreign reporter. White House correspondent is considered a plum position, but it wasn't something Bob was ever seriously interested in. He once described the times he had spent as part of the White House press corps as "glorified babysitting with spoon-fed information," despite such seductive perks as travel, access, and Easter Egg parties on the South Lawn.

"Only a few people ever get the chance to be a foreign correspondent," he would say to me, perhaps somewhat conflicted himself. "It's a dying way of life. The networks are changing so fast, shrinking the bureaus, gathering news differently. This is my last big chance in many ways." Bob's ideal was the heyday of Edward R. Murrow: London blitzkrieg, trench coats, and sneaking across enemy lines to file the story. He was a man born after his time.

"You can always go from foreign correspondent to White House reporter," he mused, "but you don't often go the other way." As he pretended to debate the merits with me, I knew where this was going. This was simply something he had to get out of his system. Part of me was excited about living overseas, but I had also decided long ago that I would never be the one to clip my husband's wings.

In the end, ABC News wanted Bob to stay enough that they created a position for him in the London bureau. We would move in late summer, when the twins were almost five months old. I would wrap up my work for Benefit Cosmetics in July before beginning a new life in England as a full-time mom for the first time.

By the end of August we had celebrated with friends, said teary goodbyes, and invited everyone we knew to come and stay with us at any time. Packing our rented minivan with enough bags to open a luggage store, we said our final farewells and drove to the airport with all the kids, the twins in car seats. Too exhausted and numb to register any serious emotion, we shoved off the East Coast and headed across the pond. Another Woodruff family adventure.

Bob

London, 2000

In the two years we lived in London, I covered only two local stories. For every other assignment I was on the road. In our first year overseas, I reported stories from the sinking of the Russian submarine *Kursk,* the fall of Serbia's Slobodan Milosevic, the downed U.S. spy plane in China, and the brutal Albanian sex trade, to name just a few. I even covered the Race Around the World, reporting from one of the biggest, fastest racing sailboats ever built. My producer Andrew Morse, cameraman Tom Murphy, and I jumped overboard into a police speedboat passing through Gibraltar when it was time to head home.

On the road I tried to talk to Lee and the kids almost every day, no matter where I was. Satellite phones helped enormously. I talked to Cathryn about her math homework while on horseback in the Egyptian desert; I reached Lee on her cell phone in the grocery store while I was huddled in a vehicle with gun-toting Afghani warlords.

Other than these phone conversations, my world at home and life on the road were entirely separate. The kinds of stories I covered as a foreign correspondent required me to be away for long periods of time, and although the conditions might have been harsh at times, the camaraderie with the cameramen, producers, and sound people who routinely made up the crew more than compensated for it.

I felt incredibly alive on the road and found it was easier to push away the everyday thoughts of being a father while working intensely. I knew I was missing important milestones and dates as well as the little things. But if I dwelled on that, I would feel extreme guilt. Although my family always came first, I found it difficult and distracting to think of them constantly while on assignment. It was as impossible as holding two simultaneous thoughts in my head or concentrating fully on two separate conversations. As much as I missed Lee and the kids, sometimes it was hard to be entirely sympathetic to her complaints of sleepless twins or exhaustion. My own circumstances, either sleeping on a hard dirt floor somewhere or laying my head on a pillow in some four-star hotel in Europe for a two-hour nap, were not always easy. I consoled myself that there were negative and positive aspects to any job. I needed to support my family and there were bills to pay.

On the other hand, I never forgot that Lee was making an enormous sacrifice for my career. And while I was determined to provide my family with a good living, I was also keenly aware that she was letting me follow my dream and had enabled me to do it. That act alone would continue to amaze me through all the years of our marriage.

Covering overseas stories for an American network

meant, among other things, rarely sleeping. The news had to be gathered and reported during the day and then written and edited at night. The time difference meant we would feed stories in the wee hours of the morning. That kind of endless work prevented me from thinking too hard about the risks I was taking, the long hours away from my family, and how my kids might be needing me that week.

There were many times, however, when I did ask myself, Is this what a parent should do? My profession had taught me one thing for sure. Danger was impossible to avoid. Bad things could happen to people everywhere, no matter how safe they tried to be. One need only ask the people who kissed their loved ones goodbye on the morning of September 11, 2001. You can take precautions in this life, but they are like seat belts; they won't necessarily keep you safe.

Knowing this made it somewhat easier to rationalize being in dangerous places. There is no question that putting yourself in a war zone increases the odds of something going wrong. But under the often tremendous pressure to get the story out on time, it just was not something I thought about very much.

One perk about traveling as much as I did was that I could occasionally take off a chunk of time to go home. These were wonderful periods where I could be involved in the kids' activities during the day, help in their classrooms, take the twins to the park, and go to breakfast with Lee. These stretches of time made it all worthwhile, although I often fell ill, as my body let down after the intensity of work on the road.

Lee would tease me that I should have gotten all this travel out of my system before we'd had kids, and I'm sure coming home as a bachelor from an overseas assignment to an empty apartment would have been easier in some ways. But I wouldn't have traded my family life for anything in the world. Walking through the door with my suitcase and seeing all those beaming faces just melted my heart. That was what life was really about for me.

Lee and I had a deal. We'd discuss it whenever we hit a rough patch. If at any time what I did was truly affecting the family in a negative way, damaging the children or our marriage, I would stop. There was nothing more important to me in the world than my wife and kids, and through the most exciting moments in the field I never lost sight of that.

Lee

London, 2002

In many ways, our life in London was pretty idyllic. England offered so much to do and see. There were lush green parks and slices of history to explore around every city corner. We made lifelong British and American friends, and the older kids blended right into the American School. Our little neighborhood in Primrose Hill felt more like a village oasis in the middle of London, and shopkeepers on the High Street soon knew our names. To most people I must have looked like an older mother paying dearly for one night of passion without birth control as I pushed the twins in their double red stroller. But I was content. Our family was more than complete. We had been blessed.

Despite all that, I felt the strains of single parenting during our two years there. Bob was having the time of his life, on the road more than he was home. Gradually, I made my peace with that. I simply tried to accept it as part of my marriage, and our home life began to take on a rhythm, even if it was an exhausting one.

Just when things felt like they were settling down, Bob and I took the twins for a routine checkup. Dr. Hecker measured each girl's head circumference, height, and weight and then moved to a simple eye and hearing test.

At first I brushed it off when Nora didn't turn at the faint silvery sounds of the rattle by her ear. "She's so interested in the bunny," I said to Dr. Hecker. "She's just like her dad, she can really focus in on things. Plus she's tired. This is her nap time." Days later we had another appointment. Nora failed the hearing test again. Then, at a different health facility, with a more complex test, the same result.

"Look how alert she is," friends said. "She heard that. It's probably glue ear or fluid." We began sneaking up on Nora to make sounds. Bob dropped pans and hid behind a pillar, calling her name at different decibels. Sometimes Nora would turn and other times she would ignore us. We were baffled enough by her inconsistency to have a goofy kind of hope.

Once, at the top of the stairs, I yelled "Nora!" and she looked right at me. See, I said to myself. Of course she can hear, she is just concentrating. She is her father's daughter. Yet things nagged at me. A mother always knows. It wasn't until weeks later that I learned about compensation: how the thump of my feet on the stairs, the movement of air, the cue to look where Claire looked could mask all that was wrong. At the time, these things didn't occur to me.

After many tense weeks and more tests, I found myself alone in another doctor's office. Bob had, once again, been called away, this time for a story in Belgrade. Dr. Sirimanna was a small Indian man, wearing black socks that had his name, *Tony*, embroidered on them. Sitting emotionlessly at his desk, he began to refer to his notes as I held Nora in my arms.

"It appears that Nora has some serious hearing loss," he began, barely looking up. "I would like to recommend that we fit her for hearing aids immediately and do some further testing. With therapy and hearing aids she should be able to develop normal speech and language and perhaps even attend a mainstream school."

I tried to understand what he was saying, but it was hard. Surely there was some operation, some way to fix this? I was unable even to come up with legitimate questions; it was difficult to know where to begin. It seemed that he was using the word *deaf*, and surely that was not my child. She wasn't deaf! Hadn't she turned at loud noises? Didn't her eyes go right to us when we walked into a room and called her name?

"Tell me about the loss," I asked. "Can it ever improve?"

"In rare instances I have seen hearing improve, maybe one child out of a thousand."

"So how long will she have to wear the aids?" I asked.

"This is a permanent situation, Mrs. Woodruff. Nora will need to wear hearing aids for the rest of her life."

Tears filled my eyes. Dr. Sirimanna squirmed uncomfortably in his chair. He was unable to think of anything comforting to say. "I'm sorry," I sputtered, feeling like a total fool. "I just . . . I thought—"

"I'd like to do a series of tests on Nora to make sure that her hearing loss isn't caused by . . . a number of factors," said Dr. Sirimanna.

"Like what?" I said softly.

"Well, there is a syndrome that can cause degenerative loss; another connection can be made with the kidneys, so we'd need to do a urine test; some blood will need to be drawn to check if this is a genetic problem. There is a syndrome that ultimately causes blindness as well as deafness. And then we'd like to do a CT scan. . . ." He droned on in somewhat choppy English.

"Wait," I cried, my eyes welling with new tears. "How many children with Nora's kind of loss have these other syndromes?"

"A small percentage. We can fit Nora's hearing aids later this week," he said, somewhat more softly. I understood that this appointment was over.

I spilled blindly back out onto the street with Nora in my arms. I recalled my very first thought when Dr. Sirimanna had confirmed the news in his office. Oddly, it was of Nora's high school prom, seventeen years away. My first thought had been to wonder if anyone would ask a deaf girl to the dance.

Back home, I called Bob on his cell phone in Yugoslavia. He was covering the war in Belgrade and would be on assignment for weeks. "Nora is being fitted for hearing aids," I sobbed into the phone. There was dead silence. My husband, who had been such a strong champion of Nora's being okay, was stunned. I could hear him fighting back tears.

"Hearing aids?" he said, in a faraway voice. "She doesn't need hearing aids."

Somewhere in the back of my mind I still wanted to believe there was some simple fix, some operation. We could clone things now, we had the capability for stem cell research, we could battle cancer and find cures. Surely there was a fix for Nora's degree of deafness. At home that night I wrote an upbeat e-mail to everyone, explaining that Nora had some hearing loss and would need to wear aids to help her develop completely normal speech and language. My heart breaking, I finished with a joke about how Nora would now match her two grandpas with their hearing aids.

The health visitors showed me how to put Nora's hearing aids in and I began what would be one of the most frustrating periods of Nora's hearing impairment: the "learning to keep them in" phase for a one-year-old. I put them in, she pulled them out. I pushed them back in, she pulled them out and put them in her mouth. I was so invested in this process, so determined for her to succeed, that I found myself frustrated and near tears as we went through this exercise a hundred times a day. By day five Nora began to keep them in for longer stretches. It was similar to what breaking a horse must feel like. How I wished Bob were home to be a partner in all of this.

I cried for weeks. Bob had gone to China to cover the story of a U.S. spy plane that was forced to land over Hainan Island. He was back in Beijing, excited at the chance to visit after all these years, and I was stuck home, a single mother, coming to the realization of how serious Nora's hearing loss was and how much we had been kidding ourselves. Just months before I had grumbled to myself at the routines of mothering: the laundry to do, the meals, the difficulty of finding a parking spot in our neighborhood. Those "so little time for myself" complaints felt like luxuries now. I'd have given anything to have my simple, predictable life return.

"Lee, I think you are overreacting, our daughter is *not* deaf," said Bob on the phone from China. "She is just hard of hearing. We will give her all the love, attention, guidance, and therapy that she needs. Nora will be her own person."

"You are in denial," I cried. "You haven't been through this week of talking to people and sitting with other crying parents. You have been to exactly two doctor's appointments. You have barely tried to put her hearing aids in." My voice began rising and I tried to control it. He was a million miles away doing his job. It was midnight there, and he had waited up to call me to find out how Nora's first therapy appointment went. I knew he felt guilty for not being there but I didn't care. I wanted him to feel the full volume of my pain. He was concerned, upset, bewildered. I thought to myself how much easier it was to be him right now.

In a slow evolution, Nora learned and hit milestones and spoke normally, and I took joy in watching it all. I got to a point where if I'd wanted to cry about Nora's hearing loss I couldn't have. There was constant vigilance required. There were therapies and more hearing aids and tests, so many tests. None of the horrible diseases Nora could have had ever materialized. With the help of dedicated therapists in London and New York, she began to speak beautifully. My life was full of speech therapy, audiograms and evaluations, and staying one step ahead of what Nora might need next. I talked and talked, I articulated, I repeated. It simply became part of our everyday life. In the end, I could see that Nora would become a person defined by her vibrant personality and love of life, not by her different ability.

Lee

London, September 11, 2001

Bob and I both looked forward to September 11. It was our wedding anniversary, and Bob was actually going to be home. He had booked a table at an expensive restaurant in London. Thirteen lucky years of marriage. Our date nights were rare. Bob had been gone more than he had been at home that first year in England.

I was with Nora and her therapist in northern London when my cell phone rang. "Hello," I said quickly, not wanting to interrupt Nora's session.

"Lee." Bob spoke fast, but I was focused solely on Nora. "A plane has

176 | LEE AND BOB WOODRUFF

crashed into the World Trade Center. I'm on my way to the house to pack for Pakistan. I think it's Bin Laden."

"Wow," I muttered, none of it sinking in on any level. I hadn't really been listening closely. There was always some news breaking somewhere. New York felt a million miles away. "Wow. Okay," I said, silently miming a clap to Nora as she successfully navigated the wooden clown down the pegged ladder, chanting "Dow, dow, dow" all the way.

"I'll call you later, babe." Bob hung up quickly, distracted, worried. I, however, was mostly oblivious.

The magnitude of what had happened would strike me only later, watching the images of the twin towers on TV once we got home. Bob left immediately for Pakistan, and I spent the next few weeks dutifully switching on the TV each morning in London to view the previous night's events on ABC. Ten-year-old Mack and eight-year-old Cathryn were aware of what had happened in the world and needed to see their father's face for reassurance. Despite the graphic images, it was comforting for them to turn on the TV, see Bob, and hear his familiar voice. Even the twins yelled "Dada!" when he came on the screen, followed by footage of violence.

While most people I knew were filtering the news for their children, my kids were watching their father reporting under police protection from the Serena Hotel in Quetta, Pakistan, penned in by an angry mob outside the gates. When the school bus pulled up in front of the house, they dutifully shrugged on their backpacks and sweetly kissed me good-bye, on some level unaware of the very real danger they'd just seen on television.

One such story involved an angry anti-American mob surrounding Bob's hotel; in another, the Taliban chased his convoy through the Pakistani desert. Although I began censoring what I showed them, Mack developed problems falling asleep. When he learned at school that four journalists had been killed in Afghanistan, his sleep issues worsened.

One night, at a total loss and exhausted myself, I decided to say a prayer with Mack for Dad's safety. Somewhere in my words and exhausted bare emotion he sensed something new. It was fear. "I thought I was the only one who was scared," Mack whispered, his confession filling him with relief and release. Through his tears and his bear hug that night I learned an important lesson. By trying to make our lives seem normal, I had left my children to carry their fears all alone.

After that I made a pact that we would talk about it all. When Bob left for a scary place, I would peer into four sets of eyes each night and ask how everyone was doing. But one night toward the end of Bob's first stint in Afghanistan, I had been so exhausted, so frustrated with Bob, that I did something for which I am still ashamed. When Claire, who had an ear infection, woke up for the third time that night, I brought her into bed with me and punched the pillow on either side of her head as I chanted, "Your father has abandoned us, stop crying, stop crying." It scared her quiet but it terrified me. Although I never touched her, I could begin to understand how single parents might be driven to do desperate things.

I'm not proud of that moment and I don't think I ever felt more ashamed than I did that night. I recall with vivid clarity how I hugged her close after that, wetting her pajama top with my tears.

The next morning, when Bob called after doing a live shot for *Good Morning America,* he made a casual comment that he had been up for forty-eight hours writing and sending his stories and he was exhausted. I bit his head off. "Don't tell me *you* are tired," I muttered. "You only have yourself to worry about and room service to go back to." He was smart enough to recognize the voice of a woman on the edge.

I think he was wise enough not to complain again for that entire stretch. He felt immense guilt during those years about leaving us, and we would talk about it often. I knew how to deftly pick that scab. "What do you want me to do, Lee, quit my job?" he would snap back sometimes, exasperated at covering the same familiar ground again. Here he was at the pinnacle of his career, doing what he had always dreamed of, and he had four kids and an exhausted wife at home, carrying the burden of their daughter's newly discovered disability.

In the end it was our family that always grounded Bob. We made it impossible for him to take himself too seriously or get lost in the story. He came back to a real life and people who depended on him. He got poopy diaper duty with our babies just like everyone else, and he would dive in, no matter what the order. During one short furlough home, he was the only dad at one of Cathryn's London Brownie meetings. One of my friends told me later that when she saw him sitting cross-legged on the floor sewing Paddington Bears, she thought, Now there's a dad doing some serious payback.

Bob

London, September 11, 2001

I was in the London bureau watching the images on TV when the terrorists flew planes into the World Trade Center, the Pentagon, and the Pennsylvania field. In the first few minutes we really had no idea what was happening, but when the second plane hit the second tower, I felt quite clearly that all our lives were about to change radically.

Our London bureau chief, Rex Granum, was standing right next to me, and we both tried to process what was happening. "This is Bin Laden," I said to Rex. "I need to start setting up to head toward Afghanistan."

"Why don't you go home to pack," he answered.

I pulled up to our house in a black London taxi, which I kept running curbside as I leaped up the steps and began throwing clothes in a bag. There was only one plane to Islamabad that day, and I had to make it. Lee walked into the house carrying Nora, and the two older kids had just gotten home. For the first time in my life I felt deeply afraid about where I was going. Things I had counted on—an immunity of sorts for journalists, a certain amount of predictability in overseas reporting—were all crumbling as fast as the Trade Center towers had fallen.

I had only about thirty minutes to pack and hold my family tight. How could I even begin to explain to them what had happened in the United States? There was not nearly enough time. I kissed them all and hugged them, said goodbye as fast as I could, and left. I had no idea when I would see them again.

Lee

Bethesda Naval Hospital, February 22, 2006

"Why do you *never* have time alone with me? Why do you *always* talk to someone else? Why are your friends *always* coming over to our house and you are not here?"

Claire crossed her arms and gave me a fake pout almost the instant she arrived in Bethesda. I knew what this was about. I stroked her belly, pushed her hair from her eyes, kissed, and snuggled, but I would never be able to make a five-year-old understand all this. Claire knew exactly where to plunge the knife. And she would make me pay for my absence dearly for the next twenty-four hours, only beginning to back off when it was time to get on the plane again. She was awful at dinner that night, howling at the table and grabbing me. She fought with Nora, and Nora fought back.

I tried hard to remind myself that each of my kids showed fear and confusion about their father's condition in different ways. At least Claire's was on the surface.

"Why do you hate me?" Claire punched me. "Why do you talk to everyone but me?" At this last outburst she curled up in a ball on the restaurant banquette next to me, and I reached down for my last bit of sanity and energy. I was walking a tightrope, trying to be with the kids for their winter break and then run to the hospital when Frannie could watch them so I could see Bob.

So many people had urged me to line up a sitter, to set up more play-dates, but what my children needed most was a steady dose of *me*. All four of them. Mack and Cathryn would arrive in two more days and have a whole different set of needs: shopping, Georgetown, restaurants.

It was February 22, time at last for the five-year-old twins to see their father. Mack had seen him on an earlier weekend, but I couldn't put this off any longer, as much as I'd hoped he would be awake for them. They hadn't asked me too many questions and we'd all been careful what we said. We had relied on the doctors to help us gauge what was right for children this young to witness. My twins have a wonderful, almost completely self-sufficient relationship with each other. The distraction that each girl provided for her twin, along with the hotel pool, had helped to stave off the moment when they would begin asking to see their dad. The fact that Bob was so often on the road made this long absence from him unremarkable. But they had begun asking questions. Their many uncles had been a helpful substitute, but they missed their father.

As we walked through the doors of the Bethesda Naval Hospital, I realized I hadn't really prepared them for any of this. Dr. M and I had agreed that she would talk to the girls first and then assess what she thought they could handle, so I hadn't wanted to *promise* a visit with their father. But when we walked into the imposing hospital lobby, their eyes became round as saucers.

"Where are we, Mommy?" said Claire.

"A hospital," I replied. I realized that if I told them this exact building was where their father was, it would open a can of worms if, when we got to his room, Dr. M didn't feel they were ready to see him in his present condition.

Just three and a half feet, my little twin dolls walked through the cold steel doors of the ICU, in their almost matching outfits, instinctively holding hands. Nora and Claire seemed to brighten the aging fluorescent-lit hallways. I averted my eyes from the doctors' stares. I could feel the residents' and doctors' eyes burning into our backs, out of both curiosity and compassion, as we walked down the hall toward Bob's curtain.

Outside of Bob's room the girls put on the same yellow papery gowns that we all had to wear. I smiled as I helped with adjustments, since the gowns came well past their feet. They looked like two little Cinderellas without a ball to attend. I looked up at Dr. M, and she nodded at me to signify that it was okay to go in. She would stay just outside the room to help me determine when it was time to go. I parted the curtain and strode toward the bed holding both girls' hands. Tentatively, they walked beside me and peered over at Bob. I lifted Nora, who was clinging to me.

"Hi, Daddy," I said in my cheeriest voice. "Guess who is here? Guess what little twin babies I've brought for you today?" I kept up my banter, and the girls stared at me as if I were crazy. They began to look from me to Bob and back again.

"You can talk to Daddy," I said gently. "He can hear you. And you can touch him too, like this." I stroked Bob's hand and then kissed it. Claire reached out her arm to touch Bob, and Nora said weakly, "Hi, Daddy, I love you."

Bob stirred slightly at the girls' voices and touch. He seemed to be sleeping more heavily than before.

Nora cupped her hand up to my ear and whispered, "How fast will his hair grow in?"

"Oh," I said, "it won't take long. Daddy's hair grows fast."

They both stroked him tentatively for a minute and then became comfortable, the way a child touches a beloved pet. I babbled on to Bob about the girls and how well they were doing in school. I described the kindergarten play, and somewhere in the middle of my monologue, Nora, whom I was still holding, cupped her hand to my ear again.

"I don't think he is handsome anymore," she whispered.

"You don't think he is handsome?" I said, repeating her words so Dr. M could overhear the direction this was taking.

From the hallway she immediately gave me the high sign that we needed to leave. "When they start asking more questions, it indicates that they are getting uncomfortable," she said to me later, out of earshot of the girls, who were fighting to be the first to push the elevator button. I was so proud of them. They appeared to have handled things well. At last they had seen their father. I could only imagine what that image would become for them as the years moved on. I could only hope that it would be a distant memory for us all, as Bob moved on through his recovery.

Lee

New York, 2002

Bob and I had stolen away to Prague from London for our first weekend alone together since the twins had been born. A short but luxurious vacation with Bob all to myself seemed like a dream. Then, on Sunday, Bob's cell phone rang.

It was Amy Entelis, vice president of talent at ABC News. Although Bob's contract had almost a year left, management was thinking ahead. They were floating the idea of Bob being the news anchor on *Good Morning America.* His profile on TV had risen with all the recent overseas coverage. He had the credibility that came with having reported serious stories, he was appealing, a strong live reporter, and he had a lighter side, which he had shown during some time as a substitute host for *Good Morning America.*

After two months of negotiating, ABC News named Bob their Saturday night anchor for *Weekend World News;* during the week he would continue to report for *World News* and *Good Morning America.* We would move to New York after the close of school in 2002. Mack would be entering middle school and Cathryn fourth grade; the twins were just two years old.

Benefit Cosmetics had been thinking about hiring someone part-time in New York to handle public relations, a perfect fit for me. So there we were, moving again.

Eight months later, as I dropped him off for his first day of school in our suburban Westchester County town, Mack gave me one of those beseeching looks that turn a mother's heart to jelly. It was another first day in a new school, and he knew no one. As he lingered for an extra moment in the security of the car, I tried to come up with a story that would help alleviate some of his fear.

"Remember last year when you kind of liked that girl in class and she liked somebody else?" I began, unsure of exactly where I was going.

"Yes," he answered hesitantly.

"Well, remember I promised that in a few months' time it wouldn't feel so bad, and you'd barely remember having your feelings hurt?"

"Uh-huh," he answered, hanging on every word, as if I had some magical wisdom that would ease him through the front doors and into this first school day. The fact was I didn't feel magical at all, just guilty that I was dumping my child into another new situation and hopeful that his dad and I had given him the right tools to cope.

"You have to trust me on this one," I chirped. "I promise you, in two weeks you will have made friends and you'll be running around the halls of this school like you own it." I watched the hunch of his back as he disappeared into a sea of unfamiliar faces and into the school. Was it just my imagination, or was he smaller than the other boys?

It would prove the hardest move yet. The older the children were, the more reluctant they were to leave the familiarity of friends. It could no longer be spun as an adventure. It was time for Mack, especially, to feel some consistency.

When I picked him up that afternoon, Mack slumped in the backseat and looked down. "No one talked to me all day," he said.

"You just wait," I retorted, not feeling as confident as I had just that morning. But the next week he was all smiles. I could rail at Bob all I wanted behind closed doors, and I did, but if your kids saw you excited about a new place, they would absorb those emotions too.

It was fitting that Bob was AWOL for this move too. In the midst of unpacking chaos, the phone rang. It was Bob calling from the Pyramids, while in the Middle East to cover the anniversary of September 11.

"Hey, babe," said a cheery upbeat voice. "You probably don't know where I am right now!"

"I can't possibly guess," I said flatly, motioning toward the living room as the 250-pound man holding one end of the couch yelled,

"Where do you want this to go, ma'am?" I was trying to match microscopic images of boxes on a form ten sheets long with the tagged numbers on the furniture and cartons coming in. The men were whipping past me at lightning speed, holding lamps, boxes, and bed parts and calling out numbers like some bingo game.

"It's sunset at the Pyramids and I'm riding beneath their shadow on horseback right now," Bob said breathlessly. "It's absolutely gorgeous. One of those moments I'll remember forever."

"Really," I said. I had a very clear mental image in my mind, too clear. "How lovely for you. Guess where *I* am?"

"Uh, where?" Bob immediately realized his error. His voice suddenly became a bit smaller. The twins writhed out of the new babysitter's arms and made a beeline for my legs.

"Surrounded by boxes with six moving men and two different trucks. I need to find a pediatrician for the kids and I don't have one local number, not one friend to write on the school forms for an emergency contact."

"Oh." Any joy Bob might have felt gazing at the sunset next to one of the seven wonders of the world must surely have evaporated. "I'm sorry, Lee. You know I want to be there helping. I just have to work. The timing sucks."

"It does," I said, motioning for an electric keyboard to head down to the basement. "I've got to go." I hung up. I felt bad but was more relieved Bob's mom hadn't heard my passive-aggressive berating of her son.

I loved my mother-in-law dearly, but all the Woodruff daughters-in-law understood that the sons came first. In Frannie's eyes, her boys could do no wrong. I would always smile, remembering a conversation we'd had when we lived in England and Bob had been covering the hunt for Bin Laden in Pakistan. He had been gone for more than a month.

"Poor Bobby," Frannie had moaned to me, as rain poured outside my window for the fourth consecutive day in the rainiest fall London had seen since they started keeping records. "I feel sorry for him. He has to be so tired." I had to restrain myself from pointing out to her that he was actually living his dream. This was Bob's choice. Moreover, at the time, he was actually staying in a five-star hotel with other foreign correspondents. Kind of like a boys' club, I imagined. As they waited for the borders of Afghanistan to open, they were being entertained by the Pakistani government at richly appointed banquets.

Bob

Egypt, September 2002

On the road for the anniversary of September 11, I was already looking ahead to my next assignment. It was obvious that there would be little time for me to settle into a routine in New York with the family. After reporting in Egypt, I would head to Qatar to help set up a news bureau in preparation for covering what seemed to be a sure conflict gathering in Iraq. It would be a base from which to cover air strikes and military strategy, although the military was mum on the subject at the time. It looked as if David Bloom would be reporting from there as well, and we spent time talking about the impending conflict as UN inspectors searched Iraq for weapons of mass destruction.

By January 2003, U.S. forces would be massed in Kuwait City on the southern border with Iraq. The tension and the military buildup felt like all of us were waiting for a whistle to blow. I was assigned as one of several embeds, becoming in essence an observer of the war while traveling up close in the ranks. Unlike the first Gulf War in 1991, when journalists had mostly ducked scud bombs on rooftops in neighboring countries or sat crammed in Pentagon briefing rooms in Saudi Arabia, the Pentagon and the media had come to terms with a way for those at home to get up-close-and-personal views of what the troops were doing on the ground.

The military was in essence gambling on winning a PR campaign, assuming the embeds would engender sympathy to outweigh whatever trauma was brought into the American living room. For the media it was a win-win situation. We had front-row seats for the war. While there would be criticism that we were protected by the soldiers and would not therefore bite the hand that fed us, it was a golden opportunity for those of us willing to be in a war zone.

When looked at from the perspective of being a father and husband, embedding with the military was not a decision I made lightly. There were risks to be weighed, and although I don't remember serious discussions with Lee about whether or not to embed, we talked about it a great deal once I had gotten the assignment. She had reservations and I tried to quell her fears. I would be traveling with the U.S. military. They would protect me.

Originally I thought I would be embedded with the Third Infantry Division of the U.S. Army, the division David Bloom had been assigned to. I ended up with the Marines Special Forces Light Armored Division Fifth Battalion, during a last-minute switch. I was traveling with ABC cameraman Matt Green and soundman James Brolan, both from London.

While David had had months to get chummy with the brass in his division and work out the particulars of his Bloom Mobile, I was thrown into a new military team and had to get up to speed very fast. David still had his *Today* show obligations and so was flying back and forth from Kuwait to New York to host the weekend show. I remained in Kuwait for three- and four-week stretches, sometimes longer, until the war. All the journalists, and the soldiers too, were tired of cooling their heels just across the border. As the weeks ticked on, the world waited to see what would happen next.

We spent most of January and February haunting the U.S. military bases in Kuwait, attending daily military briefings, equipment demonstrations, and chats with generals and foot soldiers. At night we would return to our hotel with the other journalists. There was a get-together every evening, an easy camaraderie that foreign journalists have with one another after years of meeting up on the road in the same hot spots. Man or woman, broadcast or print, everyone bellies up to the bar at the end of the day to commiserate and share stories.

The U.S. firepower, the sheer might and force of the American military poised to strike in one place, was quite remarkable. Each day more equipment and men, weapons and artillery, and amazing impregnable vehicles poured in to line up along the border. There was something altogether repellent and impressive about all these war machines glinting in the bright desert sun. So many of us were unsure how this would end. But most of us were ready for the embed to start and nervous for the war to begin.

Lee

Westchester County, New York, October 2002

I have a memory, seared in my brain, of the last joyful day we spent with David and Mel. It was fall in Pound Ridge, New York, beautiful colorful autumn in all its vivid hues. Maple-leaf red, burnt orange, and deep golden yellow streaked by as we blasted along backcountry roads in Mel's Jeep, David driving and the top off. We were headed to play tennis outdoors, and it was a glorious Indian-summer day. The Counting Crows were on the CD player because David and I had won the struggle to listen to them over Mel and Bob's vote for Prince. "American Girls" blasted from the speakers, and as we caught air in the backseat we laughed out loud.

Here were these two guys: amazingly bright, driven, passionate, and talented. Career-wise, they were on the cusp of something big; it was somehow exciting not to know quite yet what it was. There was a comfortable anticipation, like waiting for Christmas morning but not wanting it to be over yet. None of us had any desire to rush things.

We all laughed as we walked to the clay courts. Mel and I got in trouble for chatting too much on the court. David gave me a dirty look for making jokes to cover my powder-puff serve. Bob got his game face on, and finally we women retreated to the bench to watch the boys battle it out, bathed in sweat and grunting, ever the competitors. Shortly after that, our two husbands were essentially gone, traveling back and forth from Kuwait.

By spring, when the bombing began and the troops moved across the border into Iraq, the reality of war came home to our two households. Melanie and I were on the telephone every night after the kids were tucked in. We were scared and isolated, yet we had each other. It became a kind of bedtime ritual to talk to each other in bed like that. Sometimes we would watch the news together, while we were on the phone. If we'd been close before, the experience of having our husbands in a war zone brought us closer. At times it seemed there wasn't an emotion I felt that she didn't.

At the last minute, the marines had made the decision that the ABC crew could not take their vehicle, which would have allowed them to broadcast live by satellite. Bob was left with only a jerky and stilted satellite phone to feed live video back to ABC viewers. On the other hand, David was riding through the Iraqi desert broadcasting on NBC's *Nightly News* and the twenty-four-hour cable station MSNBC like some modern-day Lawrence of Arabia. With no way for Bob to see what David was doing, I gently broke it to him one night that his friend and colleague was kicking everyone's behind with the Bloom Mobile. David's gamble had paid off. While Bob and the other embedded correspondents got minor accolades for their reporting, it was David who captured the hearts and minds of the viewers. His gee-whiz boyish Ernie Pyle doggedness and his conversations with the troops on lighter formats like the *Today* show showcased the breadth of his talent. Bob, on the other hand, was having a miserable time filing stories. One piece he'd planned to do with the men in his division had to be scrubbed when the equipment failed again and they couldn't feed the tape to the satellite.

Mack had his own theory about his father's safety. He believed that because his dad was with the military, they would protect him. One day as he watched *Good Morning America* he saw an image of his father riding on a tank in full protective gear and helmet. He turned to me as he poured milk on his Cap'n Crunch cereal. "Was Dad just riding on a tank?" he asked casually.

"I think so," I replied.

"Cool," he said, and took another spoonful. I considered that a victory, in some sort of odd way.

Bob

Kuwait, January 2003

Before I left for Kuwait in January 2003, Cathryn gave me a good-luck charm. It was an old fake-gold Bedouin bracelet I had bought for her at the market in Cairo just a few months earlier. Now, less than two months before the U.S. invasion of Iraq, she pulled it out of her drawer, studied it for a moment, and gently placed it in my hand. "Daddy, I want you to take this and remember me," she said, her eyes shining with tears. "It will keep you safe." My eyes filled with tears too. I kept it in my pack the entire time that I was embedded.

As our division rolled deeper inside Iraq, my daughter wrote me an e-mail that also brought me to tears:

Dear Daddy,

How are you over there? What is it like to be in the war? Aren't you scared? I am. I have been missing you a lot and sometimes I cry. A little in class too. I love you. Do you still have my bracelet?

Love, Cathryn

After the long months of waiting for the invasion to begin, our three-man ABC News crew was ready to get moving, along with the rest of the journalists and soldiers parked just over the border in Kuwait. All of us, especially the soldiers, were tired of cooling our heels. The routine of waiting for orders to roll out had become more than monotonous.

I was somewhat disappointed when, at the last moment, it was decided by ABC News that I would embed with Delta Company, First Light Armored Reconnaissance Battalion. It was clearly an excellent group of men, but our team had spent the previous weeks getting to know the commanders and soldiers in the army division. Now I had only a few days to figure out what I needed to know about the marines in this division.

Delta was designed to be the vanguard for the larger battalion of marines, rooting out Iraq's Republican Guard as they pushed toward Baghdad and backing up the Third Infantry Division of the army, which was expected to reach the city first. Of all of the military divisions, it is the marines who are the foot soldiers of war. They see it from the ground up. An air force pilot in Kuwait summed it up: "It could be worse. I could be a marine. Very few Americans have any idea or even want to have any idea of what those guys go through. They redefine service to country every day."

Sandstorms had been a frequent problem in Kuwait, and they continued during the push to Baghdad. When we woke up in the morning, everything would be covered with a fine powder from the previous night's winds. We found sand everywhere: under our eyelids and our nails, in our underwear and socks. The gear was filthy, and it was a constant battle to keep our equipment functioning.

I was continually frustrated by mechanical breakdowns, sometimes attributable to the dust. Often when I would try to go on air there would be some technical failure. We'd been frustrated when the marines had banned the use of portable satellite dishes at the last minute. This was the one thing that made going live a reality in the war. They sent back the Humvee originally designated for us to broadcast live. This greatly limited the types of stories and the amount of coverage we could produce. The army, where David was embedded, had allowed it. I was extremely frustrated and my competitive juices were flowing. I had an inkling of what David was up to and I was even more determined to get my story across.

We ate, slept, talked, and waited it out with the marines. The major difference between our news crew and the twenty-year-olds next to us in the armored vehicle was that Matt, James, and I didn't carry a weapon. Otherwise we looked like fighters, outfitted with the same boots and chemical suits, goggles, gas masks, and T-shirts. Each day we fell into a pattern of stopping and waiting, waiting and stopping, as we rolled by the same monotonous desert horizon, bouncing hypnotically on the rutted bumpy roads that function as highways in Iraq.

Although we sensed a wariness among the grunts that we were "press" and not soldiers, our shared experiences day-by-day broke those barriers down. There was something undeniably uniting about heading into the desert not knowing from one day to the next exactly where we would be, what we would be doing, and whether or not we would get to go home. This was, of course, what critics of the arrangement had feared—that a too-comfortable relationship would prejudice reporting. I had no such concern.

Just before we crossed the border into Iraq to begin the invasion, the marines were ordered to cover a scout's advance, and two of the men in our division—Corporal Chris Stoia and Lance Corporal Jesus Suarez del Solar—made up one of the two-man sniper teams told to man a position in a lookout tower. I followed them, rolling tape as they lugged their .50-caliber sniper rifles up the stairs. For the first time, I took

Cathryn's bracelet out of my pocket and kissed it. It was my rosary and my good-luck charm.

"How do you feel about all this, Jesus?" I asked him on camera. It was some of the first action the division had seen.

"Hopefully we'll get this done soon, so we can all come home and see our families . . . safe," Jesus replied, with a sparkle in his eye.

"Are you nervous about being up here so high in the open?"

"No, not at all," he answered, as he crouched behind his weapon, aiming it at the sands below, looking for any movement.

"Can't the Iraqis get you from up here?" I asked.

"Nah," Suarez replied as he scanned the ground and horizon, looking young and serious. This would be his first combat situation. "They can't get us from this high."

On the evening of March 24, during our stop-and-start advance toward Baghdad, we saw smoke in the distance, and suddenly there was heavy artillery fire overhead. Bright flashes of light crackled in the sky and the noise was like thunder as small bombs exploded just south of us. The Iraqis fired back very close to our position and then there were more sounds, like distant firecrackers on the Fourth of July. All at once, it seemed, the explosions stopped. That night our unit was instructed to put on gas masks for three hours and try to sleep.

The mother of all sandstorms blew across the Iraqi desert on March 25. We had never seen anything like it. The closest thing I had experienced were blinding snowstorms when I was mountain-climbing in Peru and Canada. But freezing snow was more forgiving than the blowing sand and howling dust of the Iraqi desert. We put on our goggles but the sand somehow found a way to infiltrate them.

The sky took on an eerie ocher hue, almost an orange sulfur color, as the blowing sands blocked the sun, turning day into night. Then rain opened up, eventually changing to hail. It was unsettling, blinding almost. We all had the feeling *What if they choose to attack now?* By the next morning, mud had become the new enemy. It permeated everything: the weapons, the equipment. Some of the men were so covered in mud I could see only the whites of their eyes.

For working journalists, satellite phones and e-mail are modern necessities to communicate with the bureaus, file stories, and plan the day's coverage. The marines weren't afforded such luxuries. One of the greatest services that journalists did during the war was to share their phones with the soldiers so they could call home. It gave me great joy to watch one marine call a sister who'd just given birth, hear another soothe worried parents, or let men tell anxious wives and girlfriends how much they loved them. The phone offered a way to help combat some of the loneliness and boredom. A call home could make someone's day.

I was able to call Lee and the kids frequently. One phone call illustrated perfectly the difference in our two worlds. I reached her one morning as she was walking down the street in Manhattan, trying to figure out how to pay a large bill that had come in. As she spoke, annoyance crept into her voice; bill-paying was typically my department. I could hear the stress of single parenting in her voice, but frankly it was tough to be completely sympathetic.

"Lee," I said, practically in a whisper, "right now I am sitting in a tank with a bunch of guys making barely more than minimum wage who are putting their lives on the line every single day. That bill is just not important. Can't we talk about it later?"

Bob

Iraq, March 2003

Just before dark on March 27 the radio in our armored vehicle crackled. "Doc, get out to Black Six *now!*" Black 6 was the code name for the company commander's vehicle, which was at that moment parked some two hundred yards away. Marines began running toward a cloud of black smoke in the other direction. "Land mine!" they yelled. "It's a land mine!"

As I headed toward the explosion, we saw a dozen marines crowded in a circle, working frantically to save the life of a scout who had stepped on an unexploded shell. The sun was setting. They cut off his pants and boots with scissors and knives. I strained to see the marine's face.

"Who is it?" I asked.

"It's Jesus," answered the marine next to me.

I had seen some of myself in Jesus Suarez del Solar, a young man eager to make his mark. Just twenty years old, a kid, he had immigrated to the United States from Tijuana with his family. He had a sixteen-month-old child and a young wife named Sayne. We'd spent some time talking after I'd first interviewed him. His family had proudly watched him on the news.

Helping to hold lights so the men could see, I watched the marines attempt to stabilize him. I could see a dark bleeding wound on his thigh. The EMT was attempting to stanch the flow of blood from the femoral artery, and the soil on the ground was covered in a black pool. Although he also had a head wound that I could see, we later learned that the significant damage was to his legs and abdomen.

Most of the men were ordered back to their vehicles by the commander. It was pitch black outside and we were told there were cluster bombs all around. They had been dropped by U.S. troops days earlier in one of the artillery exchanges. Jesus had stepped on one of these unexploded bombs.

Because of a series of miscommunications and a broken medevac helicopter, Jesus waited more than two hours to be evacuated. He was dead on arrival at Camp Doha, after bleeding out on the helicopter. Everyone had done their best, but it had all gone horribly wrong. I was shaken and thought intensely of my own family that night.

Back in the States, the Suarez family was informed officially by the Marine Corps that Jesus had been shot in the head, but I had reported the story on *World News Tonight* accurately. Understandably, the family was very upset. After I returned home I called Jesus' father, Fernando Suarez del Solar, and we began corresponding. He ultimately became an outspoken antiwar activist. Eight months later he led a peace delegation to Baghdad, bringing clothing for Iraqi children in the hospital as part of his mission. I met him there at his request to take him to the spot in the desert where his son had fallen.

Together we walked through the dirt field two hours south of Baghdad, still rutted with fighting holes and littered with discarded MRE bags and spent artillery. Fernando placed a crucifix in the spot where Jesus fell and gathered a bag of the soil to take home and plant a flower. I read him my notes from that day. His tears flowed easily. It was an emotional moment for us both. Fernando's faith was strong, but at that moment I was questioning mine. God didn't seem to be anywhere in this desolate landscape. Jesus' death had been so random, so unnecessary. A father's, a wife's, a young baby's life had all changed in an instant.

"I am feeling very bad," he said. "My son's blood is here."

As we moved closer to Baghdad in April 2003, we began to see more evidence of what was to come. On the side of the road, we passed the bodies of dead Iraqi soldiers and civilians. They were everywhere. Who would come for them? I wondered. Would they rot in the desert? It is a tenet of Muslim culture that only Muslims can bury Muslims; we would violate that tenet were we to interfere. Once when we were stopped, I came upon a car on the side of the road; a man in the uniform of a high-ranking Republican Guard sat upright. His brains had been blown onto the glass of the back window.

The images of death are haunting, no matter how many times you see a dead body. And when you have seen so many dead, in so many places, it begins to leave you numb. But I will never get used to the look in a dead person's eyes when the soul has left the body. It shocks me every time.

On the morning of Sunday, April 6, with temperatures already climbing, I picked up my satellite phone to call the ABC bureau in New York and relay what we had already done that day. If someone had told me that within forty-eight hours I would be whisked out of the sands of Iraq and be walking through the doors of my home in New York, I would have thought they had sunstroke.

Lee

Westchester County, New York, April 6, 2003

Early in the morning of Thursday, April 6, my phone rang. Instantly I was wide awake, my heart beating fast.

"Hello?" I said.

"Lee? Hi, I'm so sorry to wake you up," said a soft voice. "This is Elena Nachmanoff at NBC." I was confused. NBC? Why was I hearing from someone at a competing network? I sat up in bed and looked at the clock: 2 A.M.

"What's wrong?" I said, with sudden clearheadedness. It was the first appearance of my inner General.

"We've been trying to reach Melanie Bloom. We've been calling all her numbers. I'm hoping that you know how to reach her." She paused. "Something has happened to David."

Lee

Bethesda Naval Hospital, March 1, 2006

David Woodruff hadn't seen his brother in a week, and when he flew back to Bethesda he was amazed by the progress Bob had made since his battles with pneumonia and sepsis. His face was much less swollen and you could see that, where the piece of skull was missing, his brain was sinking back down to a more normal size.

On this day in the ICU, Bob had a surprise in store. Although he was still heavily sedated, his eyes were open and he appeared to be trying to mouth words and communicate through his eyes.

I can't talk, he mouthed to Susan Baker and David suddenly. Both of them responded at the same time in amazement. "I know you can't talk, Bob, you have a tube in your mouth." We all looked at one another, shocked. There was something vacant, still *not there,* about Bob. His eyes were open but they were still not connected, as if there was no light on inside.

Dr. Armonda happened to show up then and saw Bob's tongue motions, his attempts to speak, and his moving facial muscles. I barely acknowledged him. I was worried this moment would be fleeting.

"I love you, honey. You're safe, the kids are safe, and I'm safe." I watched his face as I spoke. "You are in Bethesda in a hospital; you had an accident in Iraq." All at once, Bob summoned all of his energy and smiled. It was like a dog's smile, pulling both corners of his mouth in a wide, almost rictus grin. He was sending me a message. It was an amazing moment; it was, I thought, as if the sun had come out.

"Bilateral motion, he's got bilateral motion!" Susan yelped, as the doctor in her took over. Her eyes filled with tears. David began jumping up and down and squeezing Bob's hand and encouraging him. I turned to Dr. Armonda with a giant smile; I could see how excited he was.

"Are you still concerned about the nerves in his face?" I asked, somewhat impishly. I could have done an Irish jig at that moment.

"No," he said. "And the tongue looks good too." He was beaming.

Amazed, I asked myself the familiar questions. How had that rock passed all the way through the left side of Bob's neck, missing nerves, esophagus, and tongue, and come to rest against the carotid artery on the other side without doing damage?

He continued to mouth words, pointed at his trache tube as if it was a huge annoyance, and tried to hug Susan. He touched my face, bringing all his lines and tubes up off the bed, and when we sat him up he tried to get off his shoulder and back and readjust himself in the center. Susan said that his midline motions were incredible; he seemed to be functioning well on both sides of his body. Bob continued pointing at the trache, motioning for us to take it out.

When we finally adjusted the bed for him to sit up, Bob let out a huge burp, and we all laughed and clapped. He pointed at his stomach, which we assumed meant it was upset. He had been getting liquid food from a tube for four weeks and his GI tract was mutinous. I had to shake my head and marvel that, given what had happened to his head and his back, he was concerned with an upset stomach.

I kissed him all over his face, and the taste was salty and sweaty. I thought about not taking a shower for that long and how even a sponge bath couldn't take away the last traces of Iraqi dirt and sand. The scent of Bob was still Bob somehow, but it was faint, overwhelmed by hospital smells. He seemed to respond to my kisses, and I wanted to believe he knew it was me. I could tell he was beginning to feel the pain of his wounds. I was comforted when the doctors assured me again that he would remember none of this.

Suddenly, Bob brought his two hands together, to the middle of his body, and ripped off the pulse oxygen clip on his finger that was attached to a monitor. Susan laughed out loud. "Go, Bob!" she yelled. The ability to bring his extremities together equally to the midline point of the body, she explained, was another good sign.

But Bob was still not really awake. The doctors decided it was time to try to get him into a hospital chair. What they rolled in looked to me like a kind of Halloween chair of horror with arm straps and pads. It tilted vertically so that you could almost stand someone on it before getting into a sitting position.

Seeing that chair, with all its safety features, brought home to me once again how agonizingly slow this was going to be. Bob wasn't just going to wake up like Doug and start chatting. It would be a painstaking process, from bed to chair, from chair to standing, from standing to walking, from walking to . . . what? Of course I had no choice but to accept this snail-like pace. I would need to walk every step of the way with my husband. There would be no shortcuts.

Lee

Westchester County, New York, April 6, 2003

When a death happens in the military, they must tell the family before 10 P.M. or after 6 A.M. The thinking behind this rule is simple. A military family would never be able to sleep knowing they could be awakened by horrible news in the middle of the night. As civilians, we weren't afforded the same courtesy.

When my phone rang in the early morning of April 6, I was sure it was bad news for me. A part of me had been waiting for this ever since the war began. When I realized that the call concerned Melanie Bloom, it took me a few minutes to reorient myself. Something had happened to David. NBC News couldn't reach Melanie. Although I ached to know what had happened, my first thought was for Mel. She didn't know anything. We had talked only hours before and I knew her routine. She had no doubt fallen asleep with her ringer off, cell phone charging, and MSNBC on the TV so she could see David.

A wife has to be the first to know, I thought. I can't possibly ask Elena what has happened until Mel knows; it is her right. I told Elena I would try to get through and have Melanie call her. I hung up the phone and dialed Mel's private number. She answered on the third ring in a groggy, panicky voice.

"Hello?"

"Mel. It's me."

"What's wrong?" she said instantly. I recognized the tone of her voice.

"Melly, it's about David," I said softly. "Something has happened— I don't know what," I added quickly. "NBC is trying to reach you and we need to hang up right now so you can call them. And then you call me back. I'm here. I'm here for whatever you need. Okay?"

"God, Lee—what? What's wrong?"

"I don't know, Mel. I honestly don't know. It wasn't my place to ask. Maybe he was injured and is in a hospital and they need to tell you so you can go to him. I'll bet that's it. We have to hang up now. Call me back."

"Okay. . . . Okay," she said. "Stay there."

"Mel." I changed my mind. "I'm going to get up and get dressed and get in the car. My sister and brother-in-law are here this weekend and can stay with the kids. I'm going to head up to you now. Whatever it is, I want to be there."

"Okay," she said, in a small voice. She was terrified. I was too.

Only hours before, Mel had talked to David from our house. We'd been watching him report on NBC Nightly News and howled in laughter when we saw his face. It was so dark and dirty that his eyes looked like two burning white lights. "Get a shower!" I screamed in the background, as Mel left her first message on his cell. It was good-natured laughter, of course. We were worried about how tired both men were. With the eight-hour time difference, they'd been sending stories around the clock.

We had no way of knowing, at the time, that a blood clot was slowly making its way up David Bloom's leg to his lung. He'd hit his thigh on the door of a tank and had complained to Mel about it a few days earlier.

Heat, dehydration, and tight quarters would all be enemies. It had hurt so much the night before, he had risked potential danger to sleep outside, where he could stretch his legs away from the cramped quarters of the vehicle. We would have time later to berate ourselves for not knowing any of the warning signs of deep vein thrombosis, or DVT, but for now all I could focus on was that we had just talked to David.

As I drove north on the familiar route to Mel's house, my cell phone rang. It was Elena again. "Are you on the road? Are you okay to drive?" said Elena. She had no idea how calmly and rationally I was moving and thinking at this point in time. An icy clarity had dropped over me. I had to get to Mel and take care of her. I wanted to be there when she got the worst news of her life.

"I'm fine," I said, "totally fine. But you have to tell me before I get to Mel's house. What am I walking into, Elena? What has happened to David?"

"Oh, Lee," said Elena, in a voice filled with pain, "he's dead." Something inside me turned over. I had known instinctively that if David had simply been injured, she would have worded it that way when she had first called. A big part of me had known that David was gone, but a little part of me had been hoping against hope that he was still alive.

I realized I needed to call Bob. He had to hear this news from me and not anyone else. I dialed the ABC assignment desk in New York and asked them to patch me through to him.

"It's Lee, Bob's wife," I said. "There has been a family emergency."

A woman came back on the line and reported that she had been unable to reach him. "He should be calling in shortly. Can I give him a message?"

I hesitated. Rumors ran rampant in the TV world, but then again I was sure the news about David was already out and waiting to be confirmed, like a dam about to burst. But I also knew there was honor in the field, and that no respectable network would ever run with information about its competitor's employees before the family had been notified.

"Please tell him," I began, and choked on my words. "Tell him that David Bloom is dead. He can reach me on my cell phone."

She gasped for a second. "So it's true!" she blurted out, before she could compose herself. Even at three o'clock on a Sunday morning, the rumor mill had been churning.

Bob

Iraq, April 6, 2003

Dialing the number for New York, I gazed out absentmindedly at the scene before me. APCs, Humvees, and dusty hulking war machines had all halted on the sands, waiting for the next order to roll out. Our pace to Baghdad had quickened in the past few days, and we were filled with anticipation.

Hearing the voice on the other end at the assignment desk, I barely had time to identify myself before the assistant interrupted me. "I'm so glad you checked in," she said. "Your wife called. She needs to reach you." It was only 3 A.M. back home. I knew immediately that something was wrong.

I waited for the desk to patch me through. What was Lee doing on her cell phone at three in the morning in New York? I wondered. Minutes later, I felt relief flood through me just hearing her voice.

"Babe, what's wrong?" I said. The echo of the phone line made it hard to hear her. We were so far apart. Worlds apart, really.

"I have some terrible news," she said. Her voice was trembling and trailing off. "David died last night, outside of Baghdad."

My legs went weak. "Wait a minute, slow down," I pleaded with her. At that moment I realized just how scared I'd been, sure something was wrong with Lee, my parents, or our children. David Bloom, only miles from me in the desert, embedded with the army's Third Infantry Division, had been my last thought in those moments while I'd waited tensely for Lee to come on the line. "Died? What do you mean *died?* How? Was he shot?"

"They think it was an embolism. But Bob, he's gone."

I was sick with gut-wrenching sadness and guilt. My marine unit was about ten miles east of Baghdad. After I hung up, I walked to the top of a sand hill to collect my thoughts. David dead. I thought of Mel and the girls. It seemed impossible that David would never see them again, though I struggled to accept the finality of this news. Our friends' lives had crumbled with one phone call. Although Lee hadn't asked me to, I knew she would want me to come home. That wouldn't be easy. What was I going to do?

We were poised to begin the biggest part of the entire invasion story, the final push into Baghdad. It was the event that would make all the sitting and crawling along, the boredom and inactivity, the sand and sweat, worthwhile. Baghdad was about to fall in a sweep of armed forces plowing toward the city with enough firepower to level every building. But at that moment I didn't care about the story at all. My first thought was for my own family and Mel and the girls.

I thought about the last time I'd seen David, in Kuwait near the eve of the invasion. We had talked about the possibility of dying in the war, about dying on foreign soil and never seeing your wife and children again. But I don't think either one of us had ever really imagined it would happen. We'd both been afraid at moments, but we had also been undeterred. We understood, as did all the other embedded journalists, that we were putting our lives in harm's way to get the story, but I don't think we ever really believed we would be seriously hurt.

My decision to go home crystallized when I spoke to Melanie shortly after I learned the news about David. Hearing my voice on the satellite phone, Mel began to weep. "What do you want me to do, Mel?" I asked her gently.

"Please come home," she urged. "Get out of there and

come back to your family, come back to all of us. Your wife and kids need you now. We all need you."

This wasn't a request that I imagined Lee would have made. I knew her well enough to know she would have wrestled with the responsibility or burden of asking me to back out of a war. She would have left the decision to me. But Mel had instantly earned the horrible right to ask. All at once there was no doubt in my mind about what I had to do next. The question was, How would I pull out of the war, and what kind of danger would I be putting myself and others in to do so?

Before I rose to find our company commander, Captain Seth Folsom, I sat for a moment longer on the top of the hill. The landscape was dull and uninspiring, the monochromatic sameness of the desert suddenly as foreign as the surface of the moon. As I stared toward Baghdad, I let survivor guilt wash over me and braced to absorb it. Why Dave and not me?

When I called back to the ABC News desk in New York an hour later, one of the assignment editors got on the line and said they had a message for me. It was from David Bloom, dated a few hours before he died. David had asked ABC to relay a simple message to Bob when he called in next. "Tell him to stay safe and keep his head down," David had warned me. They were the last words I would ever hear from him.

I had told Lee once, a long time ago, that there were some stories worth risking your life for, possibly even dying for, if there was something greater to be gained. Watching the Bloom family changed that perspective forever.

In the weeks after David died, as we huddled tightly together in bed, Lee angrily reminded me of my idealistic remark.

"I don't believe that anymore," I replied.

Lee

Westchester County, New York, April 6, 2003

By the time I reached Melanie, she was sitting in almost total darkness, wrapped in a blanket. It was close to three in the morning. I immediately rushed to her and held her the way I held my children, enveloping her in my arms and rocking. She sobbed and moaned in a kind of trance, a symptom of shock I would recognize three years later in myself.

"Lee, why did this happen? I don't understand. Why did David leave me?" We rocked back and forth on the couch.

There were no words, nothing I could say that would be of any comfort. With my own tears brimming, I took her face in my hands and looked her in the eyes. I wanted to make sure she understood. "Whatever it is, Mel," I said slowly. "Whatever it takes, you are going to get through this. You will be okay, and so will the kids. And I will walk with you every step of the way."

That night washed into early dawn and then morning, and the day became a blur. There were immediate tasks—Mel calling David's parents and brothers—and as we huddled on her bed, each call felt like a fresh stab wound.

Mel kept calm. We turned on the TV, and images of David rolling across the desert were on all the stations. It had been impossible to contain the rumor. The news was leaking out. NBC needed to go with the story as soon as Mel had informed the family. It was a horribly public way to experience a death in the family; a horrible way for the many friends across the country to wake up on a Sunday morning, expecting to see David on *Weekend Today*, only to learn instead of his tragic death.

The Bloom girls, nine-year-old twins Chrissy and Nicole and three-year-old Ava, had been awake for hours, puzzled by the activity in the household but momentarily distracted by the television. It was time for

Mel to face the hardest thing she would ever do. She had to tell the girls that their daddy was dead.

First, Melanie spent some time on the phone with a child psychologist to make sure she had language to help deliver the news. When she hung up, we gathered the children from their rooms.

Three little girls in little flannel nightgowns looked at their mother. They were warm and soft, their hair still disheveled from bed, and when I kissed them they smelled sweet. They were happy to see me and completely accepting that I was there. We'd had many weekend sleepovers together since the fathers had gone to war. As I reached down to hug Nicole's shoulders, I couldn't shake the feeling that I was abandoning her and her sisters. My goodbye kiss felt to me like the kiss of Judas the betrayer.

"Girls, Mommy wants to talk to you," said Mel, with that false energy parents can summon. Nicole and Chrissy looked at her skeptically. Children know when something is wrong. They can read us so much better than we think.

As I left, closing the doors of the family room behind me, I thought my heart would snap in two. I couldn't imagine doing what my friend was about to do. I thought again of all of us in my kitchen the day before, happy, laughing, talking to the dads on the phone, hoping they would be home soon. There are no right words to tell your children they will never again hug their father.

In the midst of all of the sadness following David's death, there were humorous moments too. On a rainy afternoon, Mel had returned from shopping for a plot of earth in which to bury her husband and arrived back home drained and cold. I drew her a bubble bath, and in a moment that only girlfriends can truly appreciate Mel asked her sister-in-law Alison and me to jump into the huge Jacuzzi tub with her. We would soak away our collective grief together, like a coven of witches in a brew. Women have always known how to grieve. They emote, they share, they keen and wail.

We looked at one another and laughed, stripped down, and let the hot water surround and warm us. As one of three daughters, I understood the strength of being in the company of women. It was powerfully good medicine. We giggled, we poured in more bubbles, and tried to get Mel to smile. We made jokes at our own expense, and all at once, as if right on cue, the phone rang.

I volunteered to hop out of the tub and answer it. A proper businesslike female voice came on the line. "President Clinton is calling for Melanie Bloom."

"Mel," I whispered, holding my hand over the receiver, looking slightly flabbergasted, "it's President Clinton on the line for you. What do you want me to do?" There had been a lot of high-level condolence calls since David's death, but not quite at this level. I was pretty sure you weren't supposed to tell a former U.S. president that you'd call them back because you were in the tub.

Mel looked up in surprise, and the three of us suppressed a giggle. "Uh," I said into the phone, shrugging my shoulders at Mel and Alison, "Melanie is right here; please hold on." I thrust the phone at Mel and she took it, looking at me with a *What do I say?* expression.

David had covered the Clinton White House, and, while they hadn't always seen eye to eye, the Clintons had clearly respected the dogged young reporter. This was deeply personal.

Luckily for me, I had hopped out of the tub to get the phone and was free to go. I pulled on my clothes and snuck out of the room. Melanie and Alison weren't so fortunate. Mel was so afraid the sound of splashing water would reveal where she was, she and Alison barely moved a muscle for the entire conversation. Mel and President Clinton chatted warmly for at least twenty minutes as the bathwater grew cold.

Lee

Westchester County, New York, April 8, 2003

I have heard it said that when God takes something away he gives something back. Whether or not I believe that anymore, this was how the war ended for our two families.

It would take six days for David's body to get back to the States, and his two brothers would drive to Dover Air Force Base in Delaware to accompany his coffin to New York. It would take Bob only five hours, with help from the marines, to pull out of his position in the desert and helicopter back to Kuwait, and then he would fly home.

Bob's homecoming was not the joyous occasion I had envisioned. Instead, my husband was airlifted out of Iraq because one of his good friends had died there. Another family's loss was our family's gain, in a way. And because that other family was extremely close, it made his return bittersweet, intertwined with and complicated by grief: one man imperiled and another plucked to safety. After the holocaust they had called it survivor guilt.

Bob

New York, April 16, 2003

Journalism is truly the last great adolescent profession, and David Bloom attacked it that way. He was like a child with his keen intellect and boundless enthusiasm. He never lost his sense of wonder. Each story he approached warranted his complete attention and his total commitment to get it right.

"You never know," he told us once in the kitchen. "That story may be the only one someone ever sees."

I would tell Lee months later that the world of journalism seemed a little less fun without David. "Life is so much more interesting when there is someone you truly respect who is trying to kick your butt, who makes you rise to a higher level to compete. It's like playing tennis with someone better than you," I said to her. "It raises the level of your game."

On the day of the funeral in St. Patrick's Cathedral, the sky was an azure blue. Mel found the strength to stand tall with the girls, Wynton Marsalis played a heart-wrenchingly beautiful dirge, and the polished brass on the dark mahogany coffin gleamed in the sun. And when I carried that casket, with David's brothers, from that bright April day into the serenity of the church, for just a second the beauty of the ceremony lulled me into believing that all was still right with the world.

The night after David's funeral, Lee held me tightly in bed. "Don't you ever do that to me," she said, out of the blue.

"Do what?" I said.

"Don't you ever leave me. Don't ever leave us. Do you see Mel? Do you see those little kids? Promise me you will never do that to us, that you will always be careful." She was beating on my chest with her fists, almost pleading with me.

"I will. I promise," I said soberly, taking each of her wrists gently in my hands. And I meant it.

Lee

Bethesda Naval Hospital, March 1, 2006

My mother-in law had a great line about what happened to Bob. She said that almost overnight his life had gone from proud to prayers. I knew what she meant. One day people were sending cards and calling to congratulate her about her son's new position, and the next they were praying for him as he clung to life. There were still plants and food baskets in our dining room that had been sent as congratulations for Bob's new post as co-anchor of *ABC World News Tonight*. A few bottles of champagne were still chilling in the fridge. He'd had all of fifty-six days in this coveted position.

My brain had begun to freeze out certain images of Bob, and this left me with a panicky feeling. I found I couldn't conjure up the sound of his voice when I wanted to, couldn't recall the way he slept next to me and particular faces he made. His mannerisms, the very things that made him Bob, were fading in my mind after almost five weeks. The man I saw in Bethesda Naval Hospital was still so different. Now he looked even thinner. The swelling had passed, the risk of the pneumonia and sepsis had abated, but it seemed his body had shrunk, while his brain was still swollen, still jutting from his head like a giant mushroom. The sight never ceased to frighten me.

I had also begun to notice all the beautiful shapes of other men's heads: round ones, bald ones, young ones, thick-haired ones. Of course, I was practically living in a military hospital with a full supply of crew cuts and shaven heads to ogle, all perfectly rounded. Or so it seemed.

That is why, when I took the escalator in the hotel to change before a brief visit with David Westin, I found myself admiring the back of a man's head as he turned to talk to the concierge. His hair was full and just graying at the tips, and he wore a dark suit with an overcoat on his arm and carried a walnut leather briefcase. Washington is full of these stylish men, I thought. But this one has a really nice head. How low had I sunk, I mused, that I was furtively checking out the shape of strangers' heads while my own husband lay in a comalike state with only half of his.

Just as I was about to step into the elevator to my floor from the lobby, the man turned to face me. It was David Westin. "David." I choked, instantly guilty that I'd been coveting his head. We grabbed a table at the restaurant downstairs, which had become a kind of extended kitchen for our group. I brought him up-to-date on Bob's progress since I'd last spoken to him a few days ago on the phone. I filled each little baby step with a slightly inflated sense of accomplishment.

"I think your anchor will be back," I said. It felt like a bluff, a considerable one. Feeling the need to explain why Bob wasn't up to seeing visitors just yet, I told him about the pneumonia and the sepsis, and he blanched. David had never once asked to see Bob and I was incredibly grateful. In an effort to respect our privacy, he knew that if he hadn't yet visited with Bob, no one else at ABC could expect to either.

We sipped our iced teas and talk turned to Peter Jennings and how much personal information David had kept under wraps during the anchor's valiant battle with lung cancer. His wife, Kayce, had barely left Peter's side throughout his illness.

I thought about what a terrible run of luck this president of ABC News had endured and how we had both come up short. For a moment he squeezed my hand as tears brimmed in my eyes. We'd suffered different losses, to be sure, but they were keenly felt—mine of a husband and father, his of a pair of colleagues and anchormen.

The next day was a red-letter day, a day that truly made me believe that Bob was inside that shell of a body. As I sat with him, the nurse came in to inject some pain medication and all of a sudden, through his trache tube, he squawked out, "No, no, no," very clearly. She and I looked at each other, stunned. Next he asked for water, and he said the word so clearly I thought I would cry.

The nurse let me put a tiny bit of water on the tip of a swab and stick it in his mouth to wet his tongue. She had told me earlier that many times the patients get bad tooth and gum decay when they have a trache tube in their mouth over a long period of time, but she warned me that if I gave him too much water it could get down into the lungs.

He then said the word *hot* as he squirmed on the bed, his makeshift boxer shorts falling down around his hips, the tubes still snaking uncomfortably out of the leg opening. I began wiping the sweat from his brow. The mattress cover was plastic and uncomfortable, and the sheets were thin. Sweat ran down his face and eyes, and he became agitated and

tried to sit up. When he got himself up straight, he bent his head between his legs; I realized later that he was presenting his sore back to us
for a massage. He was so tired of lying in the same spot, which, aside
from his injuries, must have caused extreme pain.

All of a sudden, Bob pulled me close, eyes glazed but still incredibly
strong, and ripped off my mask. I was overjoyed. He wanted to see my
face, my entire face, not just my eyes and forehead. I just kept kissing
him, and he puckered up ever so slightly, so slowly.

In the background, the videos we had dubbed of the kids growing up
were playing and he tried to pull the hospital table closer to see. After
about thirty minutes of activity, his eyelids began to droop. I asked him
if he was tired and he croaked, "Yes."

As I kissed Bob goodbye I realized that the nurses would be putting
his wrist restraints on as soon as I left. I didn't blame them. Caring for
Bob when he was agitated was exhausting. It was like minding a toddler
or a severely retarded person in a mental hospital. Now that he seemed
to be cycling into a more "awake" state, we would need a family member to be present as much as possible.

The doctors had begun nudging me toward a conversation about
where Bob would go next. The medical staff in Bethesda Naval Hospital
had done all they could for him in the acute phase. The next step would
be a rehabilitation hospital. If he were a military person, he would go to
a VA facility. As civilians, we had choices. It hurt my head to think about
making such a big decision alone. It was time for me to come out of my
cocoon a little bit and get more information about exactly where Bob
could end up.

"Okay, Dr. M," I said, pulling the tissue box closer to me, "I need to
hear it. Tell me all the things we could be dealing with here. I think it's
time for me to know."

Dr. M began to run through the litany of possibilities. Essentially,
the main categories in the brain for cognitive damage were behavioral,
social, spatial, speech and language, and executive function, the more
logical part of the brain that controls how we order our lives and organize our activities. With a blast injury, it was hard to assess what was or
wasn't damaged because an explosion caused the brain to slosh around

against the skull. This sheared off millions of neurons and caused damage that wouldn't be revealed until Bob woke up. Even then it could take time. Sometimes the differences were subtle—slightly impaired judgment or cognitive ability, perhaps—and sometimes they were more grave, like major personality differences. One of the greatest frustrations with a head injury is that while the person might seem just fine to others, things are profoundly changed inside. These patients—with significant but outwardly subtle damage—were called "the walking wounded." Back home in America they would be a haunting legacy of the war in Iraq.

As we'd been told, Bob's focal point of injury from the blast was in his speech and language area in the left temporal lobe. He would most likely suffer from aphasia, difficulty finding words. This condition could range in severity; it often comes hand in hand with receptive or expressive behavior disorders—"language in and language out" was how Dr. M described it. Especially in the beginning, there would be times Bob might not follow a conversation if there were lots of people in the room. He would most likely ask people to repeat themselves. He would need to rely more on facial expressions and other social cues, assuming he was able to pick up on them. This meant, for example, that the telephone would be a difficult means of communication for him.

I pulled out another tissue and slumped in my chair.

"Do you want me to continue?" Dr. M asked. "I don't want to overload you."

"Go on," I said. I was sobbing. "Give it all to me now. I need to know what I could be dealing with . . . and I want to find out all at once." I stopped, as a fresh spate of tears flowed, and tried to gain my composure. "Is this likely? Do you often see these issues?" I asked. Every time Dr. M paused before she answered, I knew what the answer would be.

I read much later that more than 50 percent of marriages to brain-injured spouses end in divorce; one statistic said it was closer to 70 percent. Research showed that caregivers routinely reported feeling isolated and trapped. They felt neither married nor single; their sexual and emotional needs were unfulfilled. In another survey of wives one year after injury, they described their husbands as selfish, demanding, babyish, and dependent. The way I saw it, these wives had gained another child.

Dr. M went on. Damage to the front of the head, or the frontal lobe, often resulted in a loss of executive function. This is the part of the brain that organizes our actions without our even thinking about it. The executive function matures last in teenagers, which is the reason parents like me were often frustrated at their children's spaciness, forgetfulness, or lack of logic. It is this part of the brain that tells you in the morning to put your feet on the floor and head to the shower, pull out clothes, brush your hair, and grab your purse and briefcase before you leave the house. Your personality, the essence of "you," also resides there.

Many victims of car accidents whose heads slammed into the windshield, or the soldiers who had blast injuries, came home "flat" and unemotional. Sometimes the personality came back. More often than not, it didn't. Many also exhibited symptoms almost like Tourette's syndrome, where they would swear uncontrollably or say inappropriate things. The spouse or loved one would need to be by an arm or an elbow in social situations to smooth any potentially hurtful comments.

Depression was also very common. Once the person came to grips with his or her new—limited—capabilities (though some never realized anything was wrong), there was often profound depression. A war-zone injury would add the strong possibility of post-traumatic stress disorder to the mix. This was a very likely scenario for Bob, as Dr. M had already cautioned.

"Emotional reactions can happen later and be triggered by other things," she said. "And past reactions can have a compound effect. It is highly likely that he will have nightmares and flashbacks of the incident or other traumatic incidents from past assignments."

"Is there anything else I should know, Dr. M? This is your day; this is your window while I am feeling strong," I said. In fact, I was suddenly feeling much weaker than I had for quite a while.

"Are you sure you want this all in one day, Lee?" she looked at me hard, but I had asked for it.

I nodded.

"He will need speech therapy for sure; the tongue and the facial nerves all seem to indicate this. Speech, occupational, and behavioral therapy will also be essential at the next juncture. And we still aren't sure about the eye, are we? The one eye seems sleepy, and we won't know until he wakes up if it works. Most likely he will need to be on anticonvulsant medications to help with seizures; they can also help with mood and behavior.

"You'll eventually have to try to let him do things for himself: make his own coffee, get his own clothes, and dress himself. They will help you in rehab with the tasks of daily living. In Bob's present condition, I'm afraid he is not ready for rehab; he actively needs to be able to do rehab three hours a day."

She drew in a breath and looked at me, twirling her pen in her hands. "There is a subacute unit, but we have also been talking about the possibility of his going to a nursing home next until he can wake up more." She looked down, knowing how hard this was to hear. "He isn't responding to the doctors on command. He won't do anything for them. We will probably need to move him out of Bethesda in one to two weeks, but no rehab facility will take him in this state. We may need to put him somewhere until he is more awake."

Nursing home, I thought. This can't be happening.

And then she said it. "We are concerned about what he will do next," she began. "His vocation. He may need to learn parts of his job again or find a whole different one, and that will be part of rehab too."

"You mean like belt making and basket weaving?" I asked cynically. I could feel that my eyes held no expression.

"Well, maybe he will want to make belts and baskets," she said evenly, ignoring my sarcasm. "He may decide he only wants to work a three-day week to be with his kids more. People have a whole new appreciation for the value of life, of what it means to be spared."

"What is the worst stuff?" I asked, in a small voice. "Are these all the possibilities?"

She looked at me gently. "There are lots of worse things, but I don't think you want to know them."

"Do you ever see any miracles?" I asked softly, crying again.

"Yes," she said, with an unwavering gaze, "I do." But I knew that the miracle business was not her bag.

"Well, I guess that about sums it up then, doesn't it, Dr. M?" I said bitterly. "My husband will be the man who fondles the apples in the grocery store while drooling and spitting out swearwords at old ladies. On a good day maybe he will just tell people they are fat or ugly; on a bad day he might snap. Going out in public may be problematic, so we'll just hole up in our house and eat dog food when the unemployment check runs out. Is that about right?"

Dr. M tried hard not to smile. She was a professional to the core. "Well, I'm going to take it as a good sign that your sense of humor is still intact," she said.

Lee

Baltimore, March 3, 2006

Nothing prepared me for what I saw at my first rehab tour of Johns Hopkins. In all rehabilitation facilities there is a room that goes by different names; Easy Street or Main Street; they are all the same. It is a room where the hospital tries to simulate everyday life. There is often a "store" with plastic fruit and a cash register, a room with a bed, and a kitchen for cooking. I thought to myself that Bob had barely ever made a bed in his life. Would this really be his rehab? Would he be reborn as a housewife perfecting hospital corners on sheets and worrying about how much rinse agent to put in the dishwasher?

And then I saw it. Smack in the middle of the room was a car, a real car. It was the car that pushed me from the verge of tears into an all-out sobbing session in front of the stunned doctor who was proudly taking us on a tour of the facilities. It was the car that brought me face-to-face with the reality that once Bob did wake up, *if* he did, our life would be filled with tasks as basic as learning how to get in a car. How Bob would hate this, I thought. Look at how low we have sunk. The doctor guided Dr. M, David, and me into the family room so we could talk privately about Bob's options and what the facility could offer.

"So?" I asked numbly, thinking about the vehicle sitting on real tires in the middle of that mauve room. "I thought physical therapy wasn't going to be much of an issue for Bob. His shoulder has healed so well, they said."

"Everything has to start somewhere as his brain relearns how to give commands to his body," the Johns Hopkins doctor said, handing me a box of tissues.

"I know he is blind and deaf," I said out loud, to no one in particular. "How will I take care of everyone? How can I do this? I have to think about how I will care for everyone without a husband who can support us." I was half talking to myself.

All of a sudden I snapped.

"I made him promise me," I said, to David and Dr. M. I was sobbing so hard I couldn't catch my breath. "I made him promise me when David Bloom died that he would never do that to us. And he lied to me. How can I ever trust anything or anyone again?" Even I was taken aback by how hard I was crying, by the sudden power of an emotion I had harbored since I'd gotten that first phone call in Disney World.

"It's sad," Dr. M said. "It's sad what happened to you and your children, but I've never seen one family yet who didn't rise to the occasion. People love you and will support you. People put one foot in front of the other every day. They figure out how to do this. You, Bob and the children will be connected in ways you cannot know now."

Lee

Bethesda Naval Hospital, March 3, 2006

With Bob past the acute phase of his injuries, the doctors had decided to move him to the fifth floor, the surgical ward of the hospital, where

Doug had recovered. It was time to get him out of the ICU, even though he would still need to be watched 24/7. The danger of his falling and hurting his head meant he couldn't be left alone.

He had been given a hard white plastic hat, a climbing helmet actually, to wear anytime he got out of bed. Dr. M cautioned us to refer to it as a hat; the word *helmet* might trigger some kind of emotional trauma from the incident.

"He will most likely be disoriented and scared," she told me. "You're lucky. A lot of these guys hit people and throw punches; they can become very violent. When they start biting, that's when I really get worried about their long-term prognosis. You can take comfort in the fact that Bob has not been violent. He hasn't bitten anyone. That's a good sign."

On the way back from Baltimore, Dr. M called my cell phone and told me tersely that she had just learned that Bob had thrown some punches at some of the corpsmen who were trying to move him. He had become very agitated, screamed "Get the hell away!," and lashed out at anyone who came near him.

The children arrived for the weekend. We had decided the twins would not visit Bob again until he woke up more, but that night at dinner we had a long talk about their dad. I was quick to sanitize it a bit and leave out some of the worrisome information, like the fact that he wasn't waking up as fast as everyone had hoped. Mack looked glum and Cathryn looked skeptical. I tried desperately to catch up on their lives at home. I asked Mack question after question but got few answers. My teenage boy was suffused with a quiet anguish he refused to share.

At 3 A.M. the next morning I was wide awake. The kids were all asleep in the bedroom off the living area. The Ambien had been losing its effectiveness, and I was getting scared that I was hooked on it. Every night, somewhere around 3 A.M., I would wake up like clockwork. If I wanted to sleep again, I would have to take another half. It was all very Judy Garland, but I would have to worry about that later. Right now, sleep was the only fuel that I had.

At 5 A.M. I simply got up, still in my pajamas, and headed over to see

Bob. "I'm coming in with you," I said, not expecting an answer. I kicked off my shoes and climbed in the tiny bed with him, trying to move his tubes around so I didn't lie on them. I laid my arm carefully over his chest and nestled my head next to him, balancing against the bed rail.

For a moment, Dr. M's words about agitation and physical violence rang in my head. She had warned me not to get too close in case he became angry at me in his confusion. But I saw no violence or malice in my husband's eyes, just unending sadness and fear. I loved him more than I could imagine.

Damn the doctors and their predictions and cautions, I thought. I was unafraid. This was my husband. Somewhere inside that hurt and broken head he knew me; he loved me too but he was scared and confused. For the next two hours I whispered to him softly, pulling him back down every time he sat up. He didn't say a word the entire time.

Sometimes he would roll onto his stomach and then get up on his knees, mumbling. I snuggled him and urged him to sleep, but his eyes kept opening with a startled look, as if he was terrified. By 7:30 A.M. I was exhausted. I had to get back to the kids. Feeling dejected and low, I slipped out of Bob's room and back to the hotel.

Lee

Bethesda Naval Hospital, March 4, 2006

Mack was first that weekend to visit his dad. He was solemn, and his eyes filled with tears when he walked up to his motionless father. Bob had had a big workout the day before with the chair. Mack picked up his hand at my urging and told his dad how much he loved him. Mack's voice was breaking; it took all that he had to see his strong virile father still so incapacitated, helpless as a child.

Our son had always been incredibly proud of his father, but at age fourteen he sometimes hid it well. It hurt Bob on some level that Mack was more interested in hanging out with his friends than with us, even though he knew that an independent streak was a genetically pro-grammed part of the teenage years. But it would have hurt Bob more to see his son now: frightened, but not willing to talk about it; eager to know, but unwilling to ask too many questions. Mack's mask of stoic bravery broke my heart. He was now the man of the house. It must have been a lonely burden.

When Cathryn joined Mack next to Bob in her yellow gown and ster-ile gloves, I noticed a change. My two older children were more of a team. The sibling fighting that had been such a hallmark of our home before Bob got hurt had vaporized. They were united by the tragedy. There were cracks in the tough-guy armor Mack wore around his sister; and for her part, Cathryn, whose love for her brother had been forced underground in the past year, was able to be more herself. It was one of the tiny blessings Bob's injury brought us and I was grateful for it.

"Hi, Daddy," Cathryn said, tears glistening in her eyes. He was sleep-ing deeply, and he had grown so thin. After five weeks he looked fragile and pale, more like a vegetable than a parent. Seeing Bob again, still not really awake, was hardest for Cathryn.

We were now the family you hear about in your town or read about in the paper, the people who have been dealt a terrible tragedy. I knew how that felt from the outside. Some felt a rush of sympathy, and others made the sign of the cross and fell on their knees, praying that misfor-tune would pass them by. Watching Cathryn talk to her comatose father, I marveled at how quickly we had crossed the barrier that separated us from our old, safe, reliable lives.

That night as I undressed in my hotel room, I glanced in the mirror at my shrinking frame. I was beyond exhaustion, moving forward through sheer will. I could see ribs and a collarbone protruding and then, down by my stomach, something else. Just above my belly button was a little bubble of flesh. I pushed against it and it gurgled. A hernia, I thought glumly. Great. When can I possibly take care of myself in the midst of all of this? How would I even have time to go to the doctor? I asked Dr. Perdue to look at it the next day and he confirmed my self-diagnosis.

Lifting kids, childbirth, abdominal surgery: all these things weaken the muscles of the stomach wall over time, he explained.

I knew it wasn't serious and could wait, but it seemed to be one more giant thing on my list of things to do. My stomach had been feeling funny lately, stressed, like an ulcer even. I'd need to get a major physical once we were past the crisis stage. I'd canceled a mammogram and an OB checkup already, along with a trip to the dentist. They seemed like little things, things that could wait.

Lee

Bethesda Naval Hospital, March 5, 2006

Saying goodbye to all four children as they left to return home that Sunday with Nancy's family almost tore my heart out. Dr. Costantino had told me weeks ago that in his experience there was something special about the fifth week in a protracted illness or injury. It was some kind of a universal breaking point for families who were separated. At week five, things often began to fall apart. Doing a quick calculation as I buckled Claire's seat belt, I realized we were heading smack into the fifth week of this living hell.

"Come with us!" Claire cried. "I want to stay with you!" whined Nora. Cathryn's eyes were full. Where would I get the strength to do this for even one more week? Bob had to wake up. It was in his hands now. There was nothing more I could do. Our family was falling apart.

I couldn't bear to watch the van pull away. I turned and walked quickly back inside the hotel to prepare to go to the hospital. When I reached our hotel floor, I collapsed into David Woodruff's arms, sobbing in the hallway.

The next morning I finished my swim and headed to Bob's room for my daily early morning visit. My heart was heavy as I pushed the fifth-floor button in the hospital lobby. I thought with disgust how this had become my new morning routine. I pictured my children's sleeping faces and the smell of their sweet breath. In half an hour, they would be woken up for school. I loved that moment as they hung suspended from a dream state. Especially with Mack, they were groggy enough to let me kiss them all over their faces, rub their hair, and whisper all the silly little baby names Bob and I had given them, as I coaxed them awake. I tried to push those images out of my head as I walked past a sign on the floor that said LAUGHTER IS THE BEST MEDICINE.

When I pushed open the door to Bob's room, he was sitting up in bed, a giant smile on his face, and when he saw me he lifted his arms toward heaven. "Hey, sweetie," Bob said lovingly, with a little note of surprise. "Where've you been?"

Bob

Bethesda Naval Hospital, March 6, 2006

At four o'clock in the morning on Monday, March 6, 2006, I finally woke up. For thirty-six days I had been asleep, and for nearly all that time my eyes had remained closed. For the last week of my medically induced coma, my eyelids would open occasionally, but I don't remember seeing. I was told that my arms and legs would kick out or hit against the doctors and nurses at times, although I don't remember any of that either. I'm sure I had dreams during those thirty-six nights, but to this day I can't remember what they were. When I first woke, I had no idea how long I had been asleep or where I was. I couldn't even remember most of what I did in that initial week after I woke up, but I will never forget my first sight of Lee.

I can still see the expression of wonder on her face when she first walked in. And I remember exactly what I said to her.

"Hey, sweetie, where've you been?"

Lee hugged me with tears in her eyes. For weeks she had come in to find me asleep, but now I was awake and sitting up calmly in bed. "I've been here with you," she said, crying. "We've been here together."

I'll never forget how incredibly up she was, and it wasn't until much later that I learned how afraid she had been for all those weeks. With everything she had been through, she still had no guarantees where I would end up. The doctors did not know exactly what would happen to me. Lee smiled publicly, but inside she had been terrified.

The amount of damage to my brain was still not clear. Over the next few days I discovered that many words and names had gone away. I was not able to retrieve the name of any state in the nation, not a city in the world, or any country on earth. When I first woke up I couldn't get any of my brothers' names straight, and I couldn't even remember my children's names. Within a few days I managed to recall my two older children, Mack and Cathryn, but I'm not certain that I even remembered the twins for the first two days after awakening. On the wall opposite my bed there were blown-up photographs of my family, and just looking at them was motivating. Those pictures brought me more than happiness; they gave me a powerful will to recover.

What I remember most about waking up was the excruciating pain. It felt as if my skull were going to split open if I moved too much. It was the worst pain I'd ever experienced and remained so for almost four months, until the surgery to replace my skull. Every time I rode in a wheelchair and we hit a bump, my head would throb.

Shortly after waking up I felt a profound soreness in my back, in part from the wound in my shoulder but also from lying so long in one place. I didn't know about my back injury, and it wasn't until a day later that I realized a part of my skull was actually missing. I must have been shocked at that discovery, but I have no clear memory of my reaction. Lee tells me we looked in the mirror together for the first time. She was trying to blunt the trauma and muffle my reaction but I cannot recall the moment. I tried to keep my extreme pain and fatigue to myself. I didn't want to let anyone around me know how much or how constantly it hurt. I could tell by their faces that my family was already so worried and concerned, I thought it would be best to try to hide as much of the pain as I could.

I remember being terrified of sneezing, because a single sneeze made me feel as though my brain would literally blow out of the open part of my cranium. I was unable to lie on the left side of my head, where the skull was missing, and it was impossible to get comfortable in the hospital bed.

In those early days there were only a few things I could remember about the attack on our convoy in Iraq. Although I never saw the IED explode and I don't remember what happened around us after that, I do have a very distinct memory that was so beautiful, and so profound, it is hard even to put it into words. After I fell back into the tank, I saw what I think must have been heaven. I was bathed in a calming white light. It was soft, not glaring, and it was peaceful, enveloping. I was floating somehow. I could see my body below me as I hovered, slowly, peacefully, and completely without pain. I remember being surrounded by and immersed in pure bright light. There was no conscious feeling of urgency that I had to go back somewhere. I don't even think I knew I'd been attacked or hurt. The white light just felt good, like soft welcoming arms. I reveled in those arms.

Suddenly, the scene disappeared. I was awake on the hard floor of the vehicle and I looked up and saw my cameraman, Doug, across from me. I remember spitting blood. I remember Vinnie talking to me and someone—maybe it was the Iraqi interpreter—touching my head. More memories would come later; in those early days, this was all I could recall.

That vision of the white light was the clearest memory I had. I want to believe that "place" was heaven. To this day, because of what I experienced, I have no fear of death. Whether or not fear will creep back eventually, I don't know, but for the moment I am comforted by the thought of what will come next.

"How is the cameraman?" I asked Lee. "Is he here in the hospital?"

"Doug. Doug was here, but he is much better and has gone home to France," she told me. Although I had known Doug for years and felt very close to him, I could not remember his name, just as I had forgotten the names of Vinnie, Magnus, all my other friends, my children, and the soldiers who had worked so bravely to save my life.

I was concerned for Doug because in my mind I still saw his face bleeding. That memory had come back: me staring at him as the blood ran down the side of his head. I could picture his eyes, open and stunned, leaning over me after the attack, telling me I would be okay. The look in Doug's eyes had made me really nervous. It had made me feel as if our wounds were very, very bad.

When they told me Doug was doing well, I felt instant relief. I could not have stood the guilt if Doug had ended up worse off than I was. Lee told me later that some of the doctors in the hospital said this was a common reaction among soldiers. When they woke up after their injuries, the first thing they wanted to know was how their buddies had fared.

I wanted to turn on the television in my room to see what was happening in the world. The first story I saw that morning was upsetting. Dana Reeve had lost her protracted battle with lung cancer. There is something so much more poignant to me now about Dana and Christopher Reeve as a couple. He the handsome actor, whose life was drastically changed forever by an accident, and she the loving caregiver, her role in the marriage forever circumscribed by his paralysis. Months later, watching my own wife gracefully juggle all her emotions and duties along with my needs, I was more in awe of what Dana Reeve had accomplished in her life and marriage. Her death, falling on the day that I awoke, would strike me months later as a bitter coincidence.

Initially when I woke I had thought the injury was recent and I would be going home shortly. I hadn't absorbed the fact that my recovery would involve a lengthy run of hospitals and rehab centers. The family was careful to give me only bits of information at a time, gauging what they thought I could digest.

There is a dream I had in those early days that for some reason has stayed with me. I was living in a factory town and it was dark outside, perhaps long after dinner, and fat flakes of snow were falling gently. The people in the neighborhoods ringing the factory all had their lights on outside their houses. And in the center of town, the factory where everyone worked glowed warmly with giant industrial lights. I could tell that what they were doing inside was difficult, tedious work, yet I knew everyone in the factory was happy. They all seemed utterly content. Although I could see them, I realized they couldn't see me outside the window, and even though it was winter, my feet and hands were not cold. I woke from that dream in the dark hospital room feeling somehow comforted.

At the time, the dream meant nothing to me. But in retrospect I can see clearly what it was about. It represented the long unbroken journey I would have to take to recover. The factory work with its tedium and repetition—that would be the day-in and day-out routine of my physical and cognitive therapy. But surrounding me, embracing me, and supporting me through all that was a community of family and friends that brought me peace and encouragement. Little by little I would heal.

The solace that dream provided at the time was both welcome and remarkable, because most of my nights were actually sheer hell. All the people who had been with me throughout the day were gone, and I couldn't sleep for more than an hour at a time. I was in great pain, and I was also frightened to be alone in the dark. But there was always someone by my bed, a young corpsman from the military to keep me company and make sure I kept my helmet on. Just about every one of those kids was wonderful. They would listen to me babble about my family and my life. They talked to me, got me water, and helped me to the bathroom, because I was so dizzy I would often come close to falling over.

Those fourteen centimeters of missing skull—about five and a half inches—completely changed my sense of balance. Every time I stood I would have to lean over because I felt as if I were going to pass out. At one point, in the bathroom, I did lose consciousness, and I was not wearing the plastic helmet. A strong corpsman caught me in her arms. If she hadn't been right there the entire time, I don't know what would have happened to me.

Lee

Bethesda Naval Hospital, March 6, 2006

I have wished, so many times since that Monday morning when Bob awoke suddenly, that someone had taken a picture of the expression on my face. I would love to see what I looked like when I heard my husband, for the first time in five weeks, speak to me in a voice filled with love and look at me with eyes that were once again connected to his soul. Staring at Bob, so alive, so *present*, I was stunned. My entire face and body froze when I stood in the doorway, and it took me a few beats to realize that this was not an illusion. My husband was awake and he was calling me *sweetie*.

Half of me felt complete and total relief, and the other half wanted to wield a rolling pin in exasperation, like Lucy Ricardo, and scream, "Where have *I* been? I've been right here for five weeks, worried sick about you, you idiot!"

As I went around to the side of Bob's bed, dropping my coat and swim bag on the floor to fall into his arms, the corpsman began babbling. "He has been awake since four-thirty this morning, and he slept all through the night. When he woke up he asked me, 'Where am I? What happened to me? How long have I been here, and where is my wife?' He has been asking for you over and over again. We've been telling him you're coming. He's been speaking French with me, and I think he was speaking Chinese too. It even sounded like he was doing a broadcast at one point."

In a short time, Bob's doctors and nurses were filing into his room to get a look. I had called his parents and brothers, my family, and the Bakers, and everyone was on the way over. The whole fifth floor was excited, and the doctors seemed genuinely amazed. Going by the textbook, it should not have happened this way. This man should not be able to speak at all, let alone do so in other languages. Everyone was in awe of how quickly he had woken up.

Bob was excited, like a child on the eve of his birthday. The attention, interest, and deep emotion in the room, particularly from all those strangers in white coats, baffled him. His hands felt around on the top of his crew-cut head like two scuttling crabs until they found the raw scar and the giant depression in his skull. "What happened to my head?" he asked incredulously. "What happened to my face?"

We would need to give him information slowly, Dr. M had cautioned. "Don't tell him everything all at once."

"How are our . . . kids?" said Bob said haltingly, pointing at the giant blowups we'd taped to the wall. "Are they here?" He pointed to Mack and Cathryn. I was pretty sure he didn't remember their names, and it was clear he didn't remember the twins at all.

Impulsively, we called home and got Cathryn on the phone. Mack had already left for high school. "How are you, sweetie? I love you. Do you miss me?" he said. I almost fell off my chair. His words were halting and his voice sounded different, softer, not as authoritative, but it was him.

Little by little, Bob began putting his world together; you could see the computer in his brain working so hard to reboot. "I love you so much and then you are here," he said to me the next morning, as I walked in. He asked me to get a mirror, and I sat on the bed next to him and we both looked at our reflection together for the first time. It was a silly thing we had done throughout our marriage; hold each other in the mirror and smile back at the reflection wordlessly, seeing ourselves together. The image always showed a united front.

By inserting myself into the frame this first time, I wanted to cushion the impending shock. I couldn't imagine how it would feel to wake up to find a huge indentation on one side of my head. In this new reflection of the old us, a gaunt Bob stared back who was missing pieces.

I'd expected a devastated reaction from my husband but I got only the intellectual curiosity of the journalist. He carefully and silently studied his head where the skull was caved in, turning in different ways to examine the scars and pieces of shrapnel and gravel embedded throughout the left side of his face. Once again, we explained to him that the doctors had cut his skull to save his life. In the next few weeks, tiny rocks would work their way toward the surface of his skin as his body expelled them.

The reflection of us both, back from the mirror, showed a team. I looked happy, ecstatic, and somewhat stunned to have the man next to me alive. But the mirror revealed a glimpse of the future too. It was the very long road, the arduous journey, we would both have to take to help Bob heal.

Bob

Bethesda Naval Hospital, March 7, 2006

On the day after I woke up, I didn't want to be alone. I was petrified that if the door shut my family and friends would all go away. I asked my brother Mike to spend the night with me. That twelve-hour period was the strangest experience for both of us, and we have talked about it many times since. I can only describe it as time spent in some kind of heightened state. I would imagine it might be close to the feeling of taking hallucinatory drugs, my mind was experiencing such wild fluctuations and extreme emotions. Mike has told me since that it was a wild and terrible night. Neither of us really slept until about 5 A.M. I asked the nurse to put my pillow and blankets on the hard floor and tried to get comfortable. At times I slept in a chair just for a different position. Part of me felt crazy, yet crystal clear. I understand now how people can be out of their minds but feel as if they are completely sane and in control.

All of a sudden I had a huge desire to write, and I asked Mike for a paper and pen. Then I asked the corpsman to give me a flashlight and I began to scribble things that at the time I felt were words.

"This is incredible," I said, as if I had come up with something remarkable.

"What are you writing about?" Mike asked me. He could barely see the paper in the dark room.

"Just wait a second, I think I've figured out a story about truth." I remember it was about thirty minutes before I finished writing. On the one hand, I was exhausted. On the other hand, I had a strange electric energy. I felt intense hope.

I had no idea that I couldn't write. It felt as if my brain were filling in certain blanks and I was beginning to remember things again.

But when I woke the next morning and looked at what I had written, I couldn't understand any of it. All of it was bizarre scratching and unintelligible words. And there were only three lines. Even today I cannot read what I wrote. It would take months before I could begin to write normally, and even then the words came slowly.

That was the worst night. After that there were moments of incredible peace. The bulk of my emotions involved feelings of extreme good fortune. I felt especially lucky at my circumstances when I began to walk around the halls with my physical therapist or a corpsman and saw some of the soldiers on my floor. These guys were missing limbs or eyes. Many of their faces had been horribly maimed, others were burned. My gait, although still unsteady at times, was rapidly improving. A number of the young soldiers I saw had suffered far worse bodily injuries. Physical rehabilitation would be a big part of their recovery in addition to the blast injury. And looking in their rooms as I walked the halls, I noticed that some of them didn't have nearly the family support that I had. A few had no one with them at all.

Part of me felt guilty for that. Relieved, sad, and guilty. Not only was I physically in better shape than many of them, but I was surrounded by family. I also had options outside of the VA system and access to private care if I chose that route. Later I would come to realize how much attention my injury had received and how silently all these brave men were suffering. There was no one to tell their story.

Beyond feeling lucky, there were also moments when tears came easily. I would cry at the smallest provocation. Once I sobbed without stopping for thirty minutes. I was sad for my family, for what I had put them through, and sad for myself. I felt fear and uncertainty about what the future would bring and worried about how I would take care of my kids and my wife.

It was frustrating when the doctors came in and asked me multiple questions and tried to test my language skills. I did poorly at the exercises and was surprised by just how little my brain could handle. One of the first tests was to connect numbers spaced randomly on a page from 1 to 25. It took me almost ten minutes just to connect the dots and find the numbers.

The doctor would hold up black-and-white line drawings of objects like eyeglasses or brushes, a screwdriver or a paper clip. I could describe what they did in many cases, but I couldn't say the names. For some reason *paper clip* was one of my biggest challenges, and we had a few chuckles about that. I remember laughing a great deal because I was so happy to be alive, but I also knew that laughter was a good way to hide my fear and frustration.

I had no idea that I wasn't able to speak well. It was only gradually, when my brothers would repeat a strange word I had used and laugh or my parents would chuckle, that I realized it hadn't come out as I had intended. My speech was halting and didn't have any kind of cadence.

I will never forget seeing my children for the first time. I had been awake for a few days but had only spoken to them on the phone. Lee was in New York looking at some of the rehab options for my next step. We were talking on the phone when I broke down, on the third day of being awake.

"I need to see my kids," I cried. "Don't they want to see me?" Lee explained that she was hoping to bring them down to D.C. with her in two days so we could all be together, but I felt I couldn't wait that long. My need to see them was visceral.

She arranged for Mack and Cathryn to fly to Washington the next day. The twins would see me that coming weekend.

When I first heard the voices of my children outside in the hall, I sat straight up. I took a big breath to calm myself and tried to tamp down the pain. More than anything, I wanted to appear strong for them. My heart sped up, and when the door opened and they rushed toward me, I took them both in my arms in the biggest, most incredible hug I have ever known. Mack was crying and Cathryn had tears rolling down her cheeks as she chatted away. They stayed for an hour—the most precious slice of time I could remember in a long while, but it took about everything I had that day. We listened to some music, we cuddled, we took a walk in the hall, and I introduced them proudly to all the nurses. It sapped every ounce of energy to appear calm and happy and healthy. When they left, I collapsed on the bed, pain throbbing in my head, and fell asleep.

As I got better, I would roam the halls with my physical therapist. She helped me get my shoulder movement back with some exercises and started to build my stamina after having been bedridden for so long.

My physical abilities came back rapidly. A week after I woke up, tired of the therapist's pace, I began jogging around the nurses' station as she took off after me, yelling good-naturedly. I did have my helmet on, as much as I loathed wearing the damned thing. And sometimes, walking with the doctors or nurses, I would pretend to fall. As much as they hated it, I got a kick out of scaring them half to death before they burst out laughing. I liked to show off for the doctors too, doing a standing one-footed yoga pose to demonstrate that my balance was solid. These antics felt like the old me, the jokester, the person who liked to have fun. Just getting out of my room cheered me up.

But if my body was healing rapidly, my brain was lagging, still processing what had happened and adjusting to the new speed with which it functioned. Little by little, I became more aware of those moments when I couldn't remember a word or when I found the wrong one. There was no question that things inside my brain were now very different.

Lee asked me time and again, "What does it feel like to be inside your head?" It took me a long time to be able to answer that. What I could tell her was that everything was slower. Inside my head it felt like things moved in a lower gear. Reading was difficult, finding words took longer, and I had to listen more closely to grasp the essence of a conversation. Complex words eluded me, although I could understand everything. Lee had a term for it; she called it *swimming through Jell-O*. I thought that sounded about right.

When I think back to *how* I woke up, it felt like coming out of a kind of fog. Each day I would speak a little more clearly, feel a little stronger, and make some kind of progress, no matter how small. Some days were worse than others. If I pushed too hard one day, I paid like hell the next, with fatigue, more confusion, and a temporarily lessened ability to find the right words.

Lee

Bethesda Naval Hospital, March 7, 2006

"Where is my wedding ring?" Bob said suddenly, looking down at his hand. I pulled out the chain around my neck and showed him.

"There is no other woman in this world like Lee," he said, touching the ring.

"We'll put this back on you in a little bit," I said. "You still probably have some more procedures, and I'm not taking any chances of losing this."

Watching and listening as Bob took the jumble in his brain and struggled to build a kind of ordered tapestry was fascinating. "I can't speak very clearly" . . . "Life is so awesome and I'll have more time at home" . . . "I was working so hard this month—so hard in news" were some of the things he said to me the first day or so. "I'll feel a hundred thousand dollars better," he told one of the doctors. Once he began to speak Italian and then said to me impulsively, "Let's move to Verona."

On the third day of his awakening, the respiratory therapist came into his room and said, in a cheery voice, "Hi, I'm Peggy."

"Porky?" Bob replied.

"What did you call me?" she said, a little taken aback. Although she was in no way porcine, she did have a womanly figure.

"Porky," said Bob. I knew that somehow this was the way his brain was processing things now. He was hearing the word as *piggy* and the faulty wiring spat it back out as *porky,* which must be located in the *farm animal* category of his language center. Or maybe not. Perhaps this was the inappropriateness of the traumatic brain injury, I thought with alarm. Perhaps now he would always tell people what he thought of them, the unvarnished truth.

"Well, I do need to lose some weight," she huffed. "Can you say Peggy?" I could see that this was heading quickly from bad to worse and tried unsuccessfully to catch her eye.

Bob dutifully answered again, becoming more flustered. "Porky."

"Well," she said, loosening up a little, "my one-year-old niece called me Miss Piggy for a while. I guess that's okay."

"You do understand he has been in a bomb blast, don't you?" I explained, trying to preserve Bob's dignity by not intervening but not wanting to hurt the respiratory therapist. "Please don't take this personally." She nodded and assured me that she didn't.

Days later when we passed her in the hall and called out a hello, she wanted Bob and me to know she'd started going to the gym. She held him personally responsible.

There were other funny moments too, as when Bob was trying to tell us he was going to ace his first neuropsychiatric evaluation. He was very giddy and silly in the early days, and I wanted him to focus on those first cognitive tests. They would serve as the baseline evaluation of what was damaged.

"You need to be serious for this test, Bob," I said, like a parent talking about SATs. "How you do on this test will help determine where you go next."

"I'm going to be just like . . ." and then Bob trailed off. He couldn't think of the name. This happened so often, we became adept at finishing his sentences. The new Bob was also becoming a great charades player, using all the hand signals, body language, and sound effects he could muster. Having a conversation with Bob in the first few days after he woke up felt a little bit like watching Robin Williams do one of his highly physical comedy routines.

Bob gave up trying to think of the name and began swinging at the air with his fists like a prizefighter.

"Joe Frazier," guessed Vinnie, who was visiting that day.

"Muhammad Ali," I screamed, like a contestant on *Wheel of Fortune*.

"No," said Bob.

"Jake Lamotta?" I asked.

"No." Bob looked crestfallen. But he wasn't going to give up. About three minutes later, when we'd moved on to a totally different topic, he began to hum the theme song from the movie *Rocky*.

"Rocky Balboa!" Vinnie and I yelled out at the same time.

"Yes!" said Bob, raising his fist in victory. Vinnie and I turned to look at each other, silently marveling at that old Bob Woodruff determination. Maybe it would be enough to bring him all the way back.

Bob

Westchester County, New York, April 2006

More than a month later, after I'd gotten home from an inpatient stay in New York, I would come downstairs every morning to the kitchen, helmet on, and find I had slept so long that the children had left for school. Lee would be at the kitchen counter with Mike or Jim, whichever brother was staying with us during that time. After a quick cup of coffee I would rush to Manhattan for my outpatient therapy.

Lee had recently ordered live ants for an Ant Farm the twins had been given for Christmas. She had filled the farm with sand and then when the ants—red ones—arrived in a small vial, I tried to dump them inside the plastic farm. Some got loose and bit our fingers, and the girls squealed with excitement as we all scrambled to capture them and wrangle them back in the tiny opening.

In just one night they made inroads in the sand with multiple tunnels. Watching the ants move as a colony had become a kind of pastime for Lee. She was fascinated by them and would check on their progress throughout the day.

"Those ants are just like you," she told me one morning, when I asked her what she found so interesting about watching them. "They are so determined. And they can do amazing things, yet they move only a grain of sand at a time."

"What do you mean?" I didn't understand exactly what she was saying or why she was comparing me to an insect.

"Your recovery," she said. "Your recovery is going to be painstaking, like the way the ants are building the tunnels, one grain at a time. But you will get there. I just know it."

Even then, I couldn't have imagined how long the journey would take.

Bob

New York, October 2004–August 2005

The first time I ever filled in for Peter Jennings was on October 14, 2004. Although I had been anchoring *World News*

Tonight Saturday for a year, it was my first time actually filling in for Peter, and it was a big deal. I was grateful for any chance to sit in what is known as "the big chair."

Peter was a legendary anchor. A great writer, he could broadcast live for hours during breaking news, delivering a seamless program. He could also be intimidating at times. He did not suffer fools.

The day before my big opportunity, I walked down to Peter's office to talk with him about that night's broadcast. He was sitting at a table, surrounded by his team of writers and producers, discussing that night's program, then still a couple of hours away from air. He stared down at one of the reporters' stories, making his changes. Reporters sometimes resented Peter's editing, but we grudgingly had to admit he usually improved the piece. Although I had begun talking and laughing with some of his team, Peter did not look up. After a while, he stood, saw me standing there, and stared hard into my eyes.

"You're taking a chance at this show, are you?" he asked me, with a light smile. "Don't screw it up."

With that brief comment he went back into his office and that was it. For Peter, a compliment was not something he tossed off lightly. They were truly earned and sparely bestowed. An e-mail from Peter complimenting your story in the field was a real accomplishment. It made you want to try harder. Peter's smile and offhand remark had been his way of telling me to "break a leg."

Peter believed strongly that the best way to hone one's skills as a journalist was to stay out in the field. He had spent nearly eighteen years traveling the world and living overseas before he had been made anchor, and he had covered virtually all the major world events during that time. Before the advent of cable and the Internet, Peter, Tom Brokaw, and Dan Rather had owned the franchise of the evening news. It was this powerful triad who would enjoy the last days in the golden glow of network news's dominance.

For the rest of us in the ABC newsroom who attempted to cover the Middle East, arguments with Peter were common. His heart lay in that part of the world, and he knew more about the region than most of us put together. His experience and knowledge had been made evident three decades earlier, when nine members of the Israeli team were captured and killed by Palestinian terrorists at the 1972 Munich Olympic Games. Peter Jennings had been in the Olympic Village, and he was the lone reporter who knew the intricacies of the attackers' politics. It was a defining moment in his career.

Filling Peter's shoes as a substitute was a tall order. In the following years I would have more opportunities to fill in for Peter, in addition to anchoring my Saturday night broadcast. I was beginning to fine-tune my own skills in the anchor chair.

When Peter announced on *World News Tonight* on April 5, 2005, that he had been diagnosed with lung cancer, we were all stunned. Peter had been away from the office for a stretch and we knew he had had pneumonia, but the news was a devastating blow to the staff and the show. Although I had sent him a couple of notes, after that day I never saw or spoke to Peter again. His condition declined rapidly. He fought the cancer, surrounded by his wife, Kayce, his two children, and his closest friends. His quiet and dignified struggle against his illness, far from the public eye, would serve as a model for Lee and myself when I faced my own battle.

After Peter's announcement, most of the anchoring was handled by Charlie Gibson and Elizabeth Vargas. Terry Moran and I filled in occasionally. I felt unsure of whether or not I should be pushing to travel or throwing my hat in the ring to anchor more. At one point I had a long talk with Paul

Friedman, a former *World News Tonight* executive producer and ABC News executive who had worked with Peter for decades but had left ABC. He gave me a solid piece of advice.

"Hit the road," Paul said. "Stay away from anchoring as much as you can while Peter is out," he told me. "Peter would rather see you in the field, continuing to get the stories for the show." It would be some of the best advice I received, and in that time I covered some of the most interesting stories of my career. I was able to gain entrance into Iran, and I visited North Korea, obtaining a fascinating view of this secret society, the first Western reporter to do so since 2000.

I loved the life of a reporter on the road. It felt vital; there was something to be learned almost every day. I loved breaking stories or beating the competition to a remote place. Returning from North Korea in June of 2005, I remembered what Peter had told me about returning from London to live in New York. "I was happiest as a reporter," he said. "Don't get me wrong, anchoring is rewarding as well, but there is nothing better than getting out there."

I was on vacation in upstate New York when Peter died on August 7, 2005. I got a phone call from Paul Slavin, senior vice president, worldwide newsgathering, at seven the following morning. "Peter passed away," he said simply. Just like that. I was filled with so many emotions. A father, a husband, an icon, an intellect, and an avid reporter. So many people had lost so much. You can understand intellectually that someone is ill and will most likely die, but the actual passing of a human being that you know is hard news. Still in bed, I closed my eyes and let out my breath. I remember hoping it had been pain-free and that his loved ones had been there to ease this passage.

ABC News had been wonderfully quiet and respectful of Peter during his decline. There had not been a word and no discussions regarding successors. I knew now that the speculation mill would be running full tilt, and I dreaded all that would imply for the staff and the evening broadcast. I continued to stay on the road and keep my head down. Although I filled in occasionally, I was never very adept at playing politics. The best thing I could do, I reasoned, as the weeks and then months dragged on with no word, was to continue to do good work.

Lee

Boston, August 29, 2005

The weekend before Labor Day, Bob planned to fulfill a lifelong dream of Mack's—to see his beloved Boston Red Sox play in Fenway Park. Somehow, in the New York suburbs, Mack had grown into a rabid Red Sox fan in a sea of Yankee devotees. Bob had bought the tickets a month earlier.

A storm named Katrina had been brewing in the Gulf of Mexico that week, and as it approached and grew in strength, there was panic from New Orleans to the Gulf Coast of Florida about potential damage. Bob had covered many hurricanes in his career and he had the gear to prove it. Our basement was littered with wading boots, rain slickers, and waterproof pants, all hastily purchased on the eve of large and not-so-large storms.

ABC had initially called Bob to see if he could go down to the story, and for the first time in his career he had said no. I couldn't help but be overjoyed when I heard him tell the person on the other end of the line, "I've promised my son I would take him to his first Sox game, and I'm not going to break that promise."

The hurricane hit. It looked as if it was a serious storm, promising major damage, but initially not too different from many other devastating gales the region was known for. After the game, Bob had his eye glued to the news, and I could tell that not being at the story was killing him. As his knee jiggled up and down, he stood and began pacing, as if he were having a physical withdrawal.

When the levees broke in New Orleans, a big story turned into disaster on a vast scale. Bob knew he had to get down there fast. He had made it through the game with his son, and that was the most important thing.

Later Mack would understand what his dad had sacrificed to take him to see his beloved team in person. "Dad never canceled anything for me before," Mack said to me, with a mixture of awe and pride. Bob would wince when I later relayed the comment to him.

Bob

New Orleans, August 30, 2005

I jumped on a plane, after the levees broke, and knew I had some ground to make up. Brian Williams was already reporting from the New Orleans Convention Center, and CNN's Anderson Cooper was roaming the streets broadcasting emotionally powerful pieces. What happened next, according to others who weighed in on my time in New Orleans, would help to determine my future at the network.

When I arrived in New Orleans the next morning, the ABC team of about fifteen people had evacuated the city on police orders. I met up with them in a motel parking lot about fifty miles outside the city.

The reporters and the technical crew were exhausted. They had been filing stories into the night. Listening to the police orders and the dire reports of what was happening in the city, they had left their position, fearing the flooding and the danger of being stranded. The mood was grim, and when I arrived it was clear they needed some new blood and a new perspective.

My job would be to talk the team into going back in. I knew all the reporters and most of the technical guys. Some I had worked with in other hurricanes and tough overseas assignments. I pushed and cajoled a little, I motivated the tired troops, and convinced the live truck operators to turn around. I promised everyone, that, if at any time they felt unsafe, they could leave.

I was determined to get in and the clock was running down, but in a short period of time we wheedled our way into the city by talking to the governor's office and the troopers manning the barricades. We began interviewing people and shooting video as fast as we could. There were families pouring over bridges and out of the city; there were looters grabbing whatever they could from stores. We witnessed remarkable stories of harrowing rescues in a short time, and with barely minutes to spare, standing in the filthy floodwaters, I went live that night to report on the horror and chaos unfolding in the Big Easy.

For the next two nights we slept in our cars, until ABC could get an RV down to the city to provide bunk beds and create a base of operations on the edge of the French Quarter. For the next two weeks, my crew and I would travel around the city among the hundreds of other reporters there to record the Third World horrors unfolding in the richest nation on earth.

Lee

Westchester County, New York, Fall 2005

Watching Bob reporting, that first week after Katrina struck, I sensed something new in his on-air presence. It was almost as if rising to meet the challenge of this story, or perhaps his reporting over the past few months, had taken him to a new level. In that week, watching him anchor part of the broadcast from under glaring lights in the middle of devastation, it struck me that a certain gravitas about Bob seemed stronger than ever before.

After Katrina, the autumn dragged on and still there was no decision about who would fill the anchor chair at *World News Tonight*. The newspapers were having a field day with the open-anchor position, and the tension had spilled over into our household. I was tired of the uncertainty surrounding Bob's career that always plagued our family life. I wanted to know what the future held. I was tired of people, in the grocery store and at the playground, asking me what would happen.

The indecision was hurting everybody, especially the staff at *World News Tonight*. Bob's contract would be coming up again in the spring, and he was ready to give up the weekend anchor routine. Quietly, he began to talk with other networks about bigger possibilities. Bob wanted to stay with ABC News, but he was beginning to doubt what kind of position might be in store for him there.

In the halls of ABC News, rumor and speculation ran rampant. Would it be Charlie Gibson? Diane Sawyer? Bob Woodruff? Elizabeth Vargas? Would it be a two-person format? The gossip columnists, trade publications, and Internet blogs were buzzing. It was hard for me to read most of it and, as usual, the information I got from Bob was spotty. I was used to going to other sources to get information, but this time no one seemed to know the real scoop.

Bob kept his head down and just volunteered for assignments, anything to keep busy and stay focused on the job of reporting. He knew the anchor job wouldn't be won through whining, lobbying, or ultimatums.

Thanksgiving approached, and still there was no word. It was now more than three months since Jennings's death, seven since his announcement that he had lung cancer. The wait and anticipation were excruciating. We'd lived with uncertainty in Bob's career before, but the speculation was public now, and the stakes were high.

Bob

New York, December 1, 2005

I can't remember exactly what I was doing at the moment David Westin summoned me to his office at ABC headquarters on December 1, only that I had recently returned from New Orleans. Upstairs in his brightly lit office on the fifth floor, he had Elizabeth Vargas on the phone from Louisiana and his message was simple and full of weight. "I wanted to tell you both quickly. I want you and Elizabeth to be the new anchors of *World News Tonight.*"

I sat for a few seconds, trying to absorb what he had just said. It had been nearly nine years since I had come to ABC News. For most of those years I had never thought much about becoming the anchor, since all three network icons were firmly in place. Even recently, I'd begun to feel that Charlie would be tapped to replace Peter.

I'd grown used to anchoring on Saturday nights because it allowed me to continue reporting the rest of the time. My datelines were global. From the American streets to the chaos of the Middle East, from the death of Pope John Paul II to the presidential election of 2004 and the aftermath of volcanoes and hurricanes, wherever they struck.

After twenty-odd years of the three-anchor dynasty, everything changed in one four-month period. Tom Brokaw's last day came with some fanfare on December 1, 2004. Dan Rather stepped down on March 9, 2005, after a CBS controversy over a story on President Bush's National Guard service. And Peter announced his illness on *World News Tonight* on April 5, 2005. He had hoped to return but never did. The long-familiar faces of network news had changed almost overnight.

I tried to focus on what David was telling Elizabeth and me. "We've all been through a tough period," he began. "It is going to be hard to replace Peter Jennings, very hard, but I believe you two are the key to reinventing the way we think of the evening news. I believe in the digital world, and we need to expand what we do into the digital future."

Westin's vision was that, with all of the digital demands, the drive for Internet news and the commitment to broadcast live into other time zones, it would take two of us to anchor. "You are limited when you are simply coming out of a studio," he went on. "I want to see someone on location most of the time, and someone in the anchor chair. That way we can bring the events to the viewer with real immediacy."

The tradition of Peter Jennings rested heavily on reporting from the field, Westin went on. And he wanted to continue that tradition at ABC. "I believe in you both. This is going to be a growth experience. It will be a long process with lots of adjustments."

For the next four days, over the weekend and into the next Monday, I had to keep this announcement a secret. My agent, Rick Rosen, negotiated the deal, and we worked out the details of the contract. The plan was to release the news on Monday. I took the weekend to try to think through how our lives might change.

On Monday, Elizabeth and I walked into the newsroom where everyone had gathered, and we were each asked to say a few words after David's announcement. Although my heart beat fast, I was completely comfortable. These were all people I'd worked with for years, covering stories, on the assignment desk: colleagues and friends. It felt like home. Elizabeth gave a gracious speech about coming to *World News Tonight* and working with everyone. When it was my turn, words failed me for a moment and emotion took over. I said the first thing that came to my mind.

"This is awesome."

Lee

Westchester County, New York, December 3, 2005

When Bob called me with the good news, I felt thrilled on the one hand and apprehensive on the other. I knew this new job would require a great deal of travel. "Are you ready for this, babe?" he asked, half seriously. I wasn't exactly sure how to answer.

At the age of forty-four, Bob had just been handed the brass ring in television news. How would that disrupt our family? Lying in bed during theoretical discussions, we had both talked about how we didn't want to change anything about our lives. Whatever happened, we wanted to strive for complete normalcy and as much togetherness as possible. But there was no way to know now what the actual demands on Bob's time would be, either at work or within the community as a more public figure. All we could do was take each step as it came.

Lee

Westchester County, New York, January 23, 2006

What would you do if someone told you that the next moment would be the last time you would hold or hug or converse with your husband for over a month, that he would lie for five weeks in a comatose state, clinging to life? How would you act if you knew your husband would spend the next year and beyond recovering from a traumatic brain injury, dealt by a roadside bomb powerful enough to blow open his skull? What would I have changed about that moment, that morning, if I had known all of our lives would be blackened, held to a flame and singed, torched by a wartime explosion?

The morning he left that last time, Monday, January 23, was like many other departures. After he dragged his bag downstairs, we ran through the now-familiar verbal checklist of things he should have packed. At the last minute he grabbed his new video iPod and the noise-eliminating headphones for the plane. I was hurriedly trying to type an e-mail, and I rose to give him a final kiss as he wheeled his bag into our mudroom.

"I don't want to go," he said to me, as he headed for the door. "I don't want to leave you guys again. This has been one hell of a month." His travel schedule had been exhausting, filled with trips to Iran, California, and Texas. He'd had a full weekend of promotional shoots and then interviews relating to his new position as *World News Tonight* co-anchor.

"It's almost over, babe," I said soothingly, frankly more interested in getting my memo out on e-mail and hitting the yoga class that was starting in thirty minutes. "And in February we'll have weekends back again at least, and the family vacation to Esperanza, in Mexico, will be coming up. It will all be good. You just have to make it through this month." I kissed him one last time and he walked out the door. Just like that.

Lee

Bethesda Naval Hospital, March 9, 2006

Driving to the hospital on the morning of the third day after Bob's awakening, my cell rang. It was an unfamiliar area code, and out of curiosity and given the early hour, I answered it.

"Hi, there," said a man's voice.

"Hi," I said, tentatively. My new life had made me wary of almost everyone. "Who is this?"

"It's Bob." He sounded ticked off that I hadn't recognized his voice.

"Oh, sweetie!" I said, with a mix of incredulity and relief. "I—uh, I just didn't expect *you* to call *me*. It's been so long since I picked up the phone and it was you."

"Well, I hope I'm not bothering you," he said, annoyed, completely missing the importance of the moment. "Where are you? When are you coming?"

"I'm on my way," I told him. "I'll be there in four minutes."

"Well, I was just looking for the . . . well, I'm trying to cut . . ." and then he trailed off, unable to think of the word. The amazing thing was that I knew he was looking for nail clippers. I could understand how his mind was working as he sputtered out words that sounded roughly like *toe, walk,* and *foot.*

"Are you looking for the nail clippers?" I asked patiently, in a shockingly mommy-ish voice. I could see this new job was going to require a different kind of patience, as had pushing Nora's hearing aids back in her ears, over and over again, when she was first diagnosed with hearing loss. His need was sobering.

"Yes," he said, relieved. "Nob . . . shooters. Where are they?"

When I walked into the hospital a few minutes later, the doctors told me Bob was running laps around the hall. "What?" I said. I looked up and there was Bob, in his goofy white plastic climbing helmet and with a nurse by his side, slowly jogging and simulating lacrosse moves, unaided, down the long corridor. When he finally saw me he immediately stopped and stood, showing off, and put one foot on the inside of his other leg with his palms touching in front of his face, balancing in a yoga-tree pose.

"Hey," I said slowly, already hating the white plastic helmet that we would be living with, possibly for months, until they replaced the skull bone.

"Sweetie!" he said, and he put his arms out and began to run toward me in his too-short T-shirt and cutoff hospital pants like a man with a new lease on life in one of those horrible erectile dysfunction ads. The entire nursing floor and the doctors doing rounds all laughed as we hugged in an over-exaggerated B-movie clinch.

"Let's take it in the bedroom," I joked, to our makeshift audience.

With every brain injury there is always payback for the great days and the surges of energy where the patient pushes it. Especially early on, one day of feeling great and the resulting frenetic activity means the next day will probably feel like a setback.

So it was for Bob the following morning. He was tired and nauseated, but miraculously his speech continued to return. During one of his first cognitive tests, the reality of what Bob had lost was driven home to me. The neurologist held up cards with pictures of objects, and as I watched I realized that Bob could not come up with the words for *bird* or *tree*. For *broom,* for example, he would say, "It sweeps stuff on the floor." But despite the elementary nature of the tests, the neurologist, Dr. Degraba, was obviously pleased.

He asked Bob to copy two intersecting pentagons, and Bob did this almost perfectly. Then he scribbled something inside each of the pentagons. One held the word *love,* and in the other pentagon he'd written *tempest.* Dr. Degraba studied Bob's scribble for a bit and seemed to dismiss it. "I'm not sure what this is all about," he said, showing me the words when he reviewed Bob's results.

I knew instantly. Those pentagons represented the two halves of his brain. One contained the love he felt for his family and the gratitude he had for being alive; the other side was the tempest, the horrible raging fear and disorientation that lived in his brain right now, as he tried to make sense of his new world.

"It would have been better for you if I had died," he said to me, later that day. "I am so sorry." I tried hard to buoy his spirits. Bob was keenly aware of his deficits, an uncommon quality in most newly brain-injured patients. Like so many things about Bob, his self-awareness was remarkably intact. Most of the time his sense of humor was in evidence, but I knew he was using it like a mask. When that mask slipped, on those rare occasions where he was sad or just plain exhausted, he would allow himself to feel the fear and terror of what had happened to him and what he did not remember.

Dr. M read me the results of Bob's first baseline neurological test. She explained it was a snapshot of the major areas of the brain, looking for deficits and strength. "Patient is functioning at the impaired range across all domains of cognitive functioning," the March 8 report read. Bob's scores showed that 99.9 percent of all males his age did better in immediate memory, delayed memory, visual and spatial skills, language, and attention span. Although she explained that Bob would make improvements and his next test would probably show positive changes, I felt again a sense of despair at the inchworm pace at which this journey would inevitably be made.

Mike and Jim were on overlapping visits to Bethesda, Jimmy having flown in from Lake Tahoe, where he lived, on an early spring day. The brothers took Bob outside for his first outdoor walk. Dr. Degraba had decided to walk behind them and listen to Bob's speech as he talked to his brothers. As they all got in the elevator together, no one remembered to push the button, and it was Bob who reached over with his toe and hit the button for L. The other men were stunned. This kind of awareness wasn't supposed to happen so soon to someone who had been asleep, like Rip Van Winkle, for thirty-six days.

Outside, in the warm first sunlight of spring, Bob turned to Jimmy and casually asked, "So, Jim, would you choose the 415 or the 971?" We were all used to Bob's substituting words here and there or saying something that didn't always make total sense and tried hard not to laugh at those moments, so Jimmy played along. We took heart in the fact that you could see things improving a little every day.

"I'd choose the 415," said Jim, in a dead-serious voice.

"Really?" said Bob. "'Cause now I know you guys are lying to me and telling me what I want to hear."

"Why?" countered Jim warily.

"Because what I just said doesn't make any sense," said Bob. They all burst out laughing. Dr. Degraba rolled his eyes, as though he couldn't believe Bob had just done that. But Bob was constantly accusing us of hiding information or talking to the doctors behind his back.

With Bob awake and so present, it was time to make the final decision about his next step. I had realized that we could not live apart as a family any longer. We would put our lives back together in our own home and find the best place for Bob in the New York area.

Lee

Westchester County, New York, March 11, 2006

Back home in New York to tour prospective rehab facilities, I was exhausted just walking into my house, thinking about all the big and little needs that would assail me from every angle. I had a few minutes before the kids came home from school to listen to my phone messages, and there were two from one of Mack's track coaches. He had already left a message a week or so earlier, admonishing us for not returning the used school track uniform. Mack and I had discussed it, and I'd assumed it had been taken care of by now. In a neutral but scolding voice, his second of two new messages reported that Mack's track uniform was now two months overdue.

Something about this kind of attention to detail, this man's relentless mission to get one smelly T-shirt and a pair of used black nylon warm-up pants back in his supply closet, infuriated me. In that moment, Mack's track coach became the perfect outlet for my own anger and rage at what had become of our family. The old me would have had that uniform washed and returned long before the coach's deadline. The new me didn't even know track season was over.

Seething with anger, pent up from weeks of being a "good girl" for everyone around me, including the extended family, I let it rip. I called his school extension (I'd have called his home at 3 A.M. if I'd had the number) and left him a long, angry, but fairly controlled message.

"I'm going to assume you don't have any idea what has happened to this family," I stormed. "My husband was blown up six weeks ago by a bomb in Iraq, and I have left my life lying right here in this house. I haven't been much of a mother or anything else in the past few weeks. I sent your mangy track uniform to school in Mack's backpack when I was home two weeks ago, and he told me it is in his locker. You can imagine he too might have had one or two things on his mind while his father lay in a coma for thirty-six days. Do me a favor, coach. Please find him and get it back." After I hung up I felt somehow vindicated and oh, so much better.

People's reactions to someone else's tragedy are wonderful, comforting, perplexing, invasive, smothering, appropriate, and sometimes astounding. In so many cases, I had already witnessed how people responded immediately to their own needs, to their own grief and their need to process it. Sometimes people simply react first, not necessarily in a bad way, but in a way that people do when it is hard to see outside their own pain and fear to exactly what the griever may need.

Aside from the amazing gifts of dinners and food and trips to Costco and the flowers our church planted in the yard, I determined during my visit home from Bethesda that I mostly needed to be left alone. At least initially, I wanted to attempt reentry into the atmosphere of my town at my own pace. I did not feel strong enough to bear witness to an outpouring of grief and sympathy regarding our family. My world had shrunk so vastly that I wondered if I would be able to return to any semblance of my former life.

Every long-winded well-meaning expression of sympathy was a giant highlighting marker over the fact that I was different. Our family's misfortune now set us apart. More than anything I wanted people to treat me like the old Lee. I wanted to laugh, to pick up conversations where we'd left them before January 29. I wanted people to see me without well-intentioned sympathy and queries about the kids, without their kind offers to help. I longed for friends to tell me about *their* days, their little normal struggles with elderly parents or kids who needed glasses. I longed for the mundane world of carpooling, soccer practices, and dentist appointments. I wanted people I knew to acknowledge my pain and then move on, with the speed of a wedding receiving line. I wanted, more than anything, to be one of them again.

In the midst of a weekend of rehab tours and away soccer games, as I lamely tried to help Cath with her math homework, it dawned on me that I would soon be living at home again while Bob was an inpatient at the rehab facility. How would I fill in the gaps? I wondered, not just in parenting but in all the areas where Bob was so helpful. I could barely even reduce fractions for Cathryn; that was the point at which we had always called Dad. Who would pay the bills, keep track of when insurance premiums were due, or make college fund contributions? Without my partner what would life look like? Everything would rest on my shoulders, but for how long?

I had morphed from a confident wife and parent into a woman fearful of everything, especially of my kids getting hurt: slippery sock feet on the hardwood stairs, biking with no helmets. I saw potential head injuries everywhere. Even driving my car felt scary now. All I ever seemed to say as a mother was, "Don't do that, stop it, be careful there." I had become a coiled spring, waiting for the next injury or accident.

After looking at many wonderful options, we chose New York's Columbia-Presbyterian Medical Center for the inpatient phase of Bob's rehab. It had the privacy we needed and the doctors and rehab staff seemed warm and caring, as they had in every place we visited. Bob would have a room overlooking the Hudson River; I knew it was important for him to see the sky and have some space. Because of his sloping head and helmet and his visibility, he would be trapped on that one floor for however many weeks it took for him to get to the stage when he could move home. They had estimated this phase might last six to eight weeks, and I knew my husband was going to feel like a caged animal. As the zookeeper, I would have a new set of worries.

Before we left Bethesda on March 16, Bob said goodbye to the staff, promising to return, walk back down the halls in the months to come, and say hi to everyone. Bob's parents left for their home in Detroit that day, after a five-week vigil with their son. I was extremely proud of them, and I was grateful. They had been there every single day, sticking it out through the lowest moments and never losing their sense of humor. We had lived next to one another for five weeks in the hotel, sharing meals and sorrow, hashing over the day's events and the tedium of running laundry in the hotel machines. We had seen sides of one another, revealed in crisis, that we might never otherwise have known. We had seen one another at our lowest moments, stripped of the veneer so many in-laws wear, but in the end we had all pulled together, like pioneers in a wagon train on the plains. My in-laws were wonderfully solid and loving people, dedicated to their family. Frannie and "Big" Bob had truly raised some amazing boys.

Security would be a concern in New York. We learned there were possibly two photographer bounties out for a picture of Bob. Certainly a photo of the anchor, frail, with half a skull, and in a climbing helmet, would make good tabloid fodder. The security team advised us to check him into the hospital under an assumed name.

As I sat filling out reams of discharge paperwork, the social worker came in to ask me what Bob's alias would be. Bob's brother Dave and I realized at that moment that we could have a real field day at Bob's expense. We kicked around some funny names, some to do with Michigan, some inside jokes, some nondescript options, some that sounded more like porn stars, but in the end we settled on Steel, John Steel. There seemed no more fitting name. My husband truly was the "man of steel."

Settling into the new hospital was disorienting for both John Steel and me. There were mostly older people in wheelchairs, with a smattering of younger people who looked like they had been victims of car or sports accidents. The doctors we met were all new, and it felt in some ways like starting over again, to build trust in a whole new team.

Tucked among the vast skyscrapers of Manhattan, as the sun set brilliantly over the river, Bob's new hospital room felt lonely and isolated, like a beautiful prison.

Lee

Westchester County, New York, March 19, 2006

Bob was in capable new hands at the rehab facility in New York City, and he was now only a forty-minute car ride from our home. We had made the transition. Another change, one of so many. My body was letting down. By day two of our homecoming I felt utterly and completely exhausted. My inner General had retreated. Scratch that. My

inner General had completely abandoned me. I needed to crawl somewhere quiet for an overnight. Anywhere. I needed to sleep, to recharge,
but it seemed impossible.

My first punishment for having abandoned hearth and home to care
for Bob came from the twins, Claire in particular, who knew just where
to plunge the needle.

"How come you don't like to play with us anymore?"

"Well, honey," I began in my measured kindergarten-teacher tone
(which belied the fact that I wanted to kick them all downstairs and lock
the basement door), "it's been really hard for Mommy too. I haven't
been here."

"You used to be fun in our old life, and now it's not fun anymore.
You're on the phone all the time, making calls, and you don't *ever* play
with us."

And so it continued in our household. Chaos masquerading as normalcy. Everyone needed me seemingly at the same time. Mike was with
us, staying for a month or so to help care for Bob and fill in at least some
of the gaps as the man of the house. Jimmy, the youngest, would rotate
in for a few weeks after he left. I was so grateful. Without their steady
presence I would have felt desperate. Mike woke in the mornings with
me and helped with the daily routine, waking the children three times
before their feet hit the rug, packing lunches, and driving kids to school.

Mack had retreated from me silently. Cathryn was moody and glum.
She just wanted her father back and she asked me over and over if he
would be the same. Would life be normal again? Nora was clingy and
nervous. Claire seemed to speak in a high-pitched whine. Once I overre-
acted, pushing her into her room and slamming the door, all my nerves
jangling. I didn't want my kids to feel as if they were being punished for
their father's injury, but I could touch my breaking point as clearly as a
knot on a rope.

Dr. Costantino and Dr. Sen came by to see Bob in his new hospital
room at Columbia-Presbyterian the next morning. They began to talk
to us about the next surgery, the big one. This would be the cranioplasty
operation to replace Bob's skull, and they had decided on May 19. Bob's
spirits fell. Another nine weeks of living with the hated helmet and with

pain and disorientation. But they had to be sure Bob was well past the risk of any infection from the pieces of dirt and rock shrapnel that had been embedded in his scalp.

At that time the surgeons would do some more work on smoothing the jagged scars on Bob's face. They would try to make his tracheotomy scar look better and remove the many dozens of tiny rocks that still peppered the left side of his face. Although the surgery would take place in New York, Dr. Rocco Armonda from Bethesda Naval would be there as well. Once again, it would be the dream team in the operating room. The presence of these men would make me feel calm and in capable hands.

The army's Walter Reed Hospital had already created a state-of-the-art model of Bob's new acrylic skull plate from high-tech 3-D CT scans. A specially created bone epoxy, developed by Dr. Costantino, would fill in the seams where remaining skull met acrylic. The combination of these two procedures was brand-new. After Bob's "joint venture" surgery, future military cranioplasties at Bethesda Naval Hospital would use this method.

The ophthalmologist in Bethesda, and later in New York, was amazed at how Bob's left eye had been spared. It was another miracle. Small rocks were scattered all around the eye socket and in the upper and lower eyelids, but nothing had hit the eyeball itself, even though he hadn't been wearing blast glasses. Later, Bob would joke that he had his deep-set eyes to thank; they receded so far in his head, the eyeball had been spared.

Now that Bob was awake we could also deal with the issue of his hearing. The audiologist found, amazingly, that he had lost only about twenty decibels. "Most of his hearing is there," the doctor told me. The IED had exploded just feet from Bob in a flash of white light with what must have been the sound of an apocalypse. I remembered first seeing his ear, bloody and mangled, like a piece of pink cauliflower oozing fluid; surely, I'd thought, Bob would be deaf in his left ear at least.

The doctor explained that there was a hole in the tympanic membrane; if it did not heal on its own, he would sew it up during the cranioplasty.

"When I blow my nose," Bob said, "I can feel air coming out of my ear."

"That's normal," the doctor said reassuringly. "When people with this injury smoke cigarettes, the smoke can escape out of the hole too."

"Now that is gross." Bob laughed. "But maybe I can put a cigarette in my trache hole and smoke out of that and then one in my mouth and let smoke come out of my ear."

On a few occasions I spent the night with Bob in Columbia-Presbyterian on a skinny cot, falling asleep holding hands through the bars of his hospital bed. Staring at my husband, all I wanted to do was to hold him the length of my body and touch his face. The miracle of his presence made me suddenly hungry, and I longed to fill myself with him, to make up for those many weeks when I had watched him helplessly trapped within the sedation, wondering if we would ever be intimate again. I couldn't take my eyes off him, my husband who still looked so breakable. Holding his now-slack hand as he snored lightly in the bed next to mine, I felt like a teenage girl with an urgent need to connect.

I remembered all those times as a wife when I'd been *too tired,* when the thought of conjugal duty had felt like just that. I would have bartered years off my life, forgone untold luxuries, traded fingers and toes like coins to steal some of those nights back. We'd squandered all that time together, I thought now in retrospect. It was as though we'd used up precious oxygen in a room we'd never known was airtight.

By the end of March, as Bob was gradually putting things back together, I was sliding into a depression. I had finally hit my wall after eight weeks. Like a boxer in the ring, I had taken it and taken it, absorbed all the blows. I had been in go mode, always moving forward, making decisions, not allowing myself to feel very much. I had cleansed my body of alcohol, soda, coffee, anything that might dull my senses. But I had not allowed myself to grieve and to feel deep down in my nerve endings. And now here I was, the floodgates were crumbling, and I was a mess.

Most days, just getting through until bedtime felt as though I were swimming through Jell-O. Even the kindest word from someone simply asking "How are you?" would send me into a weepy tailspin.

As the bulbs and blossoms of spring were pushing their heads up from the cold ground, my reserves of calm, control, and optimism were disintegrating. I was left dealing with my own trauma, crumpled in a pajama-clad ball at home, oozing black thoughts and hopelessness, whipsawing between faith and anger.

Bob could tell I was sad as I pushed open the door to his room one morning, steeling myself for another day of rehab.

"You've been crying, babe," he said. "What's wrong? Did you get some bad news about me?"

"No, I'm just sad today," I said, smiling weakly. "It's all hitting me. This is all so much."

Bob folded me in his arms the way he always had and held me. There was strength there, a familiar support. A voice inside me began to say this might all be okay in the end. It would all be all right. I looked at his eyes, his deep-set sea-green eyes, the scars on his cheeks where the rocks had shot into his flesh, and the blasted gravel all over his face. I looked at this man, in his goofy white plastic helmet, and saw an amazing person, the man I would love forever. If he made it back only to 35 or 50 or 79 percent, wherever his recovery would ultimately end up, I would accept this Bob Woodruff in any form and take whatever he had to give me.

After just three weeks, Bob had cycled through the inpatient phase of his recovery and was ready to come home. I was terrified. The medications, the constant fear he might fall and hit his head—these concerns had all been in the hands of nurses until this moment. Now Bob was going to be my responsibility. It felt like carrying an egg on a spoon.

Progress was still measured in baby steps, in all those little things we used to take completely for granted. A man in a hospital bed had now been transformed into a dad who could tuck kids in at night, a person who could sit at the dinner table, a husband to give me a good-night hug and kiss. Underneath his fatigue and his pain and his need to lie down in order to gather his energy was a man moving slowly forward. We were placing great weight on May 19, the date when Bob would get his cranioplasty, his "new head" as we called it. That would be the real beginning of rebirth, when he could go outside again, when he would throw away the hated helmet and retake a big chunk of his life as a person.

A few weeks after Bob's homecoming, Mack announced, the night before the event was scheduled to take place, that he had a choral concert. If I'd been a mother on top of her game, I would have seen the flyers, read the e-mails, or heard about it from other moms. Instead I was playing catch-up. "We need to bring a salad for the party after," said Mack offhandedly. I felt a little boost. Buying salad in a bag was a thing I could do these days. It was a small but wonderful realization. I now had the ability to do my share. This felt more like the old me.

Mack scrambled after dinner to find his chorus tuxedo and figure out how to make the bow tie look right. He came downstairs holding the pair of brand-new leather lace-up shoes we had bought him in November for church and special occasions. "They're too small, Mom," he said, throwing me one of those looks that assumed I could fix everything.

"I'm sorry, honey, your feet have really grown. Maybe a pair of Dad's shoes might fit." Mack came down the stairs a few minutes later, carrying an older pair of Bob's dress shoes. They looked a bit big but we were out of options; his ride was in the driveway. I didn't see him again until he walked up the auditorium steps to take the stage.

One of the last ones in line, Mack had that self-conscious shuffle of generations of teens before him, head bowed, wishing it could all be over quickly so he could take off his uncomfortable polyester tuxedo. But it was his shoes that broke my heart. His father's shoes. As I stared down at Mack's feet I could see that they were way too big, probably at least three sizes too big, just shy of circus clown shoes. He seemed to be taking extra effort not to have them flop as he clomped up carefully on the wooden steps. Here was my boy, on the cusp of manhood, literally trying fill his father's shoes.

Each day I got through seemed a monumental triumph. There were days I wanted to rejoice, days I wanted to let someone else crawl into my skin and hold up my bones, days I could take a deep breath, and days I wanted to stay in bed and turn back the clock. There were—and still are—days I worry intensely about what this experience will mean for my children and how they will absorb it into their own lives and outlooks. There were nights when the sight of them asleep in their beds broke my heart. On other days I tried to focus on the tiny pleasures life offers—a tall hot latte with extra foam, the smell of my twins' hair after a bath, a good report card for my son, the amazingly horrible way I got to learn how many people loved us.

As I lay in bed, it was hard to feel any kind of ballast in my life. I didn't know if I'd ever have my man back again. I knew it would never be quite the same. "Say goodbye to the old Bob," Dr. Mary Hibbard, his neuropsychologist at Mt. Sinai, had said when we first met with her in late April at the outpatient rehab hospital. "Meet the new Bob." I knew the new Bob wasn't supposed to be better or worse, just different.

Bob

Columbia-Presbyterian Medical Center, New York, March 2006

Although I was still in pain and would often have to lean against walls and door frames for balance, there was a definite shift in my abilities.

The biggest difference was that the constant pain was receding. In the beginning, at Bethesda, I had been able to sleep for only an hour or two at a time. Part of that was the initial excitement of being alive. I was thinking about so many things. But much of my discomfort was due to the ongoing pain in my head and back. It was hard to focus.

Although I was often hard on myself and on the slow pace of my progress, I could see small changes. More words were coming, though I tired so easily it felt like failure sometimes.

I had occupational, physical, speech, and recreational therapy almost every day, and by dinner I found myself exhausted. Often I would have to nap to get through the day.

Initially, Lee had accompanied me to some of my sessions, but increasingly I didn't want her to see the plain truth of how little I could do. I was missing so many words. While I was learning to get around this in conversation, or rely on others to fill in the blanks, there was no going around things in therapy. As much as I loved and respected my therapists, they were not there to give me a break. It was their job to help me put it all back together, to teach me coping skills for my deficits. In the early days, the grueling nature of these sessions was like a cold shower. The therapists kept telling me that all the words were in my head somewhere; it was a matter of building the new neural connections that led to them. Much of it was time. The brain takes longer to heal than any other organ.

Once, in therapy, we were reviewing the names of fruits and vegetables and my therapist was holding up plastic replicas, similar to the ones my twins used when they played house. I could say *apple* and *banana,* but names like *broccoli* and *asparagus* eluded me. Even *potato* floated around in my head, unable to crystallize. The connections had failed.

I watched Lee's face once while I was fumbling for the word *lettuce* in the therapy room. She looked scared and very small. She was exhausted and she had lost too much weight. Her broad swimmer's shoulders hunched forward. I remember feeling how much I wanted to make this all right with her. Just then, I wanted so badly to come up with the word *lettuce* and I couldn't. I was using every bit of energy I had to get through my own days. Just one day on the rehab floor in the hospital felt like a whole week in what had been my former life.

Lee

Westchester County, New York, April 2006

It was another Saturday of schedules: soccer games and birthday parties and craziness. Though there was a familiar and welcome rhythm in our house, something was not quite right. Life appeared fairly normal on the outside, and only I really seemed to see the big holes in our family's infrastructure. The delicate balance of four children, household duties, and an injured husband was wobbling badly.

Scrambling that day for soccer cleats and water bottles, I looked down at us and saw a family that was messy but whole. I saw dynamics that were in place. I saw a woman who was trying to be strong while she dealt with many layers—layers of grief and loss for what had been, layers of caretaking and layers of fear and unease and, more than anything else, the absence of any central vision of what our lives might look like going forward. Fear had a taste, I noticed. It was metallic.

Lee

St. Luke's-Roosevelt Hospital Center, New York, May 19, 2006

After so many agonizing days, hour after hour of waiting and worrying, of watching Bob weak and in pain, the date for the cranioplasty surgery had finally arrived. Bob was nervous. This was the first surgery that he would be aware of after his injuries, and the thought of someone carving his head like a pumpkin made him incredibly anxious.

More than four hours later, the surgery was a success. Dr. Costantino and Dr. Armonda had shaved the acrylic skull plate a little to make it more symmetrical and then molded the soft hydroxyapatite cement into the edges. It would fuse to the bone like real bone, filling in the ridges around the skull plate. It had taken a few tries to render it the way they wanted, but like a pair of Renaissance sculptors they were pleased with the symmetry that resulted. In the recovery room, Bob's head was covered in bandages with a drain coming out, to collect the liquid draining off his scalp.

After almost four months, Bob finally had a rounded head again. There would be one more operation later to fill in the left temple where the muscle was shattered and then reattached, but the doctors needed to wait to make sure he was past the risk of infection. Some of the black spots we had thought were rock turned out to be dirt, blasted into the skin around his cheek, nose, and eyes. It would be impossible to take these spots out surgically and they might never rise to the surface to expel themselves. This was of no concern to Bob. He refused any future surgeries just for aesthetics. "I've earned these scars," he would joke.

After the anesthesia wore off, when Bob was more fully awake, he couldn't seem to keep his hands off of his new head, touching it the way people fondle melons and cabbages in the grocery store. There was an expression of wonder on his face that I found extremely satisfying. And in the days and weeks that followed, little by little, bit by bit, his words and fluidity of speech kept coming back.

In the meantime, there were all kinds of family jokes we made about Bob's speech, and Bob could always laugh at himself. He'd say *I can't read* when he meant he couldn't sleep. The word *deodorant* eluded him, no matter how hard his brother Jimmy quizzed him. And then there were the absolutely nonsensical mix-ups, much like the early days after he woke up and would simply manufacture new words. He commanded the twins to put on their *sleep puffers* instead of pajamas, offered Cathryn and her friend Caitlin some *cuddles* instead of cookies. A *swipe* was a beach towel, and he mentioned that the *skiing* was great at the U.S. Open tennis tournament. But those were little things. His tone and cadence and inflection were all returning.

In the beginning, when he first woke up, Bob mixed up units of measurement, using dollars instead of percentages or talking about twenty acres of gas instead of gallons. "I feel a hundred thousand dollars better," he would say. My all-time favorites were when the Verizon man became the Viagra man and when Bob saw a woman friend who, he thought, had gotten some chest enhancement. "I think she had a breast explosion," said Bob in all seriousness. It really was a much more apt description when you thought about it.

Bob

Westchester County, New York, May 27, 2006

It was the heart of Memorial Day weekend, and the drain and tight bandages had just come off. I'd had a rough recovery from the surgery and there was a great deal of fluid building up under my scalp, which was uncomfortable and scared me. I hated the dreaded bandages; it took all the self-restraint that I had not to claw them off at night. Dr. Costantino explained that they were wound so tightly around my head to counter the fluid buildup from the operation. But it felt like a cruel turban, and I was tired of the pain.

Day by day, week by week, I crawled out of this phase of recovery and began to feel better. With my new head and no more helmet, I felt like a man let out of prison. I'd had daydreams of crushing the helmet with my car or smashing it with a hammer, but once the surgery was over I didn't feel any anger or need for release. The helmet ended up in the basement as what I hoped would be a relic of this time in our lives.

Mostly I felt overwhelming relief that it had all gone so well. The new skull plate meant an instant stabilizing of the fluctuating pressure in my head. I no longer felt as if I were going to pass out every time I stood up. There was stability now; my brain was back in its house, as the doctors explained. I was looking forward to a surge of progress.

When the discomfort from the operation itself began to lift, I was like a kid on the last day of school before summer. I went to soccer games and movies and out to dinner with my family. I still experienced fatigue, but I began to feel better and stronger each day.

On Monday, Memorial Day, May 29, four months to the day from when the roadside bomb blasted into our convoy, the phone rang. Jimmy walked upstairs and handed it to me. It was Vinnie, and he had some news that he wanted to tell me personally.

A car bomb had exploded at a military checkpoint in Baghdad as a CBS News crew was getting out of their vehicle. Reporter Kimberly Dozier had been critically wounded, and cameraman Paul Douglas and soundman James Brolan were dead, killed instantly by the bomb. James and I had been embedded with the Marines Special Forces Light Armored Division in Iraq during the 2003 invasion. He and I had spent countless hours together, humoring each other, surviving the sandstorms and boredom as well as the surges of adrenaline. His traveling Scrabble board and sense of humor were legendary.

"Oh, God." I sat on the edge of the bed and wept, my face in my hands. "No. Not again. Not James." Jimmy and Lee glanced quickly at each other, worried, no doubt, about how this news might affect me. Post-traumatic stress disorder was an obvious concern; certainly news of this kind could stimulate such stress. We were devastated for all of the families. Kimberly Dozier was clinging to life; in fact, she had been medevaced to the very same hospital in Balad where Doug and I had been taken four months earlier.

My stomach turned over as I imagined another family at the starting line of our same hideous journey. But my heart broke for the families of James and Paul. I knew they had kids and wives. I knew they must be experiencing the pain of grappling with a finality that my family and I could only begin to comprehend. While I knew I had put everyone around me through hell, I had at least had the good fortune that spared them the ultimate loss.

Lee

Lake George, New York, Summer 2006

Spring slipped into summer and we planned to head up to the Adirondack Mountains for two months. We were ready to unplug from the world. I needn't have worried about anything, about easing back into a small summer community where everyone would see us and ask the same questions. Heading into the arms of our little life at Silver Bay, where our children were the fifth generation on my family's side to spend summers, was like slipping into the cool lake waters off the dock. It was as natural as my daily swim to the point, and we were embraced—tentatively at first, then respectfully, and then openly—by people who had known me since I was a little girl.

I was healing too. A routine ob-gyn checkup in May had revealed the reason for some of the discomfort I had been feeling in my abdomen. A nine-centimeter fibroid, the size of an apple, had somehow sprung out of nowhere over the course of the year. I could read the concern on the doctors' faces. There was an almost fifty-fifty chance it was cancerous, a statistic I did not want to share with Bob or many others at the time. My doctor, Dr. John Quagliarello, and the oncologist, Dr. John Curtin, were baffled at how quickly this fibroid had grown, but I wasn't. Inside that mass lurked all the stress, fear, and grief I had been stuffing down for the past four months.

It was a grueling surgery with a slow and painful recovery, and when I woke in mid-June from the anesthesia to learn it was benign I understood for the first time what it truly felt like to shed tears in utter relief.

Mercifully, God had chosen to spare us again. My gratitude felt insufficient.

My need to heal gave Bob the chance to rise to the occasion and care for me. He made me sleep, snuggled me, and held me tightly as I cried tears of helplessness, high on multiple medications. He soothed all my erratic emotions and painted a picture of our family's future with his words. Together we reveled in what I called his glorious payback.

The summer of 2006 in the northern mountains of New York State behaved about as perfectly as any summer could. The skies were blue for weeks at a stretch, and when it did rain, it was often at night, a gentle tapping pattern on the tin roof and gutters. The occasional rainy day felt just special enough to drive everyone inside for a change, to bake cookies or play a board game. Once, I had a watercolor day with my daughters and nieces, painting a flower arrangement.

Most nights were cool enough to use a down blanket, and the moon rose waxy and fat over the mountains, shimmering on the bay below like a million little fingernails. Bats swooped in the night; by day I planted flowers and watched them grow. We three sisters picked vegetables in Nancy's garden. Nora finally learned to swim, and there were campfires with s'mores and the big nodding heads of colorful dahlias growing in my kitchen garden. And for me, who anticipated finding my zen at the local berry patch each year, it was, for the first time in my memory, an endless summer of berries and jam making. We picked succulent strawberries well into July and dusky fat blueberries for a month later. Even the fall raspberries came in well before Labor Day. In the late days of August and early September, the monarch butterflies paused before migration to warm their wings on the sun-drenched dirt roads by the lake, rising like fall leaves as we approached. It was almost as if God and Mother Nature were conspiring to show me that they could produce the perfect summer. It was a gift of healing for our entire family.

My parents, who lived a few houses away in the Adirondacks, were with us all summer, and finally I was able to spend some uninterrupted time with them. They had recently moved from California to Boston, and I'd been unable to help in the wake of Bob's injury, leaving my two sisters to be their dutiful and devoted daughters.

It was my parents who had given me the greatest gift during this time by expecting absolutely nothing of me as a daughter. Among other things, they had respected my wishes that they not come to Bethesda during such a time of crisis. It must have taken an extreme act of sacrifice to have hung so far back, with only an occasional phone call from me. They had gotten their information mostly from my sisters, helping to pass news along to a chain of relatives and friends. Keeping my mother and father at arm's length had felt sad and unnatural on some level, but my parents had understood that the last thing they wanted was to be one more demand on me. They had done what I'd asked and subverted their own instinct to care for me. Now, in the throes of summer, they could grandparent with abandon, taking the twins for "school" in the boathouse with Grandma or for ice cream and rides to camp with Grandpa.

On Labor Day weekend, looking around a campfire on the beach at my children's contented faces, I reflected on the fact that they had all made journeys of their own. Mack was cheerful between teenage monosyllables and hours spent in his room blasting music. His dad would be able to attend most of his soccer games in the opening season that fall. Cathryn was back to smiling again and was no longer listening around every corner. The searching look of concern that had crossed her face constantly in the spring was gone. The twins were growing and assuming their own personalities. It will be many years before we can assess what they really know or remember about the horrors of 2006. Thankfully, they had been the most insulated, the most blissfully unaware of the gravity of the situation, and in some ways they had seemed the most resilient, taking their father's mere presence back home as a sign of normalcy. People got sick; people got better. Exploring the gray areas in between would come as they got older. For now I wanted them to remain happy first-graders, longing for a puppy and content to ride bikes and color pictures on the family room coffee table.

We've had more than our share of happy times, wonderful times, laughter to fill buckets and joy enough to burst a human heart. When I really think about it, life is not so unlike the evening news. It's nice to end the story with a happy kicker, a piece that makes us all feel good inside, like the boy who beat leukemia or the baby panda who survived. But the moments that define us, that strip us down to raw bone and cartilage and build us back up: they are the tough ones. They are the stories of grief or tragedy, stories tinged with sadness and sorrow. They are the leads on the nightly news, the ones that grab our attention and glue us to the screen. I believe how we attack those curve balls is the stuff of life; they count just as much as the good times. Perhaps there are lessons here, lessons for others who will inevitably hit the gritty pavement of life, often when they least expect it.

"Please, God, don't let anything happen to my children." Bob offered up this simple prayer one September night in bed, as we have uttered it since the miracle of parenthood happened to us. It is a parent's deepest desire to be the human shield, the lightning rod, the four-leaf clover, and the lucky rabbit's foot. "Let me absorb all the pain for them," he says again, with an unwavering gaze at me. But we both know it doesn't work that way.

You can't make deals, barter, or trade to spare one another. You can only do your damnedest to try to fathom the power and simple beauty of "for better or worse." You can hold faith and hope in equal measures in your heart, and in the end you can teach yourself how best to endure and then to survive and overcome. There is a Chinese saying that compares the human spirit's capacity to bear the weight of hardship to a simple bamboo stalk. It can carry a far greater burden than the naked eye can see.

And so we have to choose to laugh and to keep smiling. We have to hope that there is always something better around the corner. We doubt our ability to rise to meet hardship, and we do everything in our power to avoid it. We have to dig down, to believe unfailingly in the ability of the human spirit to triumph in ways we didn't think possible. To make the choice to be resilient, ultimately to bounce back, is to make the choice to be grateful, as grateful as possible for the cards you've been dealt. As we continue our journey of healing as a family, I look to Bob for inspiration. I look at the man I chose to walk through this world with, and I feel only love. Love and unending hope.

"I love you so much," Bob says to me, as he has always said, through all the years of our marriage, through all the amazing moments and the incredibly hard ones too. "I can't believe I got you as my wife," he says, and I know that there is no response required. None expected. When I look in his eyes all the lights are on, he is so very much Bob again. He is that same boy I first saw in college bouncing on his toes, an armload of books under his wing, ready for any adventure, curious about it all. His life was spared, and I know there must be a reason why. His work is unfinished in so many ways. He is a miracle man, my lucky man. And when he takes me in his arms to hold me, I can once again let him be the strong one.

"You healed me," he says to me lovingly. "And I will always love you for that."

"We healed one another," I answer. "All of us. And now we are home."

Afterword

Lee

December 2006

While a year has a beginning and end, our story still continues. Grieving a living person and then learning to hope again is not clean.

Advances are measured in tiny increments, too small, on some days, for the naked eye to see. But there are moments that I use to mark the progress. There was the day Bob casually used the word *unsettling* in a sentence. A small thing, perhaps, but I heard it, a more complex word tossed into the conversation. My spirits rose.

And as much as I hated the elementary analogy the doctors offered us, comparing this long journey to a roller coaster, I have to admit they were right. I can glide for long periods of time feeling normal and then something will happen, some little setback, and my spirits will plummet again. Gradually, I feel those dips and drops evening out.

As Bob grew stronger physically, I began to abdicate certain responsibilities. The first time he carried a wallet again and handled the waiter's tip was a tiny milestone. His first solo plane trip back to see the family in Michigan felt like sending off an unaccompanied minor. Bob was fine; I was the nervous wreck. The first time he drove, alone, down the street to the grocery store felt like turning the keys over to a newly licensed teen. I'm not sure I really exhaled until he returned with the milk twenty minutes later.

Little by little I absorbed the fact that he really was healing, that all the horrible possibilities that had been enumerated by the doctors in Bethesda had, thankfully, not come to pass. Gradually, inexorably, Bob is making his way back toward "the old Bob" at a pace as slow and painstaking as the injury was sudden and breathtaking. When I watch Bob move and talk now, it is my Bob, maybe a word glitch here and there, a name forgotten, but his expressions, his laugh, his cadence— they have all returned.

In late fall I went back to work for Benefit Cosmetics. Bob is hard at work in cognitive therapy and heading into ABC News most days to work on a documentary about his journey and the similar struggles of so many soldiers in this war. It is an important story to tell and an important part of Bob's journey to reclaim his professional life.

There were moments in the news this past year I ached for Bob: the bombing of Beirut, North Korea announcing they had a nuclear bomb, the midterm elections. My husband itched to get back into the fray. But he has made a deal with himself. He will not go back until he feels ready. He wants to be comfortable with his words and his abilities.

Bob's indomitable spirit makes it impossible to feel sorry for myself. Living with Bob is an inspiration. I have never once heard him say a bitter word or feel ripped off or cheated. A few months after he woke up, he turned to me and said simply, "It's not the end of the world if I don't get enough words back to be a reporter. I can do lots of things. There are many jobs that would make me happy." I love him for that outlook, even if I don't share it every day.

While I fully understand that the anchor chair couldn't wait for Bob's long recovery, I would be lying if I said it didn't hurt a little bit to turn on the evening news and not see my husband there. I am, after all, only human.

But if I move too far from the light, I remember to thank God for where we are today. Bob has been spared the blackness and the mental trauma that so many endure on their journeys with brain injury. For that I am eternally grateful.

Bob and I visited Bethesda Naval Hospital together for the first time in early November. It was a powerful day. I showed Bob the room where he lay sedated for almost five weeks, and he met many of the ICU staff, of whom he has no memory. We visited other soldiers with traumatic brain injury and their wives and families. Bob was a true inspiration to them, and we vowed to use our experiences to help others in similar situations.

And everywhere we went, people supported Bob and surrounded him with gratitude.

I believe there are many tools on the road to recovery—family above all, exercise, music, and even the reassurance of touch. But they are mere handmaidens to the healing powers of hope and faith. There is no question in my mind that prayer, faith, and spirituality offered up on Bob's behalf contributed mightily to his healing.

The pictures of our family and of Bob on bulletin boards in churches, synagogues, and mosques, YMCAs and community centers; the prayer lists and mass cards; the chants uttered, the candles lit, the prayer shawls knitted, the little angels sent, the rosaries, the healing stones: I believe all that collective faith helped Bob fight. When he lay, for a second time, precariously close to death with pneumonia and sepsis, those prayers formed a force field around his soul. They were the line of first defense, his body armor. You all brought him back to us.

At the same time, there was something else at work. There was hope pushing in from the margins. Maybe our family was messy at the edges that spring, but we were intact at the core. The center was holding, some days better than others, but it held. It isn't tragedy that can break families apart. It is how they respond to it. I could only hope we were responding in the right way.

And so we all keep healing. We keep putting the miles between ourselves and the IED that hit us all on January 29, 2006. Conventional medical wisdom has always held that after two years the brain with a traumatic injury is done healing. But they aren't so sure now. Bob's doctors tell us that the war in Iraq is rewriting the book on what we know about head injuries, blast injuries, and the brain's amazing ability to repair and recover. There is growing evidence that the brain continues healing years after an injury. The learning and growth that we all do throughout our lives can only fuel that regeneration. I believe in the interconnection between the resiliency of the human body and the human spirit. I see it at work every day.

Afterword

Bob

December 2006

Since the explosion that ripped through our lives on January 29, 2006, my family and I have experienced many powerful changes. We've all endured a crisis. And we've survived to feel the miraculous force of recovery at work.

What I do know is that I have been blessed. I have been very, very lucky—more lucky than so many doctors, nurses, military personnel, and my own family really believed I would be. The exact extent of my injuries is still difficult to measure, but I see improvements every day. With the help of intense cognitive rehabilitation, the healing powers of the human body, and the profound support of friends and family, I have come closer to my old self, little by little. But I will never be the same.

No one can undergo a life-changing event and be the exact person they were before it happened. I am a more grateful person now, on so many levels. I truly appreciate the depth of friendships and I'm thankful to have had this time to be more of a presence in my children's lives.

I've also had to relearn how to do certain things I once took for granted. A big part of recovering from a brain injury is to adopt different ways of doing the same thing—"coping strategies" to attack the same problem in a new way. I write down far more things than I used to,

I'm better at keeping a schedule, and I'm learning my limits when it comes to fatigue.

After I woke up from my comalike state, I would search for a word or memory, and it would evaporate before me. When I tried to read, I could barely keep a sentence in my head. By the time I got to the fifth word, I couldn't remember the first three. Now I am able to read faster, write better, remember and process information more quickly than I could have imagined in March.

As I began to think more clearly, I understood that my brain worked in slightly different ways. The only way I can describe this process is like seeing the top of a mountain from a path but without the ability to find the way up. I can still see the top, but I've forgotten the exact way. I may not always remember precisely where the path is but by taking one step at a time, little by little, I realize I can still get there, even if I sometimes take a slightly different route. I find the word, locate the answer, and formulate the question as my brain heals, rewires, and reconnects.

My vision and hearing were affected in the blast. It's much harder for me to hear conversations when there is background noise—at a restaurant, for example, or in a crowded room. And the blast, or the fall afterward, damaged a nerve that has left me with a black pie-shaped wedge in my field of vision. I can no longer see objects in the upper right quadrant of my sight. So again, I've learned to compensate. I move my eyes and head around more to see. I turn the newspaper at an angle to view it all. But I am no longer very effective at the net in tennis and basketball is out. I have no problem driving, but I miss weekend soccer with the old-guy league in my town. Those sports run the risk of potential damage a person with one head injury cannot afford.

But if I begin to feel sorry for myself, there is an image that snaps me right back to attention, and immediately reorganizes my priorities. On October 11, 2006, Lee and I sat in St. Bride's Church of London for the memorial service for CBS News cameraman Paul Douglas and soundman James Brolan, who were killed by an IED in Iraq in May. It was my first overseas flight since the injury and Lee and I came to England to honor the lives of my dear friend James, with whom I had spent so much time in Iraq in 2003, and my colleague Paul, whom I had met a number of times overseas. During their funerals in June, I was too ill to travel. This time, I was determined to be there.

As friends and family spoke eloquently on the gray, misty day, remembering James's passion for Scrabble and his disarming sense of humor, shards of sunlight suddenly filtered through the beautiful stained glass windows of the church, illuminating the families. I watched Gerri Brolan, Linda Douglas, their children and grandchildren. Lee and I were seated directly across from them and could see their grief and pain, raw and open. The little children buried their heads in their mothers' chest and cried. Looking at those two families, I felt gutted, guilty, and confused about why I had been spared. I was here, next to Lee. Those fathers and husbands were gone. "It was not your time," Linda Douglas said to me later that day, to absolve me of my guilt. But why not? I wondered. Why had it been Paul's or James's time? Why had I been spared?

On June 13, 2006, I returned to the ABC newsroom for the first time since my injury, accompanied by Lee, David Westin, and Charlie Gibson. It was just a month after the surgeons had given me a new skull. My hair was still shaved close to my head, my scars visible. I was tentative at first and then I felt the wave of love and good wishes of my colleagues. I was overwhelmed. There were tears and hugs and stories shared of the places we'd been together, the hours logged in the edit room, the time spent gathering news. I'd missed all of these people and it was clear they'd missed me too. It felt like coming home.

I have to say that I have spent very little time looking back at what was lost. I sense that people have wanted to ask me what it feels like to lose the anchor chair, to grab the brass ring and then to have it slip from my grasp. It had been the job I had wanted, and in that short period of time, despite the increased number of work hours and the pressure, I felt excited, purposeful, committed. And then it ended. In an instant.

I know that in any recovery it helps to have a goal. Right now my goal is to return to reporting the kind of news I used to cover every day. It was always my dream to go to the places where the important stories were unfolding, to dig up as much information as possible and present it in such a way that the American public might better understand what is happening in the world, within and beyond our borders.

As I work on my recovery I grow more and more hopeful that I can return to the profession I love. If I can make it back to the newsroom in any position, I will be happy. It was a dream and an honor to anchor *World News Tonight*. I had exactly twenty-seven days in that job. But I say, with all my heart, that there is no better person to sit in that anchor chair than Charlie Gibson. I admire him immensely as a journalist and a friend.

Each day the words come more easily. And each day I feel that I move toward my goal of going back on the air, as close as possible to the way that I used to work and sound. If my brain can keep putting itself back together, and I get to do what I love, I'll be a very contented man.

I've been told that if my injury had happened in an American city or in an earlier war, I would most likely have died or have suffered serious permanent brain damage. Even in America, there are few trauma centers that would do a hemicraniectomy without hesitation; this is attributable to the number of skilled surgeons available to do the procedure, as well as to the fear of litigation in our country.

During the Vietnam War it typically took the wounded about forty-five days to get from the battlefield to a U.S. hospital. Men with blast injuries as severe as mine probably would not have made it home. Now, due to incredible advances in medicine, technology, and battlefield know-how, so many more of the severely wounded are being saved.

The wounds of Doug or myself are easy to identify. But many soldiers' injuries have gone undiagnosed. Men and women who may have just been near a blast are also at risk. The concussive effects are damaging, and in the beginning of the war, these people were sent back to the battlefield—unsure of why they couldn't think straight or why their judgment was off. Many had memory problems or suffered from depression.

As I write, there is no exact count of soldiers with traumatic brain injuries. One estimate states that as many as 10 percent of the roughly 1.5 million soldiers who have served and are serving in Iraq and Afghanistan as of December 2006 may be at risk for a brain injury. But diagnosing the problem is just the beginning. The real work takes place in rehab. Each of these injured soldiers needs professional cognitive rehabilitation to help connect those neurons, to work with any individual deficits, and to develop coping strategies as they heal. There is so much more to be done on this front. This is where the battle rages once our soldiers get back to the United States. Traumatic brain injury will be a tragic and desperate legacy of the Iraq War here at home.

I had a huge advantage through every step of my journey. I had the resources of a major corporation to provide the best help, pay for my skilled medical care, and allow my extended family to always be near. I had loving family and friends surrounding me at all times. Others are not so lucky. Lee has told me stories of soldiers she saw in Bethesda with no regular visitors, their hours logged alone without the powerful balm of love, laughter, and the connective joy of family.

Visiting the Tampa Veterans Administration Hospital in December, where many of the traumatic brain injured are sent, I was speaking with the mother of a young marine. He had been so severely injured by an IED that they had removed 40 percent of his brain. He lay on the bed, unresponsive, mouth wide open, with his quilt from Landstuhl draped over his propped body. As I walked out of his room, I suddenly felt weak. I needed to sit down. The enormousness of my good fortune, my medical outcome, hit me full force. I could so easily have been that soldier. The loving, broken mother standing vigil by his side could so easily have been Lee.

From the time I embedded with the marines during the initial invasion until my fateful trip to Iraq in January 2006, I watched war move from conventional battle to terrorism and insurgency. From the days of rolling across the desert in tanks and APCs engaging in the occasional traditional battle or firefight until the moment the IED exploded just feet from Doug and me, the rules had changed dramatically. For soldiers who have been trained in conventional combat, this new warfare is disorienting and the tactics take an obvious toll on morale.

In the fall, working on a documentary about my journey and the journey of other injured soldiers in this war, I had the chance to return to Bethesda Naval Hospital and talk to doctors and nurses and personally thank them for all that they had done on my behalf. I was so grateful to be able to tell them that myself.

But I also had a chance to meet with other soldiers and some of their family members on the fifth floor of the hospital, and this gave me a better opportunity to understand firsthand the magnitude of the problem. It also helped me to fathom what my own family had gone through during those many weeks when I lay there, comatose and unresponsive.

There is one person above all to whom I really owe my life. I will never understand the full extent of anything that Lee did or endured on my behalf; the depths of her grief and fear, the reserves of energy she had to draw on, the constant love and hope she continually showered on my unresponsive self. I cannot imagine what it must have felt like to stare at my wounds and my partial skull for five weeks while I slept, and to hold my hand, praying that I would wake up and someday recover. When I awoke and saw her face, I loved her even more than before. I had not thought it possible.

She has told me numerous times that it is much harder to be in the waiting room than on the operating table. I understood what she meant in June, waiting for the results of her own abdominal surgery. I felt the passage of every minute, every agonizing second, until the doctors emerged and told us the tumor was benign.

Lee and I have shared so many experiences. We have been tested by life, perhaps more than others we know. But we have lived it as well, full throttle. I could not have chosen a woman more perfect for me and, after eighteen years of marriage, I remain in awe of her.

Writing our story, for Lee, was a way to work out her grief, to make sense of our lives. For me, writing this book was something I could begin only many months after my injury. It was slow and painful. I searched for many words. Lee was a great partner and editor. This process, for me, was in essence a part of my recovery, an exercise for my brain.

In the end, we hope that our story will help—help the soldiers and their families, help anyone with a brain injury, any family or couple or individual who has had to face a tragedy and overcome a crisis. We are no longer those two young people in my mind, running out of the church on our wedding day, our faces open, free of the grief and loss that waits just up the road. But that pain of life, the "grittier surface," as Lee calls it, is really a crucible. It's a hot fire with the power to forge couples and families together. And in this way, I've gained even more than I already had.

———

Because of our journey over the past year with traumatic brain injury (TBI), we felt compelled to make something positive come out of something so negative. Goodness and healing needed to emerge from such a devastating event.

Our immediate and extended family became committed to helping the members of the military who have suffered brain injuries from the widespread use of improvised explosive devices, many of whom are not receiving appropriate cognitive rehabilitation for whatever reason. An overwhelmed Veterans Administration hospital system, lack of funding, and a dearth of professionals trained in TBI in areas outside of larger cities have all meant that the very people who need them most are unable to access services at a critical juncture in their healing.

We established the Bob Woodruff Family Fund for Traumatic Brain Injury, administered by the Brain Injury Association of America, a twenty-five-year-old national organization dedicated to research, information, advocacy, and support for this silent and misunderstood affliction. Brain injury affects an average of 1.4 million Americans a year.

The money we raise will go to various established organizations helping individuals and families who have survived brain injuries as a result of service to their country, as well as their families, who must cope with the overwhelming consequences each and every day. These are the men and women who have sacrificed so much. They carry the scars of a life-changing injury with cognitive and behavioral impairments that are often invisible because so few Americans are aware of TBI. To learn more or to make a donation please go to www.bobwoodrufffamilyfund.org.

Acknowledgments

Writing this section was so much harder than writing our story. The names of everyone who touched our lives and the friends who supported us—and still do—could have filled another book. Fearful that we might inadvertently leave someone out, we have chosen to thank you all globally. You know what you did. There were no small acts of kindness: a meal cooked, a ride for a child, a card, an e-mail, a shared tale of personal trauma. Loyal viewers, friends, and acquaintances from college and law school, at the workplace, in New York, Beijing, San Francisco, Redding, Richmond, Phoenix, Chicago, Washington, D.C., London, and Westchester County—we are fortunate to know so many precious people who are part of our story as we lived it. So many of you generously circled back after Bob's injury to reconnect, share a memory, or cheer us on. Each of these blessings was a step toward recovery for us all.

We owe a huge debt of gratitude to the U.S. military for all they did on Bob's behalf. Their quick action, skilled hands, and loving care are the reasons Bob is with us. You all redefine service to your country every day. We are just one family among thousands who have suffered injuries in this war, and we can only hope that our story sheds some light on what these brave men and women endure every day.

Unending love and gratitude goes to our two families: the Woodruffs—Bob and Frannie, David and Lee Ann, Mike, Jimmy, and Amanda; and the McConaughys—Dave and Terry, Nancy and Shawn McLoughlin, and Megan and Mark Lucier, plus all of our nieces and nephews who held down the fort while your parents pitched in. Words on paper are not sufficient to tell you all what you mean to us.

To all of the doctors, nurses, corpsmen, and rehabilitation therapists who worked with Bob in Balad, Landstuhl, Bethesda Naval Hospital, Columbia-Presbyterian, St. Luke's-Roosevelt, and Mt. Sinai. We are in awe of all that you do.

We are so grateful to the people of Rye, New York. As relatively recent arrivals to the community, we were overwhelmed by all that you did for our family, from food to yard work, to the movie gift certificate, from Osborn Elementary, the guidance counselors' and teachers' collective eagle eyes on our kids' well-being to, finally, respecting our wishes for Bob to heal in private. We could not have chosen a better town in which to live.

We'd also like to thank the communities of Bedford, Silver Bay, Colgate University, Michigan Law School, Cranbrook School, and the Convent of the Sacred Heart in Greenwich. Your selfless acts of friendship, prayers, and roll-up-your-sleeves attitudes made a huge difference.

A special thanks to David and Sherrie Westin, for supporting us in every way—emotionally, professionally, and as friends. You did absolutely everything right and you always put our family's interests first.

Our gratitude to everyone at ABC News; you are so much more than just co-workers. Your notes, memories, movies, CDs, photos, books, e-mails, and calls, your gifts of food, ice cream, flowers, you name it, reminded us that you were cheering for us all the way. You enabled our family to mend quietly and to take the reentry at our own pace.

To Bob Iger, Anne Sweeney, and everyone at the Walt Disney Company, you all provided an amazing example of a caring and concerned corporation.

Undying gratitude to Doug Vogt, Vinnie Malhotra, and Magnus Macedo, the boys in the tank—you always had Bob's back. On that day in January, you saved his life too.

Special thanks to Vivianne Vogt, Lee's seatmate on the TBI roller coaster. You taught me how to touch the light.

To Random House editor and friend Susan Mercandetti, who took Lee out to lunch early on and assured her that we both had an amazing story to tell. She took a nine-hundred-page tome and made it lean and meaningful. Many thanks also to the sharp eye and gentle hand of Jonathan Jao. Special thank-yous to Gina Centrello, Tom Perry, Sally Marvin, Carol Schneider, Dennis Ambrose, and Dana Blanchette.

To Bob Barnett, without whose guidance, counsel, and sense of humor we would be lost.

To Tom Nagorski and Peter Balakian, accomplished authors and friends with eagle editing eyes and expertise.

To Lee's extraordinary colleagues at Benefit Cosmetics, Jean and Jane Ford, Julie Bell, Alison Haljun, and the rest of the gang, who let her drop out of work, no questions asked, when David died, and then let her disappear for nine months to help Bob heal. And for the generous care packages of makeup they sent to the nurses' and soldiers' families in Bethesda.

To the sorority of beauty editors Lee worked with daily who sent love and support.

We would like to thank the many friends who have surrounded and embraced us over the past year. From Alan Chabot and Andrew Swank, who cleaned and reorganized our entire garage, to the Lacks, who sent boxes of music CDs for the soldiers in Bethesda Naval Hospital, to the legions at Bethesda, neighbors, and friends who baked and cooked and dropped off food at our hotel, and the many folks who sent iPods to the soldiers, you have all made a difference every step of the way.

Special thanks to the Landstuhl Survivors, Susan and Robin Baker, Melanie Bloom, Lauren "Steel" Lipani, Cathie Levine, Bob Murphy, Mimi Gurbst, Dr. Peter and Laurie Costantino, Dr. Rocco Armonda, Dr. John and Lolly Quagliarello, General Peter Chiarelli, Jim Wooten, Andrea Owen, Patience O'Connor, Andrew and Anne Louise Parlin, Rob Leary, Matt and Mary McCoy, Rebecca Boucher, Rick and Hope Rosen, the Fisher House, Rene Bardorf, and Alix Kennedy and the Family Fun folks. We are grateful to Kevin Cullen for sharing his story on the CCATT flight and to Michele McDonald and nurse Deb Muhl for sharing the only existing photos of Bob before he woke up.

To Kayce Jennings, Tom Yellin, Keith Summa, Gabrielle Tenenbaum, Meena Hartenstein, Susan Schaefer, and Daisy Wright for their tireless efforts and valuable guidance on the ABC News documentary about the important subject of traumatic brain injuries among those returning from Iraq.

To Nora Leary, Alicia Chabot, Diana Dantes, and, again, Lee's sisters, Nancy McLoughlin and Megan Lucier, the surrogate "mommies" who ran our household for five weeks while we were in Bethesda; and kept it up and running once we got home.

To Devon Lamont, J.R., and Julie, who kept a watchful eye on John Steel.

To all of the wonderful people who have told us, throughout the years, that we ought to write a book. We did it.

Last, we want to thank our children, who will be more loving, more empathetic, more wonderful human beings than they already are for having taken this unexpected journey together, as a family. May you always remember that there are no perfect parents, just mothers and fathers doing the very best they can. And there are no perfect spouses either, just those who love each other enough to stand by "for better or worse." Don't be fooled: that kind of endurance is, perhaps, the greatest expression of love.

Lee and Bob Woodruff

About the Authors

LEE AND BOB WOODRUFF live in Westchester County, New York, with their four children. Bob Woodruff was named co-anchor of ABC's *World News Tonight* in December 2005. On January 29, 2006, while reporting on U.S. and Iraqi security forces, Bob Woodruff was seriously injured by a roadside bomb that struck his vehicle near Taji, Iraq. Lee Woodruff is a public relations executive and freelance writer.

About the Type

This book was set in Monotype Dante, a typeface designed by Giovanni Mardersteig (1892–1977). Conceived as a private type for the Officina Bodoni in Verona, Italy, Dante was originally cut only for hand composition by Charles Malin, the famous Parisian punch cutter, between 1946 and 1952. Its first use was in an edition of Boccaccio's *Trattatello in laude di Dante* that appeared in 1954. The Monotype Corporation's version of Dante followed in 1957. Though modeled on the Aldine type used for Pietro Cardinal Bembo's treatise *De Aetna* in 1495, Dante is a thoroughly modern interpretation of that venerable face.